READING TO LIVE

This book is a bridge. You cross alone.
The landscape entered is your own.

—From "Over the Bridge"
by John Loveday

With thanks to the staff and children at Moonee Ponds West
and Spensley Street Primary Schools

READING TO LIVE

How to Teach Reading for Today's World

Lorraine Wilson

HEINEMANN
Portsmouth, NH

Heinemann
A division of Reed Elsevier Inc.
361 Hanover Street
Portsmouth, NH 03801–3912
www.heinemann.com

Offices and agents throughout the world

The author and publisher wish to thank those who have generously given permission to reprint borrowed material:

"Over the Bridge" by John Loveday is reprinted from the anthology *Over the Bridge* edited by John Loveday. Copyright ©1981. Published by Penguin, in Krestel and Puffin editions. Used by permission of the author.

Questions from *Smash Hits Magazine*, November 1998, by D. Godley and F. Wright. Published by Emap Australia.

T-Shirts is reproduced by permission of the publishers Learning Media Limited, P.O. Box 3293, Wellington, New Zealand. Copyright ©1997.

Library of Congress Cataloging-in-Publication Data
Wilson, Lorraine.
   Reading to live : how to teach reading for today's world / Lorraine Wilson.
      p. cm.
   Includes bibliographical references.
   ISBN 0-325-00423-4
   1. Reading (Primary). I. Title.

LB1525 .W55 2002
372.4—dc21
                                                    2001039698

Editor: Danny Miller
Production: Elizabeth Valway
Cover and interior photos: Jaqueline Hendrey
Typesetting: Argosy
Cover design: Linda Knowles
Manufacturing: Steve Bernier

Printed in the United States of America on acid-free paper
06 05 04 03 02   RRD   1 2 3 4 5

CONTENTS

FOREWORD

Lorraine Wilson has given literacy educators a remarkable gift—a road map through the crazy, contradictory, confused world of literacy policy currently dominating most English-speaking countries. Her directions are simple and uncompromising: focus on the destination, keep your eye on the road, remember whom you're teaching to drive, and above all, don't be distracted by the dazzling array of billboards tempting you to take one of those beguiling side roads (which turn out to be cul de sacs).

Lorraine's road map for literacy instruction is grounded in two equally important endeavors. First, Lorraine is a teacher of young children. She has spent years in classrooms, her own and those of her colleagues; thus her understanding of both the challenges and joys of teaching shines through every chapter and every page of this book. Readers will always enjoy and sometimes marvel at the rich and endearing student work that exemplifies the instructional points she wishes to make. Second and equally important, Lorraine is a student of the professional literature; her suggestions for practice are all the more powerful for their connection to grand theories, most notably Luke and Freebody's (1999) Four Resources Model.

She uses the Four Resources Model to organize her ideas both within and across chapters. Thus we frequently encounter the reader as Code Breaker (outside the text, using the cipher and other resources, such as context, to get inside the text), as Text Participant (making meaning from inside the text), as Text User (emphasizing purpose, asking what this text can do for me), and as Text Analyst (stepping outside the text and adopting the stance of critic, asking who wrote it and why and whose interests are served by the intended messages). As we move through these chapters, we encounter all of these stances again and again, but each chapter highlights one of them.

For example, Chapter 3 emphasizes strategies for helping students acquire the cipher (the map between letters and sounds *and* between sounds and letters) but always with an eye toward making meaning. Lorraine talks about phonics, even phonemic awareness, but always in the context of making sense of the text at hand. In her approach, the real job of phonics is to help kids understand words, not just decode them. Similarly, in Chapter 4, on making meaning, comprehension takes center stage, but the purposive perspective of the text user and the critical perspective of the text analyst stand in the wings ready to play a supporting role. And so it goes throughout this excellent book as we continue to encounter these four resources as recurring themes. This feature points up two important aspects of good literacy teaching: it is always theory based and it is always functional (it helps kids learn that they can use reading and writing to get things done).

There are other important groundings in Lorraine's book. One is a clear commitment to an integrated reading–language arts curriculum. Nowhere does this shine through more clearly than in the chapter on the reading-writing connection, where she demonstrates how reading helps writing (by providing good demonstrations of good writing) and how writing helps reading (by providing a powerful means of demonstrating our understanding *and* by rendering the making-meaning metaphor for reading completely transparent). This integrated perspective also comes through in the literature chapter, where she shows us how to use literature to bring together a host of reading, writing, and oral-language activities, and in the final chapter, where she gets down to the nitty-gritty of how we can plan for the functional uses of reading, writing, and oral language she wants all of us to promote in our classrooms.

A second clear commitment is to authenticity. And here Lorraine does not suffer foolish practices. She points out the serious costs (mainly to the model of reading students infer from their daily practices) of creating special texts to practice decoding. She is equally critical of the increasingly popular practice of leveling texts, pointing out that they tend to instill, both within teachers and students, a narrow view of what constitutes competence and progress toward mature reading. Her standard is straightforward for both texts and tasks: is this something that real people would read or do if we did not force them to?

All the chapters in this book contain much for us to learn and many suggestions for what we might do in our classrooms. But I have some favorites, which I want to highlight. Chapters 5, 6, 7 and 8, are devoted, respectively, to the role of purpose, critical literacy, literature, and the reading-writing connection. The purpose chapter (5) reminds us to balance genres and focus on the value of being able to move flexibly from one type of text to another. The critical literacy chapter (6) privileges the Text Analyst stance in the face of the popular temptation to revert to a simpler view of reading (that reading comprehension is the product of oral language and decoding ability). We need to remember that literacy programs that fail to help students become critical consumers of ideas, intentions, and cultural practices also fail to educate students to participate in democratic societies. The literature chapter (7) demonstrates how we can use literature as a magnet to attract and hold together that very range of activities characteristic of quality, integrated literacy learning. And I find the reading-writing chapter (8) especially important because of my own investment in emphasizing this relationship and because of Lorraine's powerful depiction of how we can help students see these important connections.

One foot propelling her through practice, the other through theory, Lorraine Wilson moves in a single direction—away from the idea that reading and writing are ends in themselves, and thus things to be learned because we (as authorities and teachers) say so, and toward the view that reading and writing are tools for communication, learning, enjoyment, and personal insight, the means to help us live our lives more productively, more honestly, more graciously, and with greater personal satisfaction. Hence her prophetic title, *Reading to Live*. Food may be the fuel for our bodies, but reading—and the ideas, emotions, and insights we encounter in the process—is the fuel for our hearts, souls, and minds. Fittingly, you will find this book to be a delectable treat for your teacherly soul!

P. David Pearson
Berkeley, California

NICHOLAS AND THE BEGINNINGS OF READING

Nicholas

With fair curls
and dark eyes
he enters my house
clutching the doorbell.
He explores everywhere
on small fast feet.
Tiny hands
touch precious treasures.
Nicholas brings the sunshine
into my house.
When he leaves
the sun goes down.

—LORRAINE WILSON

Nicholas is my great-nephew. He, with his mom and dad, and I live in the same city, so I know Nicholas rather well. His parents value literacy and have read aloud to Nicholas since birth. Books are always a part of his Christmas stocking and birthday presents. It has been interesting for me to witness his literacy development from a young age. I include some anecdotes.

When he was two years old, Nicholas and I were out walking and passed a stop sign. He stopped and pointed, saying, "That says 'stop.'"

A few months later we were driving down the Geelong Freeway in Victoria, Australia. Nicholas was strapped in his car seat. As we approached a large green freeway sign with white print, he pointed and said, "What does that say?"

Nicholas, at two years and nine months, was in the supermarket with his mother.

"Mum, can I get some eggs?"

"I don't think 'eggs' is on my shopping list," his mother replied.

"Let me look," he said. He took the shopping list from his mother's hands and ran his finger down the list. "There it is." He was pointing to "eggs."

The next day his proud mom came to visit me. She pulled the shopping list from her bag and said to Nicholas, "Find 'eggs' on the list."

Nicholas again ran his finger down the list and this time stopped at a different word.

The point of this story is not that Nicholas could or could not read the word *eggs*. The point is that at this early age, Nicholas already knew there was a purpose for reading and for writing. He knew the purpose of a shopping list.

Yet again, at three and a half years, Nicholas was riding in his car seat in the back of my car. He asked for the flashlight to play with. Since it was a very wet day, he was wearing rubber boots, and it was not long before he had his boots off and was looking inside one boot with the flashlight.

"I can see a teeny-weeny spider," he said.

"When I haven't worn my boots for a while," I said, "I always turn them upside down and tap them in case there are any spiders inside."

A pause.

"We could write on my boots, 'No spiders to go in,'" he said.

At this young age, Nicholas knew what print is. He knew it is to be read and he knew that it serves different purposes. Did he believe that spiders can read?

At three years and ten months, Nicholas wanted to speak with me on the phone. His mother made the call. "Aunt, how do bees make honey?" he asked me.

Searching in the deep recesses of my mind, I tried to answer him but realized I did not actually know how bees make honey. "Nicholas, I will have to call you back. I don't know how bees make honey, but I will look in some books to see if I can find the answer."

I busily looked in books and so did some of my friends. It was Nicholas' dad who found a satisfactory answer that evening on the Internet and sat and read and explained it to him.

Periodically he calls with other questions, the latest being "How is the moon different to a planet?" (at four years and four months old). Each time, someone refers him to a book. He watches as the table of contents or glossary is used to retrieve the information and then the appropriate pages are found.

Nicholas is a lucky child, for his parents have read to him since his birth. He loves storybooks. When he visits my house, he heads for a pull-along cart filled with children's books that lives under a table in the family room. He quickly finds a current favorite and brings it to me. I have to read it to him then and there, and then I have to reread it. I cannot count how many times I have read at his request *Rosie's Walk*, *Hattie and the Fox,* and two factual texts, *Snails* and *Spiders*.

At Birth

For many children, reading begins at birth, for at that time the baby joins a group of family members who value literacy in varying degrees and practice reading and writing in particular ways. From birth the child is immersed in a variety of literate practices that are necessary for and valued by the particular family of which the child is a member. The young child of course joins in. In Brian Cambourne's (1988) words, the child "approximates." That child wants to do what the people around him do.

Recently I waited in a long line at my local bank. While waiting, I observed a young mother enter the bank accompanied by her toddler. She went to a side counter and filled out a withdrawal form. As she wrote on a form, so did her toddler. Because caregivers such as this young mother demonstrate to their children literate practices on a daily basis (reading the traffic signs, reading bedtime stories, reading and writing letters, poring over sale catalogs, etc.), at age five, the children come to school with much understanding of literacy. Some children may even be reading.

Young children absorb family values and practices. Some families may not read storybooks but read religious texts such as the Bible and prayer books, or read newspapers and magazines. It is a fact, however, that school literacy programs are generally built around storybooks. It follows, then, that where there is a match between home and school literacy practices, the acquisition of literacy at school is facilitated.

Whether or not families actually read books regularly, it is important that they convey to their children that they value reading and writing, they themselves engage in reading and writing practices, and they want their children to learn to read and to write.

They therefore should engage their children in the literacy practices of their home and community. Examples include reading the following:

the TV guide

the Bible, hymnals, and prayer books

horse-racing guides

maps

letters, birthday cards, other greeting cards, and postcards from family members

all sorts of environmental print (street signs, advertising signs, section signs in supermarkets)

restaurant and take-out menus

zoo, gallery, and museum display signs and maps

household product print (toothpaste packaging, breakfast food packaging)

T-shirts

sports trading cards (basketball, football)

sports programs and magazines

electronic texts

storybooks

encyclopedias

car insignia and license plates

e-mail and the World Wide Web

Upon School Entry

It is imperative that teachers find out what each child knows about literacy upon entry to school and then plan to build upon this knowledge. During early interviews with the parents of newly enrolled students, teachers should find out as much as possible about the reading and writing understandings and practices of each child. Following are some possible interview prompts:

Tell me about your child's reading and writing.

What does your child enjoy being read? (football programs, birthday party invitations, storybooks)

Which languages are spoken at home?

Which languages does your child speak?

Does your child attend a community language school?

Do you read to your child?

In which language is your child read to?

What drawing and writing materials does your child use at home?

Does your child have experience with a computer? What experience?

Does the family borrow from a community library?

Does your child know the alphabet?

What does your child write?

When children enter school at age five, they are at all different points along a literacy continuum, largely because of their prior literacy experiences. Some may be reading quite independently, others may be able to write their names and identify several words and letters, while others may not be able to distinguish between print and pictures in a picture storybook.

There is no single level of magical reading ability that five-year-old children have gained before entering school. They all have differing understandings about reading and writing. The job of their first teacher is to find what they know, to value that, and to build upon it. What a child at age five knows about reading and writing tells more about the child's prior literacy experiences and his family's literacy practices than about the child's intelligence. To set a minimum expectation for new enrollees is to create failure for some children before they ever enter the classroom, unless that minimum level matches the understandings of the least experienced five-year-old reader in that class. Age/grade standards are for politicians. They are not helpful to children.

Back to Nicholas: As I write, he is four years and four months old. He called me yesterday. The phone conversation went like this:

NICHOLAS: Aunt, I've got a joke for you.
LORRAINE: What is the joke, Nicholas?
NICHOLAS: Which card game do crocodiles play?
LORRAINE: Which card game do crocodiles play? I don't know. I give up.
NICHOLAS: Snap!
LORRAINE: That's a good joke.
NICHOLAS: You could tell your friend Louise.
LORRAINE: So I could.
NICHOLAS: You could write it down.
LORRAINE: You want me to write out the joke for Louise to read?
NICHOLAS: No. Write down the joke so you don't forget to tell Louise.

Yet another example of Nicholas being very clear about different purposes for writing.

He will start school next year. I wonder now what the approach to literacy will be in the school he attends. I hope it will continue to nurture his joyful inquiry of life and the world around him. I hope it will equip him to live a productive, happy life and allow him to participate in and contribute to his society in the new millennium. I hope it will be one that maintains and nurtures his current passion for books and reading. I hope it will be a curriculum beginning with his current attitudes, knowledge, and skills, not one that will place him and his classmates on a conveyor belt and jerk them all along the same linear path through the same levelled reading books.

In the chapters ahead, literacy development is described as more than learning to read or learning to know letters and words; it is described as a set of practices centered on meaning that equip the reader to live and survive and exercise some control in a global society where powerful interests increasingly use texts to seduce and manipulate readers.

Teaching reading is seen as *teaching for living*.

References

Cambourne, B. 1988. *The Whole Story: Natural Learning and the Acquisition of Literacy in the Classroom*. New South Wales: Ashton Scholastic.

Children's Books

Back, C., and B. Watts. 1991. *Spider's Web*. London: A & C Black.

Fox, M. 1986. *Hattie and the Fox*. Sydney: Ashton.

Hutchins, P. 1970. *Rosie's Walk*. Great Britain: Puffin Books.

Olesen, J. 1991. *Snail*. London: A & C Black.

Chapter 1

The Scope of a Reading Program

Schooling today is drawn into a socially divisive process where individuals develop their intellect for personal gain. The current curriculum aims to produce "flexible workers" for future economic activity, rather than focusing on educating the person. Success is tied to notions of "basics" and "competencies." But what is needed is to assist the hyper-individual to assimilate with the wider social group—to become a socially responsible person?

Such a curriculum would focus on the development of cooperation, reciprocity and trust—while the students learn literacy and numeracy—defined in the broadest possible sense to promote analysis of all society's texts—oral, visual and written.

—Jane Pitt (1999, 39)

Before proceeding to describe the breadth and the scope of the reading program, I first outline a view of reading as the construction of meaning, drawing upon nonvisual as well as visual information.

Reading as Meaning Making

Late one night I lay in bed reading *Angela's Ashes* by Frank McCourt. Various emotions consumed me as I engaged with this narrative: anger and sheer frustration with the alcoholic senior McCourt, shame at the landlords who preyed on the poor and leased them such pitiable premises, disgust and scorn for the priest who refused young Frank admittance to secondary school, and hope for young Frank's future, summed up in the one and only word of the final chapter, *Tis*. Reading this book at the end of the day was a roller coaster ride as I participated in the lives and the struggles of the McCourt family in Ireland.

At this same period of my life I had purchased a modem and gone online. In the early months of experimenting with electronic mail, my modem spent more time at the suppliers than it did in my home. As my confidence in technology dipped further, I attempted to solve the problem of the modem by reading the modem manual. Following is a quote from the manual.

Data Compression

The Banksia MyFast Modem can provide data compression protocols v.42bis and MNP5. That means the sending modem will compress the modem on-the-fly to greatly improve data throughout. (Note: a modem cannot support data compression without utilizing an error correction protocol.)

—*MyFast Modem QuickStart Manual*, Banksia Technology

While I could pronounce each of these words correctly and read them aloud fluently in sequence, I had no idea whatsoever what this text meant. In other words, reading this passage was a word-naming activity for me. It served no purpose for me. It gave me no joy, just extreme frustration. If I were asked to retell the passage in my own words, I could not. I could make no meaning from this text. I could not engage with it. In short, I could not *read* this text

These are two contrasting reading experiences of a mature literate adult. In the first, I was constructing meaning and interacting with the text; that is, I was reading. In the second, I was not succeeding with my reading, for I could not make sense of the text. I could not achieve my purpose of trying to understand why the modem did not work. Similarly, one might read aloud a foreign language text that has regular correspondence between letters and sounds without understanding it. An example is the Italian language. While the oral reading may sound fine, if the reader does not speak Italian, no understanding will be possible.

La mia casa non e vicina alla scuola, cosi ogni giorno prendo l'aotobus.

—LORRAINE WILSON, 1979
IL GIORNO CHE HO PERSO I SOLDI PER IL BIGLIETTO DELL' AUTOBUS,
THE DAY I LOST MY BUS FARE
TRANSLATED BY MARIA TRIACA AND JOE ABIUSO

These examples illustrate that being able to name all the words of a text correctly is not necessarily reading. The percentage of words read accurately is not a measure of reading competence.

Therefore, throughout this book, *reading* means *meaning making*.

The Reading Process

I address the nature of the reading process early in this book, for the beliefs one has about the reading process determine the scope of the class reading program. What teachers believe about the reading process determines the reading materials in the room, the activities and the purposes for reading with which the children engage in the classroom, and importantly, the classroom attitudes toward errors and risk taking.

If naming all the words correctly is not necessarily the key to successful reading, then what is it a successful reader does? It is many years since Kenneth Goodman (1969) unravelled the process readers engage with as they read to make meaning. His research identified three main cue systems that inform the reader:

- graphophonic (using letters and sounds)
- syntactic (using sentence structure or syntax)
- semantic (using experiential knowledge on life meanings)

The graphophonic cue is a visual one. The eye samples the text and takes in some letters and word shapes. Building upon the visual input, the brain takes over and predicts the text, drawing upon syntactic and semantic knowledge, or nonvisual information. "Readers select from graphophonic, syntactic and semantic cues. These cues are within the text and within the reader. Readers must have schemata for the orthography, for the syntax of the language, and for the concepts presupposed by the writer in order to select, use and supply the cues appropriate to a particular text" (Goodman 1985, 813–39).

This view of the reading process involves the reader sampling the text by drawing upon the visual information, or what the eye sees, predicting the text by drawing upon nonvisual information the reader has about language and about the world, and finally, confirming that the meaning made fits with the overall meaning being constructed within the whole text. This interaction between eye and brain in constructing meaning makes use of what is called redundancy in text: the reader uses the minimum amount of visual information necessary to make meaning. In other words, when the brain is able to predict the text satisfactorily, the eye need not scan every letter or word on the page. When the reader is lacking in related language or experiential knowledge and hence cannot satisfactorily predict the text, the reader is forced to reread or slow down and look more closely at the text. If the language and the content of the text are beyond the reader's experience, close visual scanning or processing of the print will not bring meaning. Because reading involves readers using their world knowledge and their language to interpret a text, reading is not the retrieval of *the* single meaning. Differing life experiences will result in individual readers interpreting the same text differently; that is, different readers will make different meanings of the same text.

> Reading is a matter of readers using the cues the print provides and the knowledge they bring with them (of language subsystems, of the world) to construct a unique interpretation. Moreover that interpretation is situated: readers' *creations* (not retrievals) of meaning with text vary, depending on their purposes for reading and the expectations of others in the reading event. This view of reading implies that there is no single "correct" meaning for a given text, only plausible meanings. This view is in direct contrast to the model of reading underlying most reading instruction and evaluation. (Edelsky, Altwerger, and Flores 1991, 20)

The Value of Studying Reader Miscues

Goodman's (1969) work threw a whole new light on oral reading errors. Rather than being seen as mistakes, many oral reading errors are now thought to reveal a reader hard at work constructing meaning, by bringing her knowledge of language and the world to bear upon the text. Goodman introduced the term *miscue* to replace *error* because of the negative connotations associated with the word *error*. It is now appreciated that many miscues are very positive indicators of a reader making meaning successfully.

Following are examples of miscues made by a six-year-old as she read a storybook called *T Shirts* (Corney 1985). I include an explanation of the symbols used to mark the reader's miscues on this running record.

o: omitted

c: self-corrected

substitutions: A word or words written above the text are those substituted by the reader (e.g., for line 21, the child read, "In the sun we have . . .").

The full text of T shirts follows:

T Shirts

I've got a T shirt,
A yellow, yellow T shirt,
And on that yellow T shirt
There's a great big ME.

Dad's got a T shirt,
A big orange T shirt,
And on his orange T shirt
There's a great big HE.

Mum's got a T shirt,
A big purple T shirt,
And on her purple T shirt
There's a great big SHE.

My brothers all have T shirts,
Little red T shirts,
And on their little T shirts
They have ONE, TWO, THREE.

Now we've washed the T shirts,
The big and little T shirts,
And, hanging on the line,
In the wind, we see . . .

ONE, TWO, THREE,
HE, SHE, ME.

Here is how the child, Tess, read the text *T Shirts*.

Dad has   (o)

5. Dad's got a T shirt

      yellow (c)
6. A big orange T shirt (picture of Dad wearing pale orange T shirt)

      y _ _(c)
7. And on this orange T shirt

      (o)
8. There's a great big HE.

19. And hanging on the line,

    sun   have
20. In the wind we see

Line 5: She changed *Dad's* to *Dad has* and omitted *got*. She read, "Dad has a T Shirt." Tess made some syntactic variations from the text, but the meaning was not changed. Her substitution of *has* is not visually similar to the text *got*. Tess was allowing her brain to predict ahead for her, drawing upon her knowledge of syntax or sentence construction. She did not self-correct. There was no need.

Lines 6 and 7: Tess read *yellow* instead of *orange* and then self-corrected. In Line 7, she got out only the *y*, or the first sound of *yellow*, before she self-corrected.

What might have caused her to self-correct? The color of the artwork, a very insipid orange, may have led to her read *yellow*, and then possibly the shape of the word or the very different first letter, *o*, prompted the self-correction. This was most probably a graphophonic correction.

Line 8: Tess omitted the word *great* and did not self-correct. There was no need.

Line 20: Tess, now reading about where the T Shirts have been washed and viewing artwork that showed them hanging on a clothesline, read,

> And hanging on the line,
> In the sun we have . . .

Changing *wind* to *sun* is an interesting semantic shift: clothes do dry in the sun.

Tess did not read each word accurately, yet her retelling indicated she made good meaning of this story. The nature of her use of the syntactic and semantic cueing systems indicated that meaning was the purpose for Tess' reading, not reading each word accurately.

> Thus a good reader is quite likely to make quite conspicuous misreadings sometimes, like reading "apartment" rather than "house." And such a reader will not self-correct unless the misreading makes a difference to meaning. This is the way fluent readers read. A poor reader on the other hand might pay far more attention to visual aspects of the task and mistakenly read "horse" for "house." Such a reader will not be likely to self-correct either, although this time the error makes a considerable difference to sense, because the meaning is not being attended to in the first place. A common characteristic of poor readers at high school is that they read as if getting every individual word right were the key to reading. But the more they try to get every word right, the less they will see, the less they will understand, and the worse their reading will be on every count. (Smith 1978, 34)

Language as Social Practice

In recent years, rather than being described as communication, language has been seen as social practice. Language (listening, speaking, reading, writing) develops in social contexts as particular people engage with particular activities throughout their daily lives. Language is learned interactively as individuals engage in social contexts. People use language differently in different situations. Hence, the language that is right and proper in one context is not appropriate in another. The language that members of a soccer team use in celebrating together in the locker room after a match is not the language that would be considered right at a parent-teacher interview. To gain membership of a social group, one learns the language of the group. The language will have grown and developed out of the group activities, which arise from the group purpose. Of course, gaining membership in a group requires more than acquiring the language of the group. One must dress, act, and behave like the other group members as well as have the same values (Gee 1990).

Thus, language is not neutral. There is not one way of using language that is equally attainable by all and equally right for all in all contexts.

> A view of language as social action differs considerably from the view of language as a medium or vehicle for *communication*. The notion that language is made for communication suggests that writers or speakers simply convey or try to get across a message as "pure content" in some shape or form. This kind of view, which is very pervasive in Western thought and history, tends to imply a view of language users as transmitters and receivers of neutral information. (Hodgens 2000, 19)

An example of language growing from the needs and the purposes of a group is the language of the knitting pattern.

> Beg patt—1st row—K5 (7-9-11-11), y fwd, sl 1, K1, psso, *K10, y fwd, sl 1, K1, psso, rep from * once, K4 (6-8-10-10).

Can you read and make sense of this? I am a knitter. I find it very easy to read this language, to make sense of it as I follow these instructions to make baby clothes for new members of the family. I learned to knit as I watched my mother knit and as I approximated with many dropped stitches when she gave me needles and wool and encouraged me to try. Imagine for a moment how the language of this knitting pattern came to be. Think of the very first knitters. How did they spin their wool? What did they use for needles? What were the first stitches they used? Who first began writing down the various stitches and patterns and why? Obviously only knitters could have written down the early patterns, and the purpose would have been either to pass on a pattern to a friend or to have a record for the knitter's own personal use. Language is developed and used as it meets some social purpose.

As text purposes vary, so texts take on different shapes and use language differently. Thus, different written texts demand different knowledge on the part of readers if they are to be accessed. For example, to access the knitting pattern, one needs a knowledge of the different knitting stitches and how to do them, a knowledge of the various symbols that represent the stitches, and a knowledge of the way the different possible sizes for each garment are noted in numerals in parentheses.

Likewise, to access the "Cheats" (tips for playing video games) in the magazine *N64*, one must learn a whole new written language. Of course, this language is learned as the devotees of these games learn to play them with their friends. I find intriguing the number of middle and high school students who struggle with reading novels yet read so easily the language of instruction in *N64*. For example:

Spear: BB+B

Flame Eruption: FFBB+LK

Translation:

Spear: Back, Back, plus Back.

Flame Eruption: Forward, Forward, Back, Back, plus Low Kick.

Reading Involves Purpose

It follows from the understanding that reading is social practice that reading involves purpose. Why read something—even if we can make meaning of it—if there is no purpose to reading it? "Viewed as a social process, reading is used to demonstrate group membership, acquire status or position, control others, control oneself, gain access to social rewards and privileges, to socialize and transmit cultural knowledge, and to engage in a broad spectrum of social interactions" (Bloome 1983).

In our daily lives the texts we read serve different purposes. One may read a novel or a magazine article to relax or unwind. One reads an instructional manual to better construct something such as a dining room table. One reads a map to find out how to get somewhere. One reads a meeting agenda to be alert to items to which he wishes to contribute. One reads a cartoon in a daily newspaper for a laugh. I find one of the first sections I turn to in my daily newspaper is the letters page. To be really honest, not only am I reading people's reactions to hot topics, but I am also looking to see who has been successful in having a letter published in this prestigious paper. Do I know any of the writers?

Evaluation of reading should therefore take into account the purpose of the text and the purpose for the reader in reading the text. The purpose for reading a poem is not the same as the purpose for reading the instructions on a medicine bottle. One measures the success of the reading of these two texts in different ways. Sadly, the designers of reading tests seem ignorant of this simple fact. I see in our state reading tests the same multiple-choice test questions for poems and for bus schedules. If a reader reads a map to find out how to reach a friend's home, any evaluation of the success of that reading must establish how well the reader now understands how to find the friend's home.

Why would people who are learning to read persevere if that which they were reading made no meaning and hence served no purpose? With that in mind, teachers should ensure that classroom reading serves authentic purposes for the children in their classes. That is, classroom activities must link to the children's lives. Classroom reading activities that are ends in themselves, such as busywork, textbook exercises, or trifling activities completed at the end of a book, will never inspire children to be lifelong readers. Reading a book at level 3 because one is at level 3 is not a compelling reason to read.

A New Subject

Mum says, "What did you do at school today?"
"Sheets."
"Sheets? What's that?"
"Sheets are pieces of paper the teacher gives you.
The writing on sheets is always small.
The space for the answers is smaller.
I do messy sheets.
When you finish them you put them in the bin.

At 9:00 o'clock, the teacher says,
'Here's a sheet
for you to complete.'
After play, the teacher says,
'Here's a sheet
for you to complete.'

You never hurry to finish a sheet.
Early finishers get another sheet to complete.
Sheets sometimes tell you what to do:
'Color the pig pink.'
Why? I want a green pig.
'Color the stars yellow.'
Why? I want silver stars."

Mum says, "I didn't do sheets when I went to school.
It must be a new subject."

—LORRAINE WILSON

The Four Resources Model

Two Australian researchers, Allan Luke and Peter Freebody (1999), describe literacy education thus:

> Literacy education is ultimately about the kind of society and the kinds of citizens/subjects that could and should be constructed. Teaching and learning just isn't a matter of skill acquisition or knowledge transmission or natural growth. It's about building identities and cultures, communities and institutions. (5)

In their Four Resources Model, they described four possible sets of reader practices, each necessary to achieve the literate person described in the previous quote: the code breaker, the text participant, the text user, and the text analyst.

The code breaker is outside the text and uses code-breaking strategies to get within. The role of code breaker is ongoing in that a reader is a code breaker until he has finished reading a text.

The text participant is inside the text. Depending on the text type, the reader may be participating in different ways. A cook reading a new recipe may be participating by thinking, "I could make this. I have all the ingredients. I know my kids would like this." Someone reading a novel would be participating differently. That reader may shed tears at a sad part or smile at a humorous incident. Occasionally the reader may recall a related life experience.

A text user has some purpose for his reading. The text user reads not only to understand and participate but also to make some use of the text. For example, at the moment I am reading a travel book about Rome. I will use this book in July when I am in that city. I hope reading the book will help me make good use of my time there so I can see as many of the ancient sites as possible. Text purposes affect the shape and the structure of different texts and thus, different texts are used in different ways.

The text analyst steps back from the text to analyze the text itself from a social critical literacy, perspective. With critical literacy, the reader interrogates the text and the author's motive, examining why the author may have written the text and identifying ways the author tried to shape reader meanings.

Luke and Freebody stress that these are not four discreet practices, nor are they learned in a hierarchical sequence. "The proposition here is that all of these repertoires are variously mixed and orchestrated in proficient reading and writing. The key concept in the model is necessity and not sufficiency—each is necessary in new conditions, but in and of themselves, none of the four families of practices is sufficient for literate citizens/subjects" (Luke and Freebody 1999, 7–8).

Luke and Freebody originally spoke of four reading "roles" but now call them "practices" because they see code breaking, text participation, text using, and text analyzing as a dynamic family of practices actually "done" by humans in social contexts. As discussed earlier, language develops as part of social practices. "The notion of 'practices' suggests that they are actually done in everyday classroom and community contexts—unlike psychological skills, schemata, competencies and so forth" (6).

Beginning readers can engage in all four of these reading practices. However, it is important to note that some books written for early readers make it almost impossible for the beginning reader to be a text participant, a text user, or a text analyst. Books written with controlled vocabularies or phonic texts make text participation very difficult, for meaning is not a priority in the construction of the text.

It follows that where meaning is not a priority in the composition of a text, the text will serve no authentic purpose and therefore, there is no reason to read it. Having students read such texts (controlled vocabulary and phonic-based books) suggests to those students who have no experiences with books outside of school that reading is a pointless activity, that school life is unrelated to life outside of school.

On the other hand, we as adults can be socially critical of such books. Why are they being written? Who is benefiting from the publication of such books?

Why is such junk reading material, rather than material about real issues, being fed to children?

The Scope of the Reading Program

Luke and Freebody's model assists teachers in evaluating the scope and the potential of their class reading programs. It enables them to evaluate what their reading programs will provide for the learners. For example, will the program provide readers with decoding skills? Will it make them strong in their perceptions of themselves as meaning makers? Will it empower them to use a wide variety of texts as part of their daily lives? Will it enable them to be text analysts and to read critically? Will it make possible the full gambit of reading practices necessary for participation in this modern society? In planning the scope of their particular reading programs, teachers should be alert to the shortcomings for students if one or more of these reading practices is omitted from the program. Teachers should wonder about the impact on children's lives if, for example, they do not become text users or text analysts.

A classroom where the literacy program aims to have reading as social practice, to build identities and understanding of communities and cultures, is dynamic and alive. It engages children with the four reading practices (Luke and Freebody 1999). All reading materials are authentic, having been written for some real-life purpose, not for the express purpose of teaching reading. There are books and children's work on display and visible all around the room. The reading materials include class-made books about the students and their families to help build identity and classroom community. Some classroom signs and some of the books on display are in the first languages of migrant pupils. The children read to pursue class and individual interests. Reading in this classroom is not reading specified texts at specified reading times, but reading to check on community sports results, reading to learn about a class interest, reading the class schedule, reading in preparation for a science experiment, reading a letter from a classmate travelling overseas, reading together the words of a favorite song, reading drafts of writing before continuing, and engaging in book talk with a small group of children who have read the same book. The students choose the texts they read and sometimes engage with a shared text. The teacher as experienced reader reads aloud daily a variety of texts, all of which are demonstrations of authentic texts. The children in this classroom feel valued and welcome and so do their parents. The children's questions are sought and valued. The children feel comfortable asking questions and offering individual interpretations to literature. In this classroom, talk is valued and the children regularly work in small groups as a means of developing new understandings. The children in this classroom enjoy reading and writing. In this classroom, evaluation of each student as a reader takes into account how well the child code breaks, makes meaning, uses texts, and analyzes texts. Importantly, the evaluation also considers the overall attitude of the child toward reading.

Balanced Reading Programs

The term *balanced reading program* came into vogue in the latter part of the 1990s. Proponents of such programs purport to teach both phonics and whole language, or the explicit teaching of phonics and meaning. This is of concern, for the debate between phonics and whole language is, of course, a nondebate. If phonics isn't being taught and learned in whole language classrooms, they are not whole language classrooms. Implicit in the use of the word *whole* in whole language is the understanding that all language systems, including phonics, are part of the program. Whole language cannot be about all language systems minus one.

When a balanced program is introduced today, what makes up the balance? If we picture balances, do we see whole language on one side and phonics on the other? Are the pans level? Is phonics given equal weight with all the other language systems? Phonics applies only to written language; what, then, are we saying about the importance of oral language if phonics is given equal weight with everything else? If we give equal weight to phonics, how much weight is given to other code-breaking strategies such as the semantic and the syntactic? What is the balance between teacher- and student-selected texts? What is the balance between fiction and nonfiction? How much weight is given to something as important as critical literacy?

Reading for Living

A purpose of this book is to enable teachers to stand back from their class programs, evaluate them, and think about what they make possible for learners in relation to the literacy needs of the new millennium. What is the relationship between the class reading program and the children's lives? Is the classroom welcoming of the children's lives, their cultures, their problems, their fears? Does the class reading program enable the children to learn more about themselves, their community, and what is possible in the world? Are the teaching programs (including materials used) guaranteed to enthuse all children for lifelong reading? Are the programs designed to involve all children in a multitude of authentic reading purposes? Do the programs include having children learn how to read critically? Are the programs making possible the development of socially responsible persons?

Overall, how do we develop readers whose lives are enriched because of how and why they read, who are concerned about the lives of others, and who are prepared to use their literacies to improve the lives of all?

References

Bloome, D. 1983. "Reading as a Social Process." In *Advances in Reading-Language Research*, vol. 2, ed. B. Huston. Greenwich, CT: JAI Press.

Edelsky, C., B. Altwerger, and B. Flores. 1991. *Whole Language: What's the Difference?* Portsmouth, NH: Heinemann.

Gee, J. 1990. "Introduction". In *Social Linguistics and Literacies: Ideology and Discourses,* xv–xxi. London: Palmer Press.

Goodman, K. 1969. "Analysis of Oral Reading Miscues: Applied Psycholinguistics." In *Reading Research Quarterly* 5: 9–30.

———1985. "Transactional Psycholinguistic Model: Unity in Reading." In *Theoretical Models and Processes of Reading,* 3d. ed., ed. H. Singer and R. B. Ruddell, 813–40. I.R.A.

Hodgens, J. 2000. "Language as Social Practice." In *Deakin University Language Education 1 Study Guide*, Deakin University Australia.

Luke, A., and P. Freebody. 1999. "A Map of Possible Practices: Further Notes on the Four Resources Model." In *Practically Primary* 4 (2):5–8.

McCourt, F. 1996. *Angela's Ashes.* London: Harper Collins.

Pitt, J. 1999. "A New Literacy for a New Time." In *Practically Primary* 4 (3): 39.

Smith, F. 1978. *Reading.* Cambridge: Cambridge University Press.

Children's Books
Corney, E. 1985. *T Shirts.* Melbourne: Nelson.

Chapter 2

EARLY READING INSTRUCTION

Children come into our care having already demonstrated extraordinary ability to make sense of the world around them, to construct their own meaning and knowledge, and to create their own realities.

In the process they have an innate ability to think, to comprehend, to imagine, to create stories in their minds, to question, to talk, to learn. They bring with them their own personal "knowing," their own dispositions and a treasure of experiences, interests, strengths, and potential on which learning and teaching in school should be founded. We must create learning environments that nurture and trust children as natural learners, that foster collaboration and the notion of community, while building on the uniqueness of individuality—educational environments that are responsive to the diverse interests and learning preferences of individuals and/or groups of children. Such contexts for learning enable children to grow tall in their emotional, physical, social, intellectual, and spiritual dimensions.

—LEANNA TRAILL (1993, 2–3)

It is imperative that the early teaching program captures the young child's interest and nurtures his curiosity by valuing what he knows and planning to build on his excitement for learning. Early reading programs build upon young children's understandings about language and literacy, which have developed from the social practices with which they and their families engage. Each child's language practices reflect the language practices of his family and friends. Early reading programs must value the child's language and, in so doing, value his culture, community, interests, and life experiences. Early literacy instruction is meaning-centered and revolves around authentic texts. It engages the students with all four reading practices of the Luke and Freebody model. Code breaking is not taught first, before and isolated from text participation, text using, and text analyzing. This means that often the teacher is the code breaker, enabling children to participate in, use, and analyze texts before they can read them for themselves. By doing this, young children are able to read to live: they are able to engage with texts that are important to them, texts that are worth reading. The four reading practices are all developed simultaneously in an integrated way in early primary classrooms. Code breaking is taught and learned and nurtured as learners engage with authentic literate practices that are part and parcel of the life of the classroom.

Integrating the Four Reading Practices: *Fang Fang's Chinese New Year* by Sally Rippin

Following is an example of the integrated development of the four reading practices in a K–2 class. The work took place during integrated studies of the different cultural groups represented within the class. The teacher read the story aloud to the children; that is, she was the code breaker initially, while the children were text participants, text users, and text analysts. Toward the end of the study, the more literate students read the book for themselves and engaged with code-breaking work in a study of some of the words in the text.

In the picture book *Fang Fang's Chinese New Year* (1996), Sally Rippin tells the story of Fang Fang, a young Chinese Australian girl, and her Anglo Australian friend, Lisa. It is the time of Chinese New Year and Fang Fang's mother wishes Fang Fang to invite Lisa to join in the family celebrations. Fang Fang is very reluctant to invite Lisa but does as her mother requests. The New Year celebrations are a host of new experiences for Lisa: eating Chinese duck, using chopsticks, meeting all of Fang Fang's Chinese relatives, watching the dragon and the exploding firecrackers. At each new experience, Fang Fang quietly insists that "Lisa won't like that."

Session 1: Predicting the Author's Decision

All the children sat on the carpet with pencils and paper resting on chalkboards on their knees. The teacher read the title and the author of the book. Some children made predictions of what the book would be about. (Text Participant) Then the teacher read the book to the point where the waiter places a steaming dish of Chinese duck in the center of the restaurant table. (Teacher as Code Breaker) The teacher asked the children to write what Lisa would say. (Text Participant)

As the children wrote, the teacher moved around and transcribed underneath for those children whose writing was not yet readable so their answers could later be shared. Then the teacher finished reading the story. (Teacher as Code Breaker) She made reference to individual children's earlier story predictions.

Next, children told of their experiences in Chinese restaurants and other Chinese cultural experiences. (Text Participant) Children also told what they had learned about the Chinese New Year. (Text User)

Now the teacher had the children move into a whole-class circle, and each individual child read his or her prediction of how Lisa might respond to the duck. Next the children grouped their responses in the middle of the circle. Five alternate response types were found.

1. Lisa was prepared to eat unknown food. E.g., "It doesn't matter. I'll try it."
2. Lisa refused to eat the duck and asked for something else. E.g., "iAR iA WONSS" ("I want something else.")
3. Lisa was pleased at the prospect of eating duck. E.g., "Yum yum" sed Lisa "Tot Loks God." ("Yum yum," said Lisa. "That looks good.")
4. Lisa has had duck before and did not like it. E.g., "don't wary Fang Fang I will ate it I doddet reliy ingoy duck Bit I will and I donet like Rice ethe." ("Don't worry, Fang Fang, I will eat it. I don't really enjoy duck but I will and I don't like rice either.")
5. Lisa sidetracked and avoided the issue! E.g., "Ivh had the bstTI MOVvmiTiO Mm LF" ("I have had the best time of my life.")

Session 2: Considering the Author's Decision

The teacher began the next session by reading the story aloud to the children. (Teacher as Code Breaker) Then she wrote Lisa's response to the Chinese duck on the chalkboard: "I've never had duck before. Can I try some?"

Next, the class discussed the children's alternate predictions. Then in small groups, the children considered why the author had Lisa respond the way she did. A volunteer recorded each group's thinking. (Text Analyst) Here are some of the reasons identified by these young children:

- The Chinese people would be sad.
- It looks disgusting but it tastes nice.
- Australian people don't normally try the food of other countries, so sometimes Australian people need to try other countries' food.
- I think it is good to try something different.
- Because the author wants people to try other countries' food.

- Because the author wants to be polite.
- She's trying to tell us not to upset people.

After students shared their reasons, the teacher wrote them on a large chart and children gave further clarification and expansion for various reasons. (Text Analyst)

Session 3: Retelling the Story Using a Different Author Decision
The teacher wrote one of the children's predictions of Lisa's response on the chalkboard: "Yuk! I can't eat that!" Then she read the story up to the incident in the restaurant where the duck was brought to the table and in small groups, the children continued the story, incorporating Lisa's new response, "Yuk! I can't eat that!" The teacher listed the main events of the story on the chalkboard and asked the children to retell the story with the same main events but build upon Lisa's changed response. If Lisa responded thus, how would the story change? Here the teaching was geared to having children see that authors make decisions as they write and that changed author decisions mean changed stories. (Text Analyst)

Session 4: Word Study
(Note: The very early readers and writers in the K–2 group worked on alternate activities during this session.)

On large charts the teacher had prepared the following:

Which other words are spelled like F<u>ang</u> Fang?
Which other words are spelled like ri<u>ce</u>?

Eight charts were prepared, each with a different word from the story. Part of each word was underlined. The teacher told the children to look at spelling patterns, not listen for the sounds made by the underlined letters. Groups of two to three children worked on each chart. Each group wrote with a different-color felt pen. One acted as recorder while all helped list other words with similar spelling patterns. Every two to three minutes, all groups moved on to the next chart. Each group took its colored marker with it so in later whole-class discussions, it would be easy to identify which group had added which words. During the class, each group worked on five charts and by then they couldn't think of any more words. (Code Breaker)

Two collections were as follows:

Which words are spelled like F<u>ang</u> Fang?

Sang	kangaroo	Fang Fang	dangle
bang	zang	slang	mangle
hang	tang	rang	Chang
clang	strangle	angle	
gang	bangle	angry	

Which words are spelled like tr**y**?

Woy	Mary	Cary	Sally
by	my	Arey (airy)	Camey
fly	Hayley	Katy	Kay
bitelfly	Hatty	Haty	Pary
my	Toby	acktivity	Hery (hairy)
may	Barry	assembly	
say	Larry	Mary	

The group discussed the charts. Misspellings were generally corrected by other children. What was exciting was the variety of words listed by the children. Notice the number of children's names that were included.

How much more inclusive it is to have the children compile spelling or word lists! It allows them to include words they know and are familiar with and hence, lists include names of friends, families, and places all pertinent to the children. It cognitively stretches them. Note on the *try* list the words *activity* and *assembly*. A teacher list would most probably have been limited to *try*, *by*, *cry*, *my*, *fly*, and *why*. Also, having the children come up with the lists gives them a sense of ownership: what they know is valued in this classroom.

Session 5: Grouping Words

The teacher had rewritten all the words on the charts with correct spelling. She left the words in the same order as on the children's charts. The children worked in the same small groups as they had previously. The teacher handed each group just one of the lists and asked them to see if they could group the words into subgroups. When they had done this, they wrote their criteria for group inclusion. (Code Breaker) This was most interesting and surprising. The reasons were not always those traditionally taught by teachers.

Multiple Copies of Text   Throughout this series of lessons about the picture book *Fang Fang's Chinese New Year*, a class set of the book (six copies) was available for the children to either read at silent reading time or borrow as take-home books. This permitted the children to further pursue their individual purposes and develop personal interpretations of this text. (Code Breakers, Text Participants, Text Users, and Text Analysts)

Integrating the Four Reading Practices: Moonee Pops Come to School

The following example occurred in a K–1 setting. There were several boys who at personal writing time chose to write only about Pokémon, Digimon, and other characters all of whom are the intellectual property of their creator. While I believe that we should be accepting of children's culture in the classroom, I have concerns when I observe some children using personal writing time only to regurgitate stories created by others. Hence, in the instance I'm describing, I informed the children that it was an infringement of copyright to use other creators' characters, let alone their stories, as their own. But then I needed to address how these children could invent their own fantasy characters. Thus, at the commencement of each personal writing session, I set about demonstrating how to create some small fantasy creatures and set them in a story. I wanted to show the children how they might invent their own fantasy characters.

The characters are now called Moonee Pops. (The children's school is Moonee Ponds West.) The characters are small like the Pokémon characters. They are round and green and live in the grass along the banks of the Maribyrnong River, which is not far from the school. They are nonviolent and nonsexist (in keeping with school policy), but they have a lot of fun making mischief all around the local area once it is dark. In keeping with the children's fascination with electronic gadgetry, I gave the Moonee Pops a small, built-in electronic panel that emits a popping sound when danger is near.

The development of these characters occurred quite explicitly as I thought out loud while drafting (Code Breaker, Text Participant) at the commencement of the class personal writing sessions. I brainstormed about the characters and drafted the story on large charts as the children watched and joined in. At the commencement of each writing session I reread the draft to date, thinking out loud about whether my intentions were clear, whether the story was making sense, whether the Moonee Pop doings were true to the characteristics I had given them, and so on. In drafting the story, I asked for help from the children. They had no trouble coming up with mischief for the Moonee Pops to inflict around the neighborhood. When they suggested that the Moonee Pops play some rather cruel tricks on the school cat, I reminded them of the character outline for the Moonee Pops—nonsexist and nonviolent. (Text Analyst)

They suggested that the main plot of my first story be set in their classroom, which the Pops would enter one evening. (Text Participant) Over many weeks I completed this first adventure of the Moonee Pops. As I drafted, I not only discussed the characters and their actions but I talked about some spellings, punctuation, and capitalization, sometimes seeking the children's help. There were a lot of proper nouns in my draft, so I took the opportunity to talk about the first letter of these words, for example, *Moonee*, *Maribyrnong River*, and *Poynton's*. The children were able to explain why each of these words starts with a capital letter. (Code Breaker)

Individual Moonee Pops now have names: Pip Pop is the smallest; Master Pop is the leader; Cuddly Pop is cuddly; and Computer Pop is a computer whiz. The children are fascinated and excited by the Moonee Pops. We now have regular Moonee Pop sightings around the neighborhood. Parents are reporting sightings around their homes. The children are using the Moonee Pops to explain odd noises they hear at night.

I was in bed and I heard a squeaking. I looked out through the curtain and Moonee Pops were swinging around on the clothesline.

—ALEX, AGE 6 (TEXT USER)

I heard our dog barking, and when I looked out, the Moonee Pops were teasing him.

—ADA, AGE 6 (TEXT USER)

The first story we wrote is called *Moonee Pops Meet the Bell Tower Ghost* and has been published as a beautiful classroom book with the children as illustrators. In preparing for the artwork, each child was asked to draw and color a Moonee Pop character as he or she envisaged him. (See Figures 2–1 and 2–2.) I explained that everyone in the class would look at all the visual representations and then vote for his or her preferred representation. The winning picture would then be the model for the artwork for the book. We talked about the need for a character to look the same each time that character appears in an illustrated book. So when the children were completing the artwork for our class book, they were all encouraged to try to make their Moonee Pops look like the design that the majority of the children had voted for.

The text of the first book has been typed and copied so that each individual child has a smaller version of the book to keep. They are almost all able to read it entirely for themselves even though the language is quite sophisticated. (Code Breaker, Text

Figure 2–1 Design Submitted for a Moonee Pops Character

Figure 2–2 Design Submitted for a Mooney Pops Character

Participant, Text User, Text Analyst) Many children, quite voluntarily, are now writing
Moonee Pops adventures. (Code Breaker, Text Participant, Text User, Text Analyst)

Moonee Pops

ONE BAD time.
ONW DAY A MOONEE POP THAT WAS PLaYiNG GAMES with THE ATOR (other)
MOONE POPS AT night. He saw A PiecE of meTal ON THE RiveRBAK (riverbank) He
TORD (told) ALL THE MOONEE POPS. ONE of THE MOONEE POPS said iT'S A ARK.
ALL THE MOONEE POPS HELPD TO PURR (push) THE ARK iNTo THE RiVeR. They All
GOT iNTo THE ARK THEY TiED THE ARK with A PeRS (piece) of SADR (straw) that
THEY FoD In THE ARK. Something HAPPened! THE PERS of SAWR (straw) CAT (cut)
afteR A Far (few) minutes THEY were AT SAE (sea) THEY DiscoveR how TO USR THE
ARK They GOT off THE ARK.

—ALEX, GRADE 1

When the children voted to select a Moonee Pop design, Rhiannon's won the most
votes. In keeping with the character description from my story, her Moonee Pop
was round and green, but Rhiannon did not include feet. When several days later we all
realized this, we had to resolve how the Moonee Pops moved without feet. This was
no problem for Hugh. He excitedly jumped to his feet and demonstrated across the

classroom floor how the Moonee Pops bounced their way wherever they wanted to go. (Text Particpant) That night, Hugh worked at home and made a wonderful Moonee Pop from a tennis ball. So his Moonee Pop actually bounced! When he proudly brought this model to school, of course all the other children wanted to know how he had made it. He carefully wrote out the procedure he had followed and most of the children now have a Moonee Pop that bounces. Here are Hugh's instructions:

My MooNee PoP

I have a MooNee Pop KalD (called)
cubbly (cuddly) PoP
He lives in my Tingering. (tinkering box) I
love it.
If you want to know I
maDe it.
I mabe it with

1. TeNNis ball
2. NeWs PaPer
3. carDBoraD
4. crayoNs
5. sTicKY TaPe

—HUGH, GRADE 1

Jessica then chose to write about making her model.

My MooNee POP

I made a MOONee PoP this
is hawe you Mace (make) it you
Sat (start) with 1 a tens ball
TheN two pis of NosaPaPa (newspaper)
and some cudebod (cardboard)
for the herey (hair)
Then some paypplive (paper)

—JESSICA, KINDERGARTEN

The main purpose of devising the Moonee Pops was to demonstrate to the children a way of inventing imaginary characters. Many of the books, computer games, and comics the children read contain characters devised by a creator. Under copyright law, no one else may then use these same characters in his or her writing. However, children can create their own, maybe by drawing upon their locality, and give specific characteristics to these characters. Next, they can plan adventures consistent with the characteristics. One of the first-grade boys invented a species called Pogey. The first character we met through his writing was Gogey. Pogeys sleep through the morning and swim at night.

In what began as a teacher demonstration of writing, the children in this class engaged with all four practices of Luke and Freebody's Four Resources Model. Currently the Moonee Pops are a cause of much curiosity and joy in the classroom community, with parents and children involved. Hugh (grade 1) reported this week that a Moonee Pop has had a baby under his bed. Importantly, these characters have injected much vitality and creativity into the children's writing.

Teaching Strategies for Early Reading

Following is a list of teaching strategies that are centered in meaning and are appropriate for children in the early stages of literacy. All texts used are authentic in that they fulfill some purpose in the children's lives. The danger in organizing strategies in a list like this is that one could assume they are taught isolated from the context of a rich literacy event. This is not the case.

Reading Aloud

Rationale Whenever I read aloud a beautiful poem, a short story, or a picture book, be it to five- or twelve-year-olds, I am moved by the total involvement of the children. The silence. The stillness. I think now of one six-year-old who is currently in much trouble for the violence he has been displaying in the school yard, and yet when a story is being read aloud to his class all sitting together on the mat, his face is angelic: he does not move; he barely breathes. I sense he does not want the story to finish. He is captured by story. There is something so obviously right about reading aloud to children that it must have a high priority in our daily class programs.

The teachers I work with are feeling increasingly pressured; they say they have no time for the important things, that there is more and more to fit into the curriculum. The system is increasingly telling them how to organize their school days. Statewide testing encroaches on teaching time. What I sense happening is that time spent reading quality texts aloud is suffering as a result. In fact, quiet class community time is suffering: everything is always such a rush. How sad.

Margaret Moustafa (1997) wrote, "If a child is experiencing difficulty in learning to read, we should not ask if he or she knows the sounds of the letters but if he or she has been read to extensively" (79). Capturing children's hearts and minds by reading aloud is crucial in the literacy curriculum. It is crucial in children's lives.

Purposes Reading aloud

- demonstrates what reading is
- enables children to learn about themselves, others, and the world
- takes children to magical places
- helps build a sense of classroom community: children have shared literary experiences to talk about

- promotes interest in and fosters enjoyment of books
- introduces children to, and informs them about, all sorts of texts and writing styles
- introduces children to children's authors and illustrators
- enables children to hear authors and writing styles they may not be able to read for themselves
- enables children to give their full attention to the ideas of the writing and not worry about the decoding
- facilitates individual children being able to read that same text for themselves at a later time

Reading aloud involves children in reading for enjoyment; demonstrates reading for a purpose; provides for an adult demonstration of phrased, fluent reading; develops a sense of story; develops knowledge of written language syntax; develops knowledge of how texts are structured; increases vocabulary; expands linguistic repertoire; supports intertextual ties; creates a community of readers through enjoyment and shared knowledge; makes complex ideas available to children; promotes oral language development; and establishes known texts to use as a basis for writing and other activities through re-reading. (Braunger and Lewis 1998, 47)

Strategies   Those texts read aloud might include

invitations	storybooks	factual books
letters	the daily schedule	a daily notice by the classroom door
notes	labels	class-made books and charts
captions	newspaper articles	posters
rhymes	poems	songs
recipes	lists	items from the school newsletter

After reading a powerful story, do one or more of the following:

- Say nothing. Sit quietly and wait for the lead from the children.
- List the children's questions on a chart with each questioner's name after his or her question. Then have those children who wish to discuss a particular question form a small group with the original questioner to talk through and come up with answers. When the whole class meets back together, ask each questioner to recount whether or not he has an answer to his question and how the group arrived at that particular answer.
- Have children write personal responses (see "What's on Your Mind?" on page 77).
- Have children engage with critical literacy (see Chapter 6).

After reading aloud a factual text, do one or more of the following:

- List the children's questions. Older children might write for themselves questions that are raised while listening to the text. Then have children get in small groups to discuss questions and seek answers, possibly using other resource materials.
- Have children write something they learned while listening.
- Demonstrate note taking. With the book closed, think out loud and list some key words on the board. Then try to write several of the main points in your own words.
- Have children make notes of key points, after previously observing you make notes. Because the text has been read aloud and the children do not have a copy, they have to draw upon their own resources in making notes rather than copy directly from the book.

Language Experience Stories and Sentences

Rationale All children love to read about themselves and their doings. The language experience approach, where children's language (listening, speaking, reading, and writing) is developed from the children's firsthand experiences, means the children use language to learn about their experiences as they simultaneously learn language. Built around the children's experiences, this approach is inclusive of all children in the classroom, unlike some published materials, where the experiences and language may differ from those of the students. Because the nonvisual cue systems of semantics and syntax are so important in predicting text, it follows that the more familiar a reader is with the language and the subject matter of the text, the greater chance that reader has of experiencing success. "The amount of background knowledge children have on a topic prior to reading a passage has a powerful effect on their abilities to make sense of the passage" (Moustafa 1997, 64). Hence, language experience reading materials that are about the children and their experiences and are written in their language make success possible and offer authentic purposes for reading.

Language experience materials include class-made stories and books, charts, diaries, news sentences, songs, rhymes, classroom signs, letters, captions, and more. They are written jointly by the children and the teacher or by individual children. When reading class-made experience materials, the children are able to draw upon all three of the cueing systems, since the texts have been written in their language and are about their experiences.

All the experiences the children share at school are possible subject matter for experience books. The books may be funny, serious, factual, instructional, recount, or other various text types. Funny books that are made together are important. Humor makes the school day more enjoyable for both teacher and students. Every classroom should experience laughter.

Some ideas for experience books:

All About Us (Include a photo of each child in the room with the child's name and a caption.)

The Day We Made Kites (Recount a kite-making experience)

When the Parrot Escaped (Create a factual retelling or use part truth and part fantasy with many exaggerations and much fun!)

How to Make Gingerbread Men (Write a simplified recipe that the children have actually followed with diagrams.)

The Best Things About School (Include an entry from every child in the class.)

When Our Classroom Roof Leaked (Recount a shared experience.)

When We Had Injections (Recount a shared experience.)

The Best Football Player (Include photos and text for either the children or their professional heroes.)

When Our Teacher Was Away (This could be a fantasy!)

What Our Principal Does (Write a factual description of the administrator's duties.)

Class-made books about the children themselves are a rich incentive to get them reading. Because the children are in the books, the text participant role presents no problem. Since the language has come from the children, the syntax presents no problem either. I would prefer to see many more class-made books being used in early literacy programs than many of the early reading books being published today. Some of these new reading books, although they are glossy and in full color, are about nothing. Many are a hoax upon children!

Purposes   The purposes of this activity include

- jointly developing written texts about the children's experiences
- developing reading materials with which the children can identify and enjoy
- demonstrating what writing is
- teaching print concepts such as the directional features of written English, the concept of word, letters, and sentences
- demonstrating the writing of a particular genre such as narrative, recount, or procedure
- demonstrating aspects of the writing process such as drafting, redrafting, and editing (including spelling strategies and punctuation)
- developing the children's reading and writing abilities

Strategies   Following are two possible strategies for creating language experience materials. The first is making a class book about a class experience, such as the school festival. Before the festival, help the children follow steps in a recipe to make candy to sell in a booth. Show them a map of their playground that shows the position of the booths, the eating areas, and side shows.

On the day of the festival the children attend the event with family members. After the festival, discuss everything the children did and experienced at the festival. Ask each child to focus on just one aspect of the festival and write a sentence or two about it. Have a conference for sense with each child. Ask those children whose writing is readable to underline and try to correct three or four spellings. Then have each child draw a picture to illustrate his or her writing. Finally, type the children's writing, collate it with their artwork, and publish it as a class book for all to read.

Another possibility is to accompany a science experiment with writing. For example, as part of a study of living things, have the children plant twelve bean seeds in the twelve hollows of an egg carton. Leave bean seeds that are not planted on the science table for the children to examine through magnifying glasses. Give the bean seeds in the egg a little water every two or three days. Every two days, dig up a bean seed and examine it for signs of change, *after* asking the children to predict what might have happened to the seed. Tape the exhumed bean seeds on a chart, noting the date. Each day, write a statement describing what has happened. When comparing the state of each bean seed, read the statements from previous days. For example:

MONDAY, FEB. 1: We planted 12 bean seeds.

WEDNESDAY, FEB. 3: We dug up a bean seed. It looked just the same.

FRIDAY, FEB. 5: We dug up a second seed. It looked a bit swollen.

MONDAY, FEB. 8: The third seed has a crack in the top.

And so on.

Big Books

Rationale   Big books were first devised to be used with a group of children, not just an individual child. It was thought that by using an enlarged book with a small group of children, the preschool experience of a parent reading aloud to a young child could be replicated. In the preschool reading experience of one child with one parent, the child is close enough to touch the book and see all the book and print features very easily as the parent reads aloud. This close proximity facilitates interaction between the child, the adult, and the book.

The first big books were indeed big with big print. Unfortunately, there are now many books on the market masquerading as big books. In these more recent publications, the print is far too small for members of small groups to be able to see clearly the book and print features.

Big books can be demonstrations of both fiction and nonfiction writing.

Purposes   The purposes for reading a big book to children are numerous. These include presenting information on a topic, such as animal environments or a particular culture; presenting information about a text type, such as a fairy tale or rhyming poems; and demonstrating aspects of reading practice.

Guided Reading Strategies with Big Books   Begin by holding the book so the children can observe the print and the pictures, the directional features you will follow as you read. Then do one or more of the following:

- Have child predict the title. Point to the title on the cover and ask the children if they can read it. Encourage them to look at the artwork as a way of predicting the title. When a child suggests a title, ask, "Why do you think that?" Ask them to count the number of words in the title. "Are there enough words or too many words for your title?" Have individual children say their titles and point to the words. Do they match?

  Sometimes, you might refer to the first letters of words. For example, if the title were *The Big Bad Fairy*, and a child predicted *The Naughty Fairy*, you might praise the idea and then ask, "Which letter does *naughty* start with?" or "This word starts with the letter *b*. What might it be? The b . . . b . . . Fairy . . ."

- Have the children predict the story. There are a couple of ways to do this. First, you could have the children predict from the title what the book might be about. Write the children's predictions on the chalkboard. After reading the story, refer back to the predictions. Did any child make an accurate prediction?

  Another option is to stop at some point while reading the story and ask the children to predict what will happen next.

  Predicting makes children focus on meaning: reading is constructing meaning from print.

- Work on children's tracking skills. Before reading a new book, have the children try to construct the story by discussing each picture in the book. Different children could tell their versions of the story as you turn the pages from the front to the back of the book.

- Study the direction of print. Ask a child to come and show where you should begin reading. As you read, use a pointer to show the direction of the print.

- Have children join in refrains. Some stories in big books have refrains. When you read one of these books for the second or third time, have the children follow the text and join in the reading of the refrains. A child might try to point to the words of the refrain as classmates read it aloud.

- Practice with cloze. On later days cover some highly predictable words in the text of the big book with sticky notes. Have the children read the text, insert words that make sense when they come to a word that is covered. This strategy encourages children to draw upon context in predicting text. It shows that one does not need to see every word as one reads to make meaning.

You can list the children's insertions on the chalkboard and then after completing the story, compare them with the text words.

Discussing with each individual child his or her reasons for selecting the word he or she did, reveals much about the child's reading or code-breaking strategies. Did the words the child inserted make sense? Was each word semantically and syntactically acceptable?

Revisiting Text

Rationale Revisiting favorite texts is something pre-school-age children demand of their parents. They ask for the same story again and again. While the adult reader may become tired of the story, the young child seemingly does not. A child would not ask for a story to be repeated if he were not enjoying it. Those texts that children want to be read again and again are those that develop committed readers. One needs to ask of some classroom texts whether any reader—adult or child—would wish to hear them again.

Revisiting a text familiarizes the children with the content and the language. Hence, one will later see the children rereading these same books for themselves, often with their eyes on the pictures. Being familiar with the meaning and the language facilitates the child's reading and forms a platform from which the child can begin to unlock the mysteries of print. Knowing a story or a rhyme by heart enables a child to match the spoken text with the written text. Revisiting loved text allows time for meanings to develop and connections to be made between spoken and written words. Gradually the young reader's eyes move from the picture to the print as she reads.

Revisiting texts is a strategy commenced in children's homes and should be continued in classrooms. A regular spot could be set aside in the class schedule for the revisiting of favorite books. For example, you might inform the children that a period right after lunch each Friday will be reserved for the rereading of their favorite texts.

Purposes   When an adult rereads a child's favorite text, it

- allows time for meanings to develop
- fosters different interpretations
- helps the child critically examine themes within the text
- allows the child to make use of the text by learning through personal reflection or learning about some aspect of the world at large
- familiarizes the child with the content and the language, helping the child make connections between the spoken language and the written text

Strategies   Either have an individual child select a favorite book or let the majority vote determine the rhyme or the book that you will reread. At the end of the reading, do one or more of the following:

- Say nothing. Remain silent and let the children soak in the euphoria.
- Encourage further development of earlier interpretations. For example, ask, "What did you notice this time that you did not notice before?" "Are there any new puzzles in this story?" or "Has anyone changed his understanding of this story?"
- When children have developed personal interpretations, prompt critical literacy with questions such as

    Was that fair?

    Who had the power in this story?

    Why was the main character a boy?

    Would it have mattered if the main character were a girl?

    Could the problem have been solved in some other way?

    Why did the author write this book?

For a longer list of such questions, refer to Chapter 6.

Repeated readings

Rationale   Repeated readings are one example of revisiting text. Repeated readings occur with new texts. It is important that there is some purpose for the repeated readings other than to read by memory or read to recognize the words. The purpose might be that the students engaged with the repeated readings are to read and share their book with the whole class later. On different readings the children might have a different focus, for example, to observe how the art complements the text or to focus on how the main character feels throughout the story.

Repeated readings can be done with the whole class, a small group, or individual children. If the whole class will be working together, the text should be a big book, easily seen by all children.

Purposes   The purposes of repeated readings are to develop deeper understanding of a text and to help children become able to read a text independently.

Strategies   Choose one or more of the following strategies. Note that in the first three simple strategies, the children are learning about participating in text (predicting), code breaking (words in title, concept of word, word identification), and analyzing (discussing characters and predicting how they will behave throughout the story).

- Read the title and ask children to predict what the book will be about.
- Draw attention to the author. Have the children read other books by this author? What type of books does this author write? Who are her characters? What might happen to them in this story?

- Draw children's attention to the words in the title. Ask questions such as "How many words are there?" "Who can touch and count the words?" or "Which of the words is *Princess*? How do you know?"

- Read the story aloud. At the end have children discuss their earlier predictions.

- Read the story again, leaving some words out for children to insert (oral cloze). The words left out should be well into the sentence and easy to predict.

- Read the story together with the children. Have children discuss the fit of the artwork with the text. Does the art ever reveal something the text does not?

- Have individual children read the book aloud or individual children read a page in turn.

- If there are multiple copies of the text, have the children read individual copies silently.

- Depending on the type of text, have the children follow up in different ways. For example, they may share the funny parts, comment on related life experiences, give their opinions of the text, or discuss the story from a social critical literacy perspective.

When the children come to read individually with this strategy, many of them may be reading the book from memory. The pictures may cue the children to the story and prompt them to recall the text. On later days the big book will be reread and the small books will be available for the children to reread. This is called revisiting text. The more familiar a young child becomes with what the book is about and the more he looks at and rereads the book, the greater opportunity there is for him to make some print connections. He may realize, for example, that a large word is saying "GRRRR" or that a repeated phrase is saying "Little pig, little pig, let me in."

When children read from memory, their eyes are on the pictures. As a young child comes to make some word-print connections, you will notice that the child's eyes are studying the writing. In early reading development this switch of the eyes from the picture to the print is very significant.

Repeated Readings Using the Listening Center

Rationale   The rationale for using a listening center is the same as for regular repeated readings.

Purposes   Through repeated readings, children develop understandings of a text and become able to read the text independently. Having the children engage with repeated readings by using a listening center leaves the teacher free to work with another group.

Strategies Set up a listening center with six to eight copies of a book, a taped reading of the book, a cassette player, and a cue card. Make sure there is at least one student in each group who knows how to operate the cassette player.

For a storybook, the cue card can list the following instructions:

1. Listen to the tape and follow the story.
2. Listen to and read with the tape.
3. Talk about the book.
4. Listen to the tape and follow the story again.
5. Talk about any puzzles.
6. Read the book aloud together without the tape.
7. Read silently without the tape.
8. Make an entry in your literature journal (if the children have literature journals).

For a factual text related to classroom study, such as one that describes native Australian animals, the cue card could list the following instructions:

1. List all the native Australian animals you know.
2. Listen to the tape and follow the text.
3. Add to your list.
4. Listen to the tape and follow the text again.
5. Check your list.
6. Read the book aloud along with tape.
7. Share your list in your group.
8. Present lists to the class.

Using this organization, a small group can work independently for forty to forty-five minutes.

When recording a story for the purpose of a taped book activity, it is important to remember that the reading should not be too fast and should allow time for the children to look at the pictures before turning the page.

Story Reconstruction

Rationale When children begin reading familiar texts with their eyes moving from picture to print and back, more attention can be directed to the text. Story reconstruction involves children in sequencing the sentences from a known text, which have been written on sentence strips, into the correct order. When the pictures are not available as an aid, the children's familiarity with the text helps them identify the next sentence. They must rely on their developing understanding about sounds, letters, and word shapes to select the correct next sentence.

Purposes Story reconstruction further develops children's concepts about print (word, letter, sentence, and capital letters) and their visual processing as well as heightening their understanding about the sequencing of particular texts.

Strategies After children have experienced repeated readings (as described previously), write the text on separate sentence strips. Have the children move into a circle. Scatter the sentence strips of the text within the circle and open the big book to the relevant page. Then read aloud the first sentence and ask individual children to find the matching sentence. Continue in this manner, reconstructing the text on the carpet.

The children may need to check the strip they choose with the text on the page of the book. This develops the visual reading strategy.

At a later time, read each sentence from the book aloud, without allowing the children to see the text. Ask individual children to select the matching sentence strips and place them in sequence. Ask each child how he or she knew he or she had chosen the right sentence. Children generally reply with reference to a first letter or a word: "I know this is 'Little pig, little pig, let me . . .' because it starts with *l*." This focuses the children's attention to the surface features of the language, letters, and word shapes. (Code Breaking)

Later still, without reference to the original text, have small groups of children sequence the sentence strips in the correct order.

Sequencing is generally easier to do with narrative than with informational texts because the position of each sentence in a story is of greater significance than in factual reports. The children's conversations as they try to reconstruct text sequence will reveal much of their understandings about the schematic features of different text types.

Innovating on Text

Rationale Innovating on text occurs after children are familiar with a particular rhyme or story. The children, together with the teacher as recorder, write a new text by building upon the structure of the familiar one. In this activity, the children are explicitly learning about both reading and writing. Because they build a story on a familiar story structure, around characters and a setting they choose, and because in the process of writing the story there are many rereadings, the finished story is easy for the children to read. Allowing the children to select the characters and the setting provides opportunity for the children's cultures and communities to be legitimized in a classroom book; the children see their lives in print.

Purposes Innovating on a text furthers children's reading and writing abilities because they're building upon familiar structure. It also furthers children's understandings of the schematic and linguistic text features of a particular type of text.

Strategies

***Brown Bear, Brown Bear, What Do You See?* by Bill Martin Jr.** Begin by reading the title of the book. Have children predict who or what the bear is going to see. Then read the big book aloud and before turning each page, ask the children to predict who the next creature might be. Children may join in the repetitive text.

Read the book aloud a second time with children reading, too. Then tell the children that they are going to write a story of their own based upon Bill Martin Jr.'s story *Brown Bear, Brown Bear.* Ask them to think of possible characters for their book. (They cannot be animals as are Bill Martin Jr.'s characters.) Perhaps in this innovation, they'll be classmates or fairytale characters.

If classmates are chosen, the initial draft may be an oral one with the children all sitting in a circle. Ask, "How might our story start?" (If need be, refer to the start of the original book.) For example, the class might begin with "James, James, who do you see?"

James would then continue, "I see Mario looking at me."

The class would together chant, "Mario, Mario, who do you see?" and Mario would take up the draft, saying, "I see Jennifer looking at me," and so on.

The story may be further varied by changing the action from "looking" to other things. For example, "Jennifer, Jennifer, who do you see?"

"I see Natasha waving to me."

"Natasha, Natasha, who do you see?"

"I see Laurence winking at me."

By constructing the innovated draft, the children are very much participating in this text. What they compose must make sense. It must flow on from what came before.

Next, write out the innovated text with the children observing and helping. Highlight elements of the composing process as you go along. For example:

Who can think of a good first line?

Does that flow on?

Is that the best word?

Does that really sound finished?

***And the Teacher Got Mad* by Lorraine Wilson**   This story has a repetitive pattern and a repetitive line: "And the teacher got mad." Begin by reading the book several times to the children over two or three days so they become familiar with it. Have them identify the repeated sentence and the main character. Then ask them to suggest an alternate main character, one who also gets somewhat mad or angry on certain occasions. List their suggestions on the chalkboard and have the children vote for their favorite, for example, Mom.

Referring to the book *And the Teacher Got Mad,* have the children suggest the first episode that upsets Mom and write it down. Every other sentence should be "And Mom got mad."

When the draft is complete, read through it with the children, listening to check that it makes sense and that it is in the best possible order. Then have all the children read the draft together, listening to see if the best words have been used or that the story sounds finished. When the children are happy with the draft, brainstorm publishing ideas. For example, choose an art medium and colors to suit the title *And Mom Got Mad*. Hopefully, children will think carefully about what colors best portray someone who is often angry. Also, have children give ideas for the cover art.

In the next session, have children help with publishing jobs. Assign two children to cooperatively complete the cover art, including placement of the title and other lettering. Have two children plan and complete appropriate borders for the title page. Have two children complete art and lettering for the title page. Ask individual children to complete artwork for the text pages, which could be full-page art opposite alternate-page text. Make smaller copies of the book for each child to illustrate and take home.

Rhymes

Rationale Rhymes, with their repetitive sounds and strong rhythms, are greatly enjoyed by young children. Being relatively short, rhymes are quickly memorized, and through repeated sayings and readings, children learn to read them quite quickly. Rhymes with the repetition of particular sounds of a language help in the development of phonemic awareness.

Purposes Rhyme can be used to introduce children to an alternate text type, demonstrate that reading can be fun, develop children's reading and writing abilities, help children learn more about a particular topic, and give children an opportunity to experience and identify the individual sounds of their language. (Phonemic Awareness)

Strategies Begin by writing a rhyme on a large chart or in a blank big book for easy reference. Then choose one or more of the following strategies:

- Read the rhyme together as a class. To get things going, you can first read the rhyme aloud to the children. Then ask the children to read the rhyme along with you.
- Read the rhyme in parts.
- Have the children move in time to a rhyme. For example, they may march to the beat of "The Grand Old Duke of York."
- Ask the students to draw pictures of the images the rhyme puts into their heads.
- Have the children share their interpretations of the rhyme.
- As emergent readers begin to develop print concepts, ask them to point to the rhyme as all the class members read it. It is interesting to see if the child pointing (1) knows the directional features of written English, (2) knows where the readers are reading, (3) has one-to-one word correspondence, and (4) knows the beginning and the end of written text. Note how some children lose their place in the middle of the rhyme but know when the rhyme is getting near the end quickly move the pointer to finish with the readers.

- Draw attention to the rhyming words. Can the children identify those words that rhyme or sound the same? List the rhyming words on a chart. For example, from "Humpty Dumpty," the following words may be listed:

wall   fall

men   again

Note how the study of phonics develops from words the children can read. The children may then add other words that rhyme with *wall* or *men* to this list.

After identifying those words that rhyme or sound the same, ask the children about the sounds that are the same in these words. Note that it is more difficult to isolate and identify common individual sounds within words than it is to identify the onsets and rimes. An onset is the consonant or consonants that come before the vowel in a syllable, and a rime is the vowel and the consonants that follow.

Onset	Rime
w -	all
m -	en

Innovating on Rhymes

Rationale   When children are familiar with a particular rhyme, they can innovate upon it. That is, they can keep the rhythm and the shape of the rhyme but change key words so that the rhyme takes on new meaning. Thus the rhyme may be written about the children's locality or interests or friends. This is done as a group or with the whole class with the teacher recording.

Purposes   By innovating upon an existing rhyme, the children are learning about the writing of rhyme and coming to understand the importance of rhyme, rhythm, and rhyming patterns.

Strategies   Begin by having the children say a familiar rhyme together. Then read the rhyme aloud while the children listen for the rhyming words. List these words on the chalkboard. Ask the students to identify the rhyming pattern, that is, which lines rhyme. For example, rhyming couplets, first and second lines rhyme, or second and fourth lines rhyme.

Any simple rhyme may be innovated upon.

> Three grey kangaroos
> Cross the street.
> Hit by motor car
> Now roo meat

> —LORRAINE WILSON

The pattern of this rhyme is two beats to each line and lines 2 and 4 rhyme. The first innovation may involve rewriting lines 3 and 4. As line 2 has to rhyme with line 4, the children can list words that rhyme with *street*. For example, *heat, feet, seat, meet, wheat,* and so on. An innovation might be

> Three grey kangaroos
> Cross the street.
> They hopped to the park
> To escape the heat.

Next, the children might innovate on a new rhyming pattern. For example:

> Three grey kangaroos
> Cross the park.

Remember, line 4 has to rhyme with line 2. The children can now list words that rhyme with *park*. For example, *dark, hark, shark, spark, bark,* and so on. Then they should try to add two lines with two beats each.

> They went home when
> It was dark.
> They drink at the waterhole
> After dark

A third innovation on this same rhyme may involve leaving out more of the original text and rhyming with the new text. For example:

> Three grey elephants
> Cross the road.
> A truck driver swerved
> And lost his load!

One could continue with further variations:

> One hungry schoolboy
> Went to the deli.
> "I need some food
> To fill my belly."

Classroom Print

Rationale   In the real world, print serves many different purposes, as it does in class-rooms. Print materials that are important to classroom life make excellent early literacy texts because they are the stuff of the children's lives.

Purposes   Classroom print can be used to develop a sense of classroom community when you create necessary everyday classroom texts with the children. You can also facilitate the smooth organization of daily class routines by making such organization explicit through the use of jointly constructed texts.

Strategies

- Post a daily news sentence by the door for the children to read as they enter the room. For example, "We go to library after morning play," "School party next Saturday," or "Please put your lunch orders in the lunch basket."
- Post a list of the children's names. This is a great aid when children are writing and need to spell their friends' names.
- Write out the daily schedule on the chalkboard each morning. The daily schedule is important in classroom life. While it does not have to be the same each day, some events are scheduled regularly. Where the schedule is written on the chalkboard each morning before the children arrive, we see parents entering the rooms with their children and going to the schedule to read and discuss the forthcoming day.

9:00 A.M.	Development Activities
9:35 A.M.	Attendance, Money Collections
9:45 A.M.	Personal Writing
	Finish Draft of Our Big Book
11:00 A.M.	Recess
11:30 A.M.	Phys Ed
12:00 P.M.	Literature Groups
1:00 P.M.	Lunch
2:00 P.M.	WATER EXPERIMENTS
3:15 P.M.	Story Time
3:30 P.M.	Time to Go Home

See you tomorrow!

Refer to the schedule during the day. For example, "What are we doing after lunch today? Ah, water experiments. At lunchtime, who can help fill up the buckets with water?"

- You could also write out instructions for feeding a classroom pet or instructions for using the class computer; create a schedule for using the computer to ensure all children have equal access; or make a list of items available for lunch orders each day at the school cafeteria with their prices.

Partner Reading

Rationale   Reading to a classmate provides yet another audience with whom to share a book and provides extra reading practice for emergent readers.

Purpose   The purpose of partner reading is to have classmates read to one another and share meanings together.

Strategy   Have children read books to each other in pairs. Encourage them to help each other if problems occur, look at the illustrations, and question and talk about their books.

Take-Home Books

Rationale   Most afternoons each child should take home a book from the classroom to read. We learn to read by reading. Hence, the more reading children do, the easier will be their journey toward becoming independent readers. The child chooses the book he wishes to borrow. It might be one of the books he has read in a small-group reading session with the teacher, or it might be a title from his shared literature group, or it might be a title from the classroom library. It is important to communicate with parents the purpose of this practice and exactly what is expected of the family. A letter to parents might make the following points:

- The reading session with parent and child together should be an enjoyable time.
- The child self-selects his own take-home so that he will enjoy reading and experience some control over his reading program.
- If the child cannot read his take-home book, the parent should read it aloud to him. Later readings may involve the parent and the child reading the book together.

It is important that the children choose for themselves the books they will take home. This allows for individual interests and purposes for reading. It allows for the child who has an interest in batteries and lightbulbs to read more about them; it allows for a child who wants to read a favorite author, such as Anthony Browne, to do so. This practice of allowing children to choose their take-home books recognizes that learning to read is not an end in itself. Reading is always about something and always for some purpose. The earliest reading lessons must reflect this basic understanding. Sometimes a child will wish to take home a book he has borrowed before because it is a favorite. This should not be frowned upon. It is indicative that the child sees books as a source of enjoyment, knowledge, and satisfaction.

Purposes   Take-home books provide an opportunity for children to further practice their developing reading abilities by borrowing books they wish to read or wish to have read to them. This practice of taking books home also develops in children a positive attitude toward books and reading.

Strategy Every two or three days, have each child select a take-home book from books available in the classroom. Children who are able, enter the title of their book on a list, which is perhaps kept in the cover of the take-home book. For children who are unable to make this record, either you or a parent helper can note the entry for books borrowed. You might also leave a column on the borrowing list for a parent or a caregiver to make an entry about the child's reading or the child's reaction to the particular book.

Readers Theatre

Rationale The purpose of readers theatre is to read a text to entertain an audience. It is scripted theatre. This needs to be emphasized because sometimes the children want to act out the story without their scripts. Readers theatre is a reading activity. Therefore, the children must read their scripts and be entertaining—no boring monotone voices! Readers theatre provides an enjoyable, supportive forum in which children read.

Purpose As mentioned earlier, the purpose of readers theatre is to provide an opportunity for children to read aloud to entertain an audience.

Strategies This reading activity may occur with children of similar reading ability, but it also works really well with mixed-ability groups. The group size must equal the number of reading parts in the text. The text may be a story (preferably one with much direct speech), a poem, or a play. There should be a copy of the text for each participant. If the text is a poem, the separate reading parts must be clearly marked on each copy. When the text is a storybook, a narrator can read the text that is not direct speech. Each group should have a leader who can read the text independently. Each leader should have two cue cards; one cue card lists the characters required and the other lists the directions to be followed in preparing the script for performance.

Readers' Theatre
For a group in which all children can read the text, the cue card may read as follows.

Readers Theatre

1. Leader allots parts.
2. Read in parts.
3. Discuss: How can we improve our performance? Is our reading conveying the meaning?
4. Practice in parts.
5. Perform to class.

For a mixed-ability group, the leader must be able to read the text.

Readers Theatre

1. Leader reads aloud.
2. All read together.
3. Talk about the text. What is happening?
4. Leader reads aloud.
5. Leader allots parts.
6. Read in parts.
7. Discuss: How can we improve our performance?
8. Practice in parts.
9. Perform to class.

Brainstorming Lists

Rationale   If the content of the curriculum is to be relevant to the students, then topics studied should begin with and build upon the children's existing understandings of that topic. Such understandings may be revealed in small-group brainstorming sessions.

Purpose   Brainstorming sessions identify children's questions, existing understandings, or predictions for the purpose of planning future teaching, for example, in an integrated study of the zoo.

Strategies   During integrated topic work, beginning readers work as members of small mixed-ability groups to brainstorm questions, write down existing knowledge, make predictions, or detail information they have learned. For example, prior to a visit to a zoo, the children can list the animals they predict will be at the zoo. On return, working in the same groups, the children can now list those animals they actually saw at the zoo. They can then cross-check their two lists. Each learner can reflect upon what he or she learned about the actual animals that live in the zoo.

Alternatively, before the excursion, the children might brainstorm the questions they wish to answer during their excursion to the zoo. At the conclusion of the unit, the children can brainstorm what they have learned.

Making Learning to Read Difficult

In 1997 a symposium, titled Reaching Consensus in Literacy Education: Beginnings of Professional and Political Unity, took place at the International Reading Association Convention in Atlanta. Participants in the symposium were drawn from the full gambit of pedagogical beliefs. They put together a list of teaching practices they agreed would make reading development difficult. That list included the following:

- emphasizing only phonics
- drilling on isolated letters and sounds
- insisting on correctness
- expecting students to spell correctly all the words they can read
- making perfect oral reading the goal of reading instruction
- focusing on skills rather than interpretation and comprehension
- using workbooks and worksheets constantly
- creating fixed-ability grouping
- adhering blindly to a basal program (Braunger and Lewis 1988, 77)

Summary: Early Reading Instruction

Early reading instruction of the type outlined in this chapter is holistic in nature. The texts students read are authentic and serve real-world purposes. Throughout the teaching, the child is placed at the center of the learning. Her questions and text interpretations are valued. Individual meanings are respected. Where possible, children are given choice over the texts they read. Early reading instruction that aims to make young children passionate about reading

- builds upon children's lives—their interests and their existing knowledge about, attitudes toward, and abilities in reading
- incorporates and values children's experiential worlds
- involves a variety of authentic texts
- is meaning-centered
- values the teacher reading aloud carefully chosen texts
- makes success possible
- explicitly identifies and encourages the use of the different cue systems
- includes the revisiting of texts
- develops responsibility in each child for setting purposes for reading and choosing books
- makes possible the development of readers as code breakers, text participants, text users, and text analysts

References

Braunger, J. and J. Lewis. 1998. *Building a Knowledge Base in Reading*. Newark, DE and Urbana, IL: Northwest Regional Educational Laboratory's Curriculum and Instruction Services, NCTE, and IRA.

Moustafa, M. 1997. *Beyond Traditional Phonics: Research Discoveries and Reading Instruction.* Portsmouth, NH: Heinemann.

Traill, L. 1993. H*ighlight My Strength*. Crystal Lake, IL: Rigby Education.

Children's Books

Martin, B. Jr. 1986. *Brown Bear, Brown Bear, Who Do You See?* London: Fontana Picture Lion.

Rippin, S. 1996. *Fang Fang's Chinese New Year.* South Australia: Omnibus Books.

Wilson, L. 1987. *And the Teacher Got Mad*. Crystal Lake, IL: Rigby.

Chapter 3

CODE BREAKING: ENTERING THE TEXT

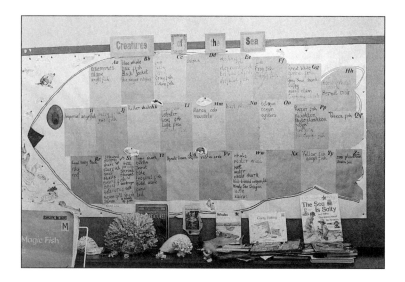

If we understand that the brain is the organ of human information processing, that the brain is not a prisoner of the senses but that it controls the sensory organs and selectively uses their input, then we should not be surprised that what the mouth reports in oral reading is not what the eye has seen but what the brain has generated for the mouth to report. The text is what the brain responds to; the oral output reflects the underlying competence and the psycholinguistic processes that have generated it. When expected and observed responses match, we get little insight into this process. When they do not match and a miscue results, the researcher has a window on the reading process.

—KENNETH GOODMAN AND YETTA GOODMAN (1977, 819)

Code breaking is what a reader does to get inside a text or to unlock the mysteries of the print to access the meaning. Code breaking continues until the reader has reached the end of the text. Code breaking is not learned first, in isolation from the other reading practices. Code breaking is learned as the reader engages with text participation, text using, and text analyzing. As discussed in Chapter 1, code-breaking strategies are integrated into all reading lessons.

> Competent readers don't learn to "crack the code" first and then come to "critical literacy" later, in fluency, as the icing on the cake. Joan Henderson, when evaluating remedial reading programs in light of this model, pointed out that readers who are successful in the first three "reader roles . . . are more prey to manipulative text than are those who can't decode."
>
> If we don't allow children to take up all four practices in an integrated way, are we teaching kids to "crack the code" and "read for meaning" just so they can be bureaucratically controlled and commercially exploited? ("Reading the Signs and Following Tracks," 1999, 3–4)

Myth: Reading Is Visual

There is a widely accepted misconception in the general community that reading is solely a visual activity, that what the eye sees is all-important. With this view of reading as visual, the correct identification of each individual word is considered of prime importance, and when the reader cannot name a word the reader is expected to convert the letters into sounds, to sound out and name each word.

However, this view of reading has no substance. The purpose of reading is to construct meaning. Meaning is made from written text directly without converting it into sound (Smith 1999). The community view that reading is naming each word correctly is erroneous, for, as demonstrated in Chapter 1, one can name each word correctly in some texts and make no meaning whatsoever.

To name each word correctly and to make no meaning is not reading. Who would bother to read if all one did was to name words correctly and make no sense? To be a code breaker and not enjoy reading or to see no purpose for reading is to waste time. To be a code breaker and not read critically is to severely limit one's capacity to act upon the world.

Reading is not working out each word and then adding all the individual word meanings together; adding individual word meanings together will not bring one to the underlying meaning of the text. The meanings of different words change in different contexts. To reach the underlying meaning or deep structure, one must interpret chunks of language. Think for a moment of the word *roll*. What does it mean? Note the meanings possible when the word *roll* is embedded in text:

The gambler is on a roll.

He's eating a sausage roll.

He has a bank roll in his pocket.

They enjoyed a roll in the hay!

Watch the ball roll.

The Reading Process

As mentioned earlier, it was once thought that cracking the code was a purely visual act. It was the research of Ken Goodman (1967) that clarified what it is efficient readers do in the process of making meaning. His work in identifying the major cueing systems illuminated the role of the nonvisual cues, or the part the brain plays, in the process of code breaking. His work showed the interactive way the eye and the brain work in the process of constructing meaning. The brain uses samples of visual information supplied by the eye to predict the text ahead, drawing upon knowledge about language structure, or syntax, and experiential knowledge, or semantics. Goodman identified three major cueing systems that efficient readers draw upon when they read:

- graphophonic (using letters and sounds)
- syntactic (using sentence structure or syntax)
- semantic (using experiential knowledge or life meanings)

Try to read the following passage. When you finish, think for a moment about what the passage was about. Could you retell it in your own words? Note that there are several missing words. Think of the words you inserted. How did you determine which words to insert?

1. The old man walked slowly up the steep _____. Every minute
2. or two he stopped _____ rested. He was breathing quickly and
3. _____ was running down _____ cheeks. I wondered who _____.
4. was. Did he _____ in the neighborhood? I wondered _____
5. anyone would be _____ if he did not make it home.

How did you know what to insert in the space in line 1? Did you insert *hill* or *slope* or perhaps *staircase*? Whichever word you inserted, you drew upon your experiential or world knowledge. You made use of the semantic cue system.

In line 3, did you wish to insert *tears*? If so, did you later change your choice to *perspiration* or *sweat*? If you had inserted *tears* you probably would have paused and reread: "tears was running . . ." The grammar is not acceptable, so you would have self-corrected. The insertion of *perspiration* or *sweat* or *tears* was informed again by your experiential knowledge, but if you changed from *tears* to *sweat* because of the singular verb, you were making use of the syntactic cue system.

At the end of line 4, you were probably thinking of a word that made an acceptable sentence, that is, you were making use of your grammatical or syntactic knowledge to insert *if* or *whether*.

To successfully read line 5, I'm predicting that you read on to the end of the sentence and then returned to insert perhaps *worried, anxious,* or *concerned.*

Redundancy in Text

Efficient readers make use of redundancy in text, that is, the eye does as little work as is needed for the brain to able to read on, or to predict the text. Consider the following thirteen letters. Look at them and then close your eyes. How many can you remember? Check and see.

d m a w u i b h o s y t e

Did you remember six or seven? Here are another thirteen letters. Look at them and then look away and see how many you recall.

Who used my bait?

I'm sure that in the second example you were easily able to remember all thirteen of the letters. Why was this? In which example did the eye need to do the most work? Obviously, the eye was busier trying to remember the first line of letters, because there was no logic to their order. There was no quick system for remembering the letters displayed. The second grouping was arranged in a meaningful sentence of words you would know, and therefore the brain was able to assist the eye in predicting and remembering familiar letter sequences. Did you notice that the same thirteen letters were used in each display? With new texts a reader generally needs more visual information at the start of the text than farther on, for at the start the reader is not able to draw upon context to the extent he can when he gets farther into the text.

As a reader takes a visual sample of print and the brain then predicts ahead, the reader often changes the author's text, using words from the reader's repertoire. Sometimes the word substitutions are visually unlike the words of the text but may not alter the meaning at all. Consider the following substitution.

goed
The little boy went up the hill.

Here a young reader predicted according to the past-tense form of *go* in his current oral language. The word *goed* is visually different from *went*. However, this child did not look at the word *went*. In the context of the story he was reading, he was seeing just enough of the print for his brain to fill in the text and make sense of it.

Phonics

The popular media uses three different terms as synonyms in discussions about phonics—*phonetics, phonemic awareness,* and *phonics.* These three terms are not synonyms; they mean quite different things.

Phonetics is the scientific study of human speech sounds. Phonetics was the scientific field of study of Professor Henry Higgins in the film *My Fair Lady.* Phonemic awareness is the ability to identify and manipulate the smallest sound units of a language. Some writers refer to this as phonetic segment awareness. Phonics is the study of the relationships between the letters and the sounds of a language. It is important to note here that letters represent sounds only in the context of words.

The study of letter-sound relationships in English is very complex. There are several reasons for this. First, there are more speech sounds in English than there are letters. While there are twenty-six letters, there are approximately forty-two to forty-four sounds in spoken English. The number is approximate because different speakers of English use different speech sounds. Think for a moment of the sounds of Scottish speech. Now think of the sounds heard in American English. Not only are there more sounds than letters in the English language, but different letters and letter combinations are used to represent the same sound. Consider the following words and note the different letter representations of the middle sound of *pot.*

pot	was	sausage	cough	honest

As well, in written English, one letter can represent more than one sound. Consider the sounds represented by the letter *o* in the following words.

pot	won	only	women	woman
pool	road	fork	loud	

Second, many different languages have contributed to the English language, hence spelling patterns reflect the spelling of other languages. For example, *cigarette* is French.

Third, English spelling sometimes carries meaning rather than sounds. The past-tense spelling of many verbs in English ends with the letters *ed.* This spelling is not representative of sounds. Rather, it conveys the meaning that the action of the verb is in the past.

walked	stopped	founded
loaned	pushed	blasted

The *ed* does not consistently represent the same sound pattern but, as illustrated here, represents three different sounds.

The spelling of the following pairs of words indicates meaning relationships.

sign - signature

medical - medicine

Note, however, the different sounds produced by the *g* in *sign* and *signature* and the *c* in *medical* and *medicine*.

The word *two*, which tricks many young spellers, is no longer a problem when the learner's attention is drawn to other words with similar meanings.

two (not *tow*)

twin

twelve

twenty

Fourth, there are many different variations of spoken English. People in different English-speaking countries spell most words in the same way and can communicate by writing without difficulty. However, English speakers do not always understand one another's spoken language with the same ease. Different accents mean different pronunciations and different speech sounds. When the Scottish film *My Name Is Joe* was shown in Australia, it was screened with subtitles, even though the film was in English!

Hence, when discussing the teaching of phonics, one needs to ask, "Whose phonics will we teach?" In other words, which set of speech sounds will we relate to the letters of the language? In the teaching of sound-letter patterns, the program must be sensitive to and inclusive of the accents of the students. For example, in a sorting activity of words with common sounds, there will be different "correct" groupings depending on the pronunciations of the speakers in the grade. I think of a Canadian pupil who spent several years in a school where I was teaching. She added much to the children's understandings about phonics, especially that letters represent sounds in the context of words and that speakers of English have different pronunciations of the same words. Even the children local to the school found variations in their pronunciations. My own name is an example. What is the first vowel sound in *Lorraine*? For some speakers it is the *or* of *born*. For others it is the *o* of *dog*. And I use the schwa vowel as is heard in the middle of *separate* and, commonly in Australian speech, at the end of *the*, *mother*, and *father*.

A further issue is that a sound within the same word may change according to the context in which the word is used (Goodman 1993). So, for example, the same speaker may use two different sounds for the letter *a* in the word *can*. Consider these two sentences:

Yes you can.

Can I help?

For many English speakers, the sound of the letter *a* in the second *can* is the short schwa vowel.

Phonemic Awareness

There is a view held by many phonic proponents that an awareness of and ability to manipulate speech sounds (phonemic awareness) is a prerequisite for learning to read. As phonemic awareness is about the sounds of the language, it relates to spoken language and not to print. Hence, its relevance for the teaching of reading holds good only for those practitioners who see reading as a sounding-out process rather than a meaning-making one, which is usually done silently.

Those readers who do perform well on tasks of phonemic awareness are generally those who can read. In other words, there appears to be a correlation between proficient reading and phonemic awareness. (Note, however, that adult readers of nonalphabetic scripts and profoundly deaf readers do not do well on measures of phonemic awareness, which may suggest that phonological awareness and reading are unrelated [Scholes 1998].) This correlation is not evidence of causation. That is, the fact that readers do well on tests of phonemic awareness does not prove that phonemic awareness causes reading. In a close examination of the research of the National Institute of Child Health and Human Development, which purports to show explicit instruction in phonemic awareness as "the most powerful weapon" for promoting literacy, Coles (2000) found that "when research data supposedly showing a predictive relationship between skills and later reading and writing achievement were re-examined, pre-school reading achievement, not skills ability, was found to be the best predictor of future reading achievement" (544).

Today there are educators and community members who argue strongly for the teaching of phonemic awareness prior to children learning to read. Such teaching involves the decontextualized practice of particular sounds and the manipulation of sounds within words. Moustafa (1997) cites numerous research studies that found that young (six- and seven-year-old) prereading children could not analyze spoken words into phonemic elements. She thus queries the relevance of phonic instruction for non-reading students: "If children have difficulty analyzing spoken words into phonemes, how can they understand instruction in letter-phoneme correspondences?" (12).

On the topic of phonemic awareness, I give the final word to Frank Smith (1999):

> Lack of phonemic awareness is a bogus construct . . . it's just not true that some children may lack phonemic awareness. Even infants demonstrate an exquisite sensitivity to the phonemic structures of speech. They don't confuse words that have a close similarity of sound, like *pat* and *bat*, or *sip* and *tip*, either in hearing someone else say them or in saying them themselves. (Young children may have articulatory problems in producing some sounds, but that has nothing to do with either phonemic awareness or reading.) No one

except a professional linguist pays attention to individual sounds of spoken words, not even proponents of phonics do this. Not being able to say what the component sounds of words are is not the same as being insensitive to them. (We can all distinguish one face from another, but we would be confounded by anyone who asked us how we do it, or requires us to be able to talk of the distinguishing features of eyes, noses and mouths.) (153)

Whole Language and Phonics

A holistic approach to learning incorporates phonics. The nature of the word *holistic* means that all the subsystems of language are part and parcel of the learning program. If one of those subsystems, namely phonics, were eliminated from the curriculum, the program would not be whole, not be holistic. In whole language progams where the learning of writing and reading are integrated and where children are expected to write whole texts from their first days at school, much of their learning about sound-letter patterns occurs as they write. Requiring children to write lets them try out their developing understandings about the sounds and the letters of the language. However, there are identifiable differences between the way phonics is learned or taught in whole language classrooms and in skills-oriented classrooms. Generally speaking, in skills programs, the sounds and the letters are taught from a predetermined sequence and are taught as isolated pieces of information, quite divorced from written context. As well, each letter is initially given one fixed sound value. For example, learners are taught that the letter *a* makes the sound heard in the following words: *cat, bag, sad.*

In a phonic reading program, children move through a sequence of graded readers. Each of these texts has vocabulary limited by the number of words containing known phonic elements. The first priority for writers of such reading books is to construct texts containing certain words rather than to compose meaningful texts.

Such books serve no real-life purpose. If one analyzes such texts against Luke and Freebody's model, one sees how they limit the literacy practices possible for the learner. Why participate in or spend time developing meaning with such a text? What is the use for the reader of such a text? What relevance do such texts have for the children's lives? It is demeaning of young children to invite them to read such materials.

In isolated skills programs, children's approximations and experimentations in writing are generally frowned upon. Hence, children are not free to write in their own codes using invented spelling; they are not free to work out the sound-letter relationships for themselves from daily reading and writing.

Teaching Skills in Holistic Classrooms

Rather than teach skills from a predetermined sequence isolated from children's existing understandings, the holistic teacher observes her students, listens to their reading, reads their writing, and finds starting points for skill instruction. One common way of differentiating between learning in skills-based classrooms and learning in holistic classrooms is the part-to-whole versus whole-to-part dichotomy. In skills-based instruction, tiny pieces of language are introduced and practiced out of context. For example, a single letter might be taught each week; a new word might be introduced every two days. The letters and the words taught come from a predetermined sequence of instruction. Eventually, when all the parts are known, the learners are expected to put them together to interpret and produce whole texts.

In holistic classrooms, teaching about the smaller components of language occurs from whole texts that the children are writing or reading because they serve some purpose in the students' classroom lives. The study of a letter or a word or an item of punctuation makes greater sense to the learner when it is embedded in a context that informs about that language item. For example, in regard to phonics, when a child can read a word and say it out loud, he then has a frame of reference for discovering the letter-sound patterns within that particular word. Asking children to sound out words they cannot read and hence cannot say out loud is almost asking them to do the impossible. Imagine if you could not read these words and you were asked to sound them out; what would you do?

was   there   one   do   love

Building on What Children Know

Last week, I was using a big book titled *The Meanies*, from the Story Box series, with K–1 children. Before reading the book, the children were discussing the title and predicting what the book might be about. When one child read the title correctly, I asked her how she did it. Her first comment was that the word *Meanies* started with the letter *m* (letter name). We continued on to enjoy the book together.

In our next session together, I referred to the word *Meanies* and reminded the children that Maddy had told us that *Meanies* started with the letter *m*. I had a large chart on the chalkboard and asked the children if they could name other words beginning with the letter *m*. They suggested many words, including their names, such as Maddy and Michael. I next asked for words containing the letter *m* but not beginning with it. Again, they had numerous words to add, even *swimming* with a double *m*. Later, when reading the words, we talked about the sound represented by *m* in these words the children could read. The next time I entered this classroom, I noticed that more words had been added to the list.

A major difference between skills classrooms and whole language classrooms is that in skills classrooms, sounds are attributed to letters divorced from words, whereas in whole language classrooms, sound-letter patterns are discussed only in the context of words.

Skills-Based Classrooms	Holistic Programs
The letter *a* is taught as having just one sound, as in *cat* and *bag*.	The sound represented by the letter *a* is discussed in words the children can read, such as *cat*, *was*, *Andrew*, and *Fiona*.

Phonics and Early Writing

From the first days at school in whole language classrooms, young children are encouraged to write as they are able, be it in scribble or strings of letters or in invented spelling. The children's approximations are welcomed, for they show the children's current understandings about writing. The children write every day, so each child's understandings about writing are very evident to the teacher. She can see in front of her eyes whether the child has directional understanding of written English; whether the child has the concept of a word; whether the child knows the letters of the alphabet; whether the child understands sound-letter relationships or punctuation; and importantly, the particular text types the child has obviously experienced. With all this evidence of a child's understanding in front of her, it is easy for the teacher to teach at the point of need.

Figure 3–1 Danny's Writing

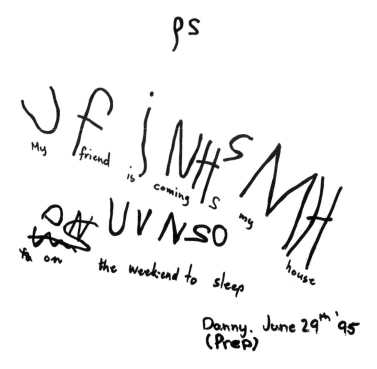

Figure 3–2 Danny's Writing

Consider Danny's work in Figures 3–1 and 3–2. Note in Figure 3–1, Danny used the numeral 1 for the word *One* and in Figure 3–2, he used the numeral 2 in two places for the word *to*. From observing Danny's writing and talking with him on completion, I learned that Danny knew the following:

- Writing conveys meaning.
- Writing can recount personal experience.
- Writing is done in lines from left to right.
- Numerals and letters are used in writing.
- There are "words" in writing. (This was a developing understanding.)
- Letters represent sounds (e.g., *m* for *morning*, *b* for *put*, *r* for *a*). (This was also a developing understanding.)
- He could spell some words correctly (for example, the automatic spelling of the word *on*).

Danny's comments as noted on his writing indicate how aware he was of what he was doing as he wrote.

Danny's writing shows how, given the opportunity, children explore letter representations for sounds. In these early explorations or experiments, children sometimes use letter names for letter sounds, as the following example from Marie clearly shows.

mi mami kam with mE to thA muZeam.

—Marie, age 6

Note the use of the letters *i* and *k* for their sounds in *mi* (my) and *kam* (came). Note also the use of the letter *a* for both the *a* sound in *came* and the shorter vowel sound in *the* and *museum*. The letter name *a* is produced in the throat quite closely to the vowel sound of *the* and *museum*. For a fuller discussion of early writing, refer to Chapter 8.

Classroom Strategies to Develop Code Breaking

Classroom strategies for developing code-breaking skills take place in the context of reading and writing. Whole lessons are not generally devoted to teaching one code-breaking strategy. Working with young children, you can discuss or demonstrate several strategies every time you read or write, listen to a child read, or talk with a child about his writing. Remember, code-breaking includes using visual and nonvisual strategies.

Reading Aloud

Rationale In the context of reading aloud to children and introducing them to the riches and the mysteries of texts, we are also demonstrating how we read and specifically how we break the code. (For a fuller argument about the benefits of reading aloud, refer to Chapter 2.) For example:

- To read, we need to look at the print.
- If there are pictures or diagrams, we may pause to look at these.
- If reading a story book, we start at the front of the book. When reading factual texts and poetry, we do not always start at the front.
- Our eyes read from the top of each page and move down, although not on a regular letter-by-letter or word-by-word basis.
- Sometimes we reread to check that the text is making sense. We may even verbalize our confusion—"That didn't make sense"—and then reread.
- We may pause at an unfamiliar word and break it into parts to attempt a pronunciation.

Purposes We can read aloud to specifically demonstrate the following:

- English is read from left to right and progressively down the page or the column.
- Written language consists of letters, words, spaces, paragraphs, and headings.
- Reading involves making mistakes or miscues, pausing, reading on, and rereading.

Strategy As you read aloud, make explicit comments like the following:

> "I start reading at the top."
> "I'll read the next line."
> "I'll read the next page."
> "I'll read this paragraph again."
> "That didn't make sense. I'll read those words again."
> "I'll read this heading, *The Three Little Pigs*."
> "Oh, look at this long word. How do I pronounce that?"

Oral Cloze

Rationale Reading involves predicting the text ahead. You can develop this ability in young learners when you read aloud by occasionally stopping and having the children fill in the next word. This encourages the children to develop the nonvisual cue systems, that is, the semantic and the syntactic systems. As the children are listening to the story, if they are understanding, they should be able to predict ahead by drawing upon the meaning of the story and their knowledge of English grammar.

Purpose Oral cloze is used to develop in readers the ability to predict text by drawing upon the context of the text they're listening to.

Strategy Occasionally when you're reading aloud to your class, pause and let the children fill in the next word. Oral cloze best occurs near the end of a sentence, ensuring the listeners have sufficient context to be able to predict meaningfully.

Cloze Reading

Rationale Reading involves the eye taking a visual sample and the brain predicting the text ahead. The reader's syntactic and semantic knowledge inform the predictions he makes. Some predictions might differ from the text but not interfere with the meaning. Where the predictions do not make sense, the reader must reread. Structure cloze around whole texts with which the children are familiar, not as isolated exercises.

Purposes Cloze reading activities allow children to

- gain confidence as risk takers when reading individually
- use semantic and syntactic prediction while reading
- understand that reading is about making meaning
- understand that naming each word correctly is not the aim of reading

Strategy Paste sticky notes over several content words prior to reading a big book aloud to the children. When you reach each covered word, have individual children predict what the word might be and list these for all to see. This encourages the children to draw upon the context of the text to predict words ahead. For each word suggested by the children ask, "Does it make sense?" When there are three or four words on the list, remove the sticky note. Read the word and have the children check if it was on their class list. Then have the children use their other suggested words in the sentence to see if they are acceptable substitutions.

Repeated Readings of Early Storybooks and Rhymes

Rationale   Repeated readings incorporate the revisiting of text. Revisiting text is important in the early stages of reading because it gives the child an opportunity to fill out his understanding and then use this knowledge of the content to make links with the print.

   Repeated readings build a bridge for the child to move from memorization of a story to actually matching parts of the story to particular print features. The child learns the text by heart and knows from the pictures which print is on which page, knows where choruses are repeated, and so on. Familiarity enables the child to read the text for himself. Initially this reading will be by memory and the child's eyes will be on the pictures, which will trigger recall of the story or the text. Knowing a book by memory provides a point of reference for the child to begin to identify particular words. Having heard the story several times, the child's understanding of the plot and other issues is more highly developed, hence he is better able to predict the text. The more the child reads the book, the more likely it is he will recognize some of the print features, such as an italicized word, a repeated line, or a word starting like the child's name.

Purpose   Repeated readings assist emerging readers in being able to read early reading materials independently.

Strategy   Either use a big book with a small group or the whole class or have a very small group use a normal-sized book.

- Begin by reading the book aloud to the class. Discuss meanings.
- Read the book aloud again using some oral cloze of single words.
- Then read the book aloud using oral cloze of two to three words (for example, *the bag*).
- Next, have everyone read the book aloud together and then ask the children to reflect upon related life experiences.
- Finally, have individual children read the book aloud.

   Note that discussion of the content and clarification of meanings should be interwoven with the repeated readings.

Text Recomposition

Rationale   Text recomposition draws upon the child's knowledge of the content and the form of a familiar text to reconstruct it in sequence. In the reconstruction of early picture books, the illustrations are not included, requiring the child to focus more close-ly on the print to complete the reconstruction.

Purpose Text recomposition develops the visual reading strategies by having children reconstruct short, familiar texts such as rhymes and stories.

Strategy When a child is familiar with a simple text, be it factual or narrative or a poem, after repeated readings, write the text on large sentence strips. The task is for the child to recompose the text in the same order as the original text. Initially, you may see the child looking at the original text before looking for a particular strip. But it does not take long before the child looks straight to the sentence strips and distinguishes between particular print features, such as the first capital letters, enlarged words, final letters, and length of lines, in selecting the right sentence.

Language Experience

Rationale Language experience is where children's experiences, both in and out of school, are the source of language acquisition and development. Children experience something firsthand and then hear, speak, read, and write about the experience. Language experience is inclusive of children's lives—their cultures, their localities, their families. Sometimes you can write down the children's oral language for them, which the children can later read back. Sometimes you can have the children write first and then you can transcribe their work. As children use language to learn about their experiences, they are simultaneously learning language and learning about language. Texts written in children's language about their experiences are easy for them to read back, for in trying to predict the text, the children have the necessary experiential and linguistic knowledge. Language experience is particularly significant for those children whose life experiences differ from those of the mainstream child.

Purposes Language experience activities

- foster positive self-images in the students by centering classroom learning around their experiences
- make learning meaningful and relevant by incorporating children's life experiences into the curriculum and involving them in firsthand experiences in the classroom
- foster meaningful use of language (listening, speaking, reading, and writing) in the classroom
- develop meaningful reading materials particularly relevant to the children who helped create them
- make possible the use of the three cueing systems in reading by having children read materials written about their experiences in their natural language.

Strategies   One option is to have each child keep an experience journal in which he or she makes entries about his or her experiences. The child might draw or write first. Where the child's writing is not readable, ask the child's permission to write the text in conventional writing. Remember to write in the child's language, that is, write what the child has said. For example, following a bubble-blowing activity in the classroom, a five-year-old's sentence might be, "I blowed a great big bubble." Later the child might look at her accompanying picture to draw meaning for the writing. The child will reread the writing using both her experiential knowledge and her own language to predict the text.

   Another alternative is to create a class experience book. Write about a shared classroom experience for a group of children and then publish it as a class book for all the children to read. Have the children help with the illustrations. Put together smaller versions of the book so that each child has an individual copy of the text to illustrate and take home to read.

Using Pictorial Information to Read Text

Rationale   When artwork accompanies a text, it is there for a purpose, for example, to clarify the text or to provide information in addition to that provided in the writing. Therefore, in the process of making meaning, the reader draws upon the pictorial information as well as the print.

Purpose   When reading illustrated texts, children make use of those illustrations in their endeavors to make meaning of the text.

Strategy   When a child is reading to you and stops at a word that is clearly illustrated on the page, point to the item in the illustration and wait for the child to name the artwork. Then draw attention to the unknown word and have the child reread the sentence in full. For example, if a text reads, "The monkey stole the keys from the man's pocket," and the keys are evident in the artwork, the child stops before the word *keys*, and keys have not been part of the story before, it makes sense to refer the reader to the artwork.

Explicitly Talking About Reading Strategies

Rationale   The context of hearing a child read aloud is a pertinent time for you to explicitly advise the child to use contextual cues in identifying difficult text. When the child is reading aloud, you are able to hear the strategies she is using. Is the child sounding out each unknown word? Is the child rereading when miscues do not make sense? Are the child's miscues syntactically and semantically acceptable? What strategy could you suggest to the child to help her read?

Purpose   Explicitly suggesting strategies helps children use both visual and nonvisual strategies in reading to make meaning.

Strategies   When hearing a child read aloud, explicitly introduce strategies for the identification of unknown text. You can do this in a number of ways.

- Say, "Put in a word that makes sense," or "Read on, then go back and put in a word that makes sense," to require the reader to draw upon contextual information, either syntactic or semantic, to predict the text.
- Advise the child to put in a space filler, for example, "something," and keep reading. Then have the child reread, getting the text to make sense.
- Refer the child to pictorial material.
- Refer to the first letter or a word within a word. Sometimes a child knows the intended sense of a passage but can tell that his preferred word is not the one in the book. For example, a child may wish to insert *horse* when the correct word is *pony* in the following sentence: "Bobby rode his pony around the farm." Here, you could say, "*Horse* makes good sense. Do you know a smaller animal that looks like a horse and starts with *p*?"
- When a child miscues while reading aloud in such a way that meaning is lost and no self-correction occurs, ask, "Did that make sense?" then have the child reread and get the text to make sense.

Whichever strategy the child uses, it is important that the reader does not take too long trying to decode one word. If the child spends too much time on one word, he will forget the meaning he was building up, or what came before. It is better to tell a child an unknown word than have him lose meaning. Of course, proper nouns, such as children's names, cannot usually be predicted, so it is best to tell these to the children.

Reading Strategy List

Rationale   Listing on a classroom chart the strategies different children use to work out unknown text is an explicit way of promoting the range of strategies available and also informs the teacher of where her teaching may need to be directed (Kadyra 1999).

Purpose   Reading strategy lists display and promote the range of strategies students can employ in the identification of unknown words.

Strategy   Begin by putting a big book on display at the front of the classroom. It can be either a factual book or a storybook. Ask an individual child to begin reading. If the child makes a miscue or hesitates at an unknown word, note the child's name and the text word on a large chart. At the end of the child's reading, have *her* describe how she worked out the difficult word or why she used particular substitutions. Then list the strategies on a chart. Have a second child continue the reading, and repeat the process, building up a list of strategies actually used by the children.

This is quite powerful because the strategies are not being talked about in isolation, but are being demonstrated by individual children as they read a text large enough for all children to see and follow.

Print Search

Rationale   Print conventions such as punctuation, the use of capital letters, and paragraphs are best learned and understood as they are met in the context of whole text. Discussion of these items in the context of a whole text reveals the children's understandings as to why the conventions are there.

Purpose   A print search can help you evaluate across a grade the children's understandings of particular print conventions and give you direction for future teaching.

Strategy   Demonstrate the strategy to the whole class first, writing on a large chart. After reading a big book with the chidren and enjoying the meaning, conduct a print search. Open the book to one particular page and ask the children to look at the print and tell about the print items they recognize and know the purpose for. Gradually introduce the term *print conventions*. Record the children's findings on a large chart. For example:

> There's an "s" like in my name in "snake." (Sam)
>
> There's two words the same. (John, pointing to "zoo" and "zoo")
>
> There's a question mark after "town" because it's a question. (Mary)
>
> "John" starts with a big "J" because it's his name. (Duc)
>
> There are commas between "apple, carrot, lettuce." They are in a list. (Sam)
>
> There are talking marks where the dragon speaks. (Michelle)

After children have experienced doing this as a grade, some children will be able to do it individually.

After listening to *Lester and Clyde* by James Reece, Alex and Ellen, both grade 3, each completed a print search from a page of the text (see Figures 3–3 and 3–4). Notice how such an activity accepts children's existing knowledge and makes it possible for the teacher to teach from and build on such knowledge. Observe the different understandings that Alex and Ellen have about contractions.

Asking About Children's Understandings

Rationale   Children's writing tells us much about their understandings about spelling and other print conventions. It also proves very informative for teachers to ask children why they have written something the way that they have. Children's answers can then inform teaching.

Purpose   Ask questions to find out which strategies a child has used and why.

Strategy   This strategy is explained by way of example. Rebekah, grade 2, wrote the following short recount, set out in lines as shown here.

> I went To Swemeing it was Fun
> I Do Diveing I Do Baksrot to
> I go wef catheRine
> my ouD techa ust to Bey
> Kule

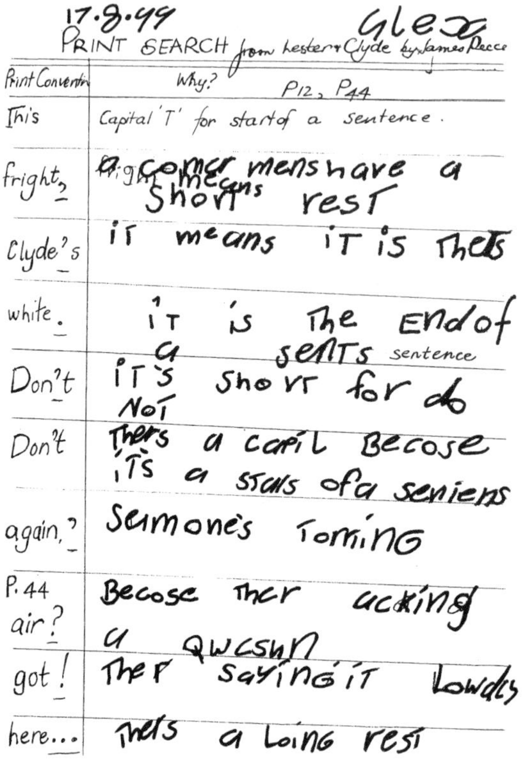

17.8.99 Alex

PRINT SEARCH from Lester & Clyde by James Reece

Print Convention	Why? P12, P44
This	Capital 'T' for start of a sentence.
fright,	comer means have a short rest
Clyde's	it means it is thers
white.	it is the End of a sents sentence
Don't	it's short for do Not
Don't	thers a capil Becose its a stats of a seniens
again, ?	Semone's torming
P. 44 air?	Becose ther acking a qwesun
got!	Ther saying it lowdly
here...	thers a loing rest

Figure 3–3 Print Search, Alex

Translation:

> I went to swimming. It was fun.
> I do diving. I do backstroke too.
> I go with Catherine.
> My old teacher used to be
> Kelly.

I asked her to try to put in the full stops. This is what she did:

> I went To Swemeing it was Fun
> I Do Diveing I Do Baksrot to.
> I go wef catheRine
> my ouD techa ust to Bey.
> Kule

Note that two full stops were inserted by Rebekah. I asked her why she put the full stops where she did and she replied, "Two lines would be a full stop." One might wonder how Rebekah came to such an understanding regarding the positioning of full stops!

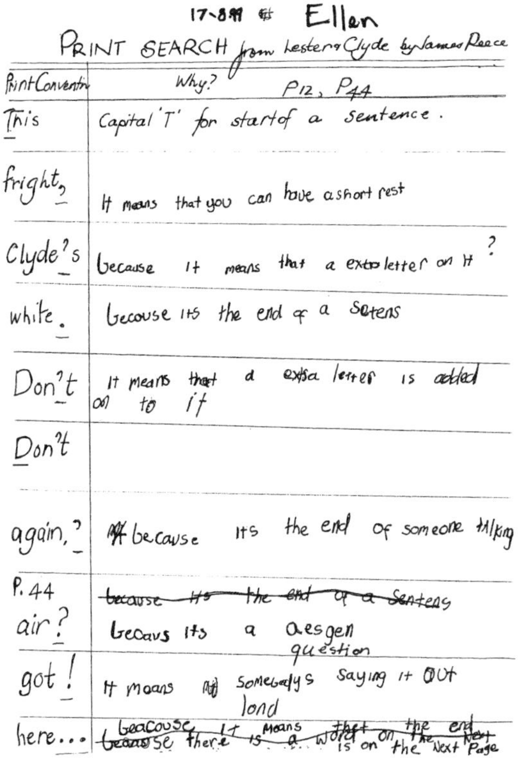

17-8-99 Ellen

PRINT SEARCH from Lester & Clyde by James Reece

Print Convention	Why? P12, P44
This	Capital 'T' for start of a sentence.
fright,	It means that you can have a short rest
Clyde's	because it means that a extra letter on it ?
white.	becouse its the end of a Setens
Don't	It means that a exsa letter is added on to it
Don't	
again,'	because its the end of someone talking
P. 44 air?	~~because its the end of a Sentens~~ becavs its a aesgen question
got!	It moans somebodys saying it out lond
here...	~~becaouse there is a word~~ is on the Next Page / Beacouse It Means ~~that on the end~~

Figure 3–4 Print Search, Ellen

We proceeded then and there to look at text in picture books, first just with Rebekah finding the full stops and checking if they were indeed at the end of every second line. I next read the book aloud to her and whenever I reached a full stop, we talked about why the full stop might have been there.

It is so important that we let children approximate in their learning and that we talk with them about what they have done, so that our teaching can start with their current understandings.

Listening to Rhymes

Rationale It is very important to read rhymes and chants aloud and say them together in any early literacy program because such texts play with the sounds of the language. In rhymes, one, two, or more sounds are repeated again and again, and hence these texts are important in bringing children to an awareness of the sounds of the language.

Purpose Immersing children in rhyme facilitates in children the development of phonemic awareness.

Strategy Introduce nursery rhymes, movement rhymes, rhymes that tell stories, noisy rhymes, funny rhymes, and, in fact, all sorts of other rhymes in the classroom. Write the rhymes on large charts and read them aloud yourself first. Then have the children join in if they are familiar with the rhyme. Read the rhymes in different ways:

- in high voices, in low voices
- in loud voices, in quiet voices
- in parts
- with actions

When the children are thoroughly familiar with a particular rhyme, ask them to identify the rhyming words. Write these words on a chart. On following days, have the children add other words that sound the same to the list.

Learning Letter Names and the Alphabet

Rationale   Becoming literate involves knowing the alphabet and making use of the letters.

Purpose   The purpose of this activity is for children to learn the alphabet and recognize and be able to name each of the letters of the alphabet.

Strategies   Choose one or more of the following strategies:

- Teach the students an alphabet song.
- Put the alphabet on display in your classroom at a height children can see easily.
- Attach an alphabet strip to each work table.
- Draw attention to the letters in a child's name. For example:
  "Who else has a name starting with the letter *s*?"
  "Who can find the letter *s* on the alphabet strip?"
  "Does anyone have a letter *s* anywhere else in his or her name?"
- If all the children's names are on cards, the children can use the pack of cards for sorting the names into groups, such as first-letter groups (e.g., all the names starting with the letter *m*) and end-letter groups (e.g. all the names ending with the letter *y*), or put them in alphabetical order.
- Keep several alphabet books in the classroom. Primary classrooms should have several attractive alphabet books for the children to peruse. Alphabet books and lists can be compiled by the children as part of integrated classwork. During a topic such as animals, all children could first compile a list of animals, then sort the animal names according to first letter, and later sequence them in alphabetical order. These could be published in a class animal alphabet book.

Study of Sound-Letter Patterns (Phonics)

Rationale   Knowledge of sound-letter relationships is one of the cueing systems used when reading and is important when spelling. Study of sound-letter patterns is done best in the context of known words or when conferencing about invented spellings with children.

Purposes   One purpose of such study is to foster understanding that

- sounds are represented by letters in words
- in English, letters may represent more than one sound
- in English, the same sound may be represented by different letter combinations
- different speakers of the one language pronounce some words differently and thus give different sound values to particular letters

It also helps children to develop knowledge about the particular sound-letter relationships of the English language.

Strategies

1. Invented Spelling   One way to help children study sound-letter relationships is to encourage invented spelling. Children should write from the day they enter school, not to practice penmanship but to convey meaning, or to compose. Of course, some children may scribble or use invented symbols or strings of letters. But given the opportunity to write frequently for real purposes, children will approximate writing conventions. Their invented spelling will show their understandings of phonics and other spelling strategies. Their invented spellings are not random and when understood show much logic at work as the young learners experiment and form and test hypotheses, all in the process of moving toward conventional spelling.

When children are first discovering sound-letter relationships, it can be very revealing to sit next to a child as he writes and after each line of writing ask what he has written. This way, you can transcribe the child's writing before he forgets the exact word order, and often, very intelligent phonic connections will be revealed.

The teachers of a double K–2 class asked me to work individually with a seven-year-old in their class. They were concerned because they were still unable to make any sense of his strings of letters. This is what he wrote in the session with me:

IMOeORDS	I'm going to the doctor's.
IDeBLe	I don't hear properly.
IMOeORSRL	I am going to a hospital
OeAORASND	to get an operation.
NVSRNVRSE	And that's the end of the story.

In this privileged situation of one teacher working beside one child, it became evident how much this child knew, despite having hearing problems. (The hearing deficiency, coincidentally, was raised by the child in this session.) There is only one letter I cannot account for in this piece of writing, and that is the *D* at the end of line 4 after ORASN (operation).

Throughout, the boy was consistently relating letters to sounds he heard. For example, he used the letter *r* for *a* (as in *a* hospital, in line 3) and for *the* in lines 1 and

5. He used the letter *d* for *don't* in line 2. He used the letter *e* for *hear* in line 2. He used the letter *v* for the *th* of *that's* and the *f* of *of* in line 5.

He knew the same words are spelled the same way. For example, he spelled *going* as *oe* in lines 1 and 3. He represented more than the first sound of some words. For example, he used *BLe* for *properly* and *ORASN* for *operation*.

Sitting next to this child as he wrote and talking with him about his writing after each line revealed much about what he knew about writing, his phonic generalizations, and his needs.

2. *Demonstrate sounding out words as a spelling strategy* Another activity is to demonstrate sounding out words as a spelling strategy. Children learn language as they watch demonstrations of language in use. As you demonstrate writing in front of young learners, you demonstrate many things, all in the context of writing for some authentic purpose. For example, you show them the directional features of written English, spacing between words, punctuation, appropriate beginnings, and much more. Writing in front of young learners is also an opportunity to demonstrate the sound-it-out spelling strategy.

While demonstrating writing in front of the class, occasionally sound out a word you are writing. Do not deliberately sound out every word as you write, but occasionally pause before a new word and say it out loud: "morning." Say the word slowly, perhaps breaking it into syllables, "morn-ing," and ask the children what it might start with. When you have the *m* written, focus on the next sound and so on. When you ask the children for help, they will often excitedly call out their preferred letters. You may notice that children will start offering correct letters for sounds needed in your writing before they begin making sound-letter connections in their own.

3. *Build on Known Patterns* A third strategy is to build on known patterns. Some spelling generalizations are transferable. Being able to spell one word may mean one can spell a group of related words. Studies show children can hear the onsets and rimes in words before they can hear each single sound. Hence, when they can read or write a particular word, you can ask them to apply knowledge about this one word in the identification of other words with like onsets or rimes. Children's spelling confidence is increased when they realize they can spell not only one particular word but also other similar words. You can also extend children's word identification and spelling abilities by having them read words with onset or rime patterns similar to those of words they know.

Either when working with an individual child or a group, select words the children can read or write and write these words out separately. Then write next to each word other words of a similar pattern. Ask the children to try reading the new words. For example:

Dad	bad, sad
car	far, bar
short	port, sort

4. Build a Word Wall A word wall can help you promote discussion of sound-letter relationships in words known by the children. Sound-letter relationships are best discussed in the context of known words, so a collection of the children's favorite words forms a good basis for discovering particular sound-letter patterns.

Pin words children are interested in (their names, their suburb) or words that occur frequently on a word wall in alphabetical order. Add words to the wall only when the children are watching. Children will suggest many of the words to be added to the wall. Once children can read the words, use a group of words for sorting. For example, remove all the words beginning with the letter *c* and have children sort them into groups according to the first sound in each word. Encourage the children to identify the differing sound-letter relationships.

car	circle	church
come	Cindy	cheese
computer		chocolate

5. Compile Class Word Lists A similar strategy is to compile class word lists. In contrast to a traditional skills program, whole language classrooms have no predetermined sequence for the introduction of particular sounds or letters into the teaching program. Rather, in holistic classrooms where children experience a wealth of language experiences, the teacher observes and builds upon children's discoveries. By developing class lists of the children's discoveries about sound-letter relationships, you can draw attention to phonic patterns.

Begin by simply listening to the children's sound-letter discoveries. Four- or five-year-old children are alert to the first letters of their names. Hence, it is common to hear a young child say, "That starts like my name," or "That's *l*. My name starts with *l*." Whenever you hear young children make observations of this kind, follow them up. For example, start a letter *l* chart. Ask all the children to contribute words that have the letter *l* in them. When you value children's discoveries and build upon them, you inspire them to be alert for new letter and word discoveries. Compile the lists with the children watching. On later days, individuals may add additional words to the list. I sometimes hear one child say to another at writing time, "You'll find that word on our animal list," or "You'll find it on the double letter list."

It must be very confusing for young children to join classrooms where the walls are covered with word lists at the commencement of the school year. Sometimes the charts are faded and dusty, having hung in the same tired positions for many years. So many words! How is a five-year-old meant to navigate all those lists? Such resources are not used by the children. It is wise to remember that classrooms are living, growing entities. They are not museums.

6 Study Rhyming Words Yet another way to develop phonic understandings is to study rhyming words. Rhyme plays with and repeats particular language sounds.

Exposure to rhyme is important in developing phonemic awareness. Reading rhymes provides opportunities for the study of rhyming words—the sounds and the letters representing the sounds.

Display a rhyme in large print in front of the children. Have the children read and enjoy the rhyme. It may be read in parts or acted out. When the children are familiar with the rhyme, ask them to name the rhyming words. List these on a chart. Then ask them to add other words that rhyme with those on the list. For example, from the nursery rhyme "Jack and Jill," the list might begin with *Jill* and *hill*. Then children might add *pill, dill, will, spill, until, mill, fill*, and *pterodactyl*. Next ask them to identify the rhyming sound of all these words. Finish by having them name the letters representing the rhyming sound in each word, for example *ill* for *pill, il* for *until*, and *yl* for *pterodactyl*.

Word Sorts

Rationale   Children's knowledge about words, including capitalization, sounds, letters, syllables, and base words, can be developed through the study and the classification of known words.

Purposes   The sorting and grouping of known words develops children's knowledge of sound-letter relationships, syllabification, and the difference between upper- and lowercase letters.

Strategy   Have the children use collections of words that are important to them to make word groups using different criteria. In early primary classrooms, the children's names may be the first words sorted by a group of children. First, allow the children to form groups of words according to criteria of their choosing, for example, long names and short names. This reveals much about individual children's print understandings. Then give them the sorting criteria. Examples include the following:

>   names with the same first letter (Sam, Sally, Stephanie)
>   names with the same first sound (Ken, Chris, Kelly, Cathy)
>   names with the same number of letters (Ken, Duc, Tom; Christine, Alexandra)
>   names with double letters (Sally, Matthew, Holly, Lorraine)
>   names that have a common sound (John, Tom, Wally)
>   names that have the same number of syllables (Ken, Duc; Andrew, Leanne; Samantha, Agatha)

Reading Organizational Print Features

Rationale   Being able to access and decode texts involves knowing about particular organizing features.

Purpose   The purpose of this activity is to inform students about particular text organizational features of the informational report genre through demonstration.

Strategy As part of integrated reading in social studies and science, discuss organizational features of relevant texts in the context of finding answers to children's questions. Demonstrate how to read and make use of features such as tables of contents, indexes, headings, labelled diagrams, glossaries, and graphs. Some of these demonstrations can occur with big books.

Evaluation

To evaluate a child's code-breaking strategies, observe a child as she reads. Note whether the child's eyes are on the print or the pictures. Then watch and listen to see if the child

holds the book the right way

observes conventional print directions

finger points, showing one-to-one word correspondence

retells the book from memory

predicts semantic and syntactic substitutions by drawing upon context

makes only visual miscues (Note: This is not positive.)

uses graphophonics as a checking strategy

self-corrects miscues that do not make sense

ignores syntactically and semantically acceptable miscues

stops and rereads if unsure of meaning

uses tables of contents, indexes, glossaries, headings, and so on appropriately in accessing text

focuses on making meaning

In addition, observe what the child does when confronted with unknown words. Does she refer to artwork? Skip the word and keep reading, or start the sentence again, trying to draw upon the context to insert a meaningful word? Sound the word out? Break the word into parts?

You must also observe the child as she writes. Note whether the child has an understanding of directional print features.

Does the writing progress in lines?

Does the writing move from the left to the right on the page?

Does the writing move from the top to the bottom of the page?

Is the writing scribble or invented symbols or letters?

Check to see if she has understanding of sound-symbol relationships. Does she:

represent the first sound of most words?

first and the last sounds?

consonantal sounds?

vowel sounds?

represent sounds for each syllable?

spell some words conventionally?

In addition, note whether she uses:

items of punctuation correctly

text features such as numbers for sequence, headings, table of contents, labelled diagrams, and so on

Summary: Learning to Code Break

Code breaking is just one of four possible reading practices. Being able to code break takes the reader into the text. Code breaking by itself has no value. Code breaking is always meant to access meaning and make text use possible. To be critically literate, one must be able to access text.

Successful code breaking involves the reader drawing upon both visual and nonvisual information and making use of redundancy in text. Code breaking is learned as children are read aloud quality texts, as they revisit familiar texts, as they observe experienced readers and writers reading and writing, and as they read and write for themselves. In other words, the teaching of code breaking occurs in the context of the teaching of reading and writing. The learning of code-breaking strategies occurs as children are engaged with reading and writing as part of their classroom investigations and daily lives.

References

Coles, G. 2000. "'Direct, Explicit, and Systematic'—Bad Reading Science." *Language Arts* 77 (6): 544.

Goodman, K. 1967. "Reading: A Psycholinguistic Guessing Game." *Journal of the Reading Specialist*: 126–35.

———. 1993. *Phonic Phacts*. Ontario, Canada: Scholastic.

Goodman, K., and Y. Goodman. 1977. "Learning About Psycholinguistic Processes by Oral Reading." *Harvard Educational Review* 47 (3): 317–33.

Henderson, J. 1993. "Anabranch or Billabong." *Australian Journal of Language and Literacy* 16 (2): 119–35.

Kadyra, M. 1999. "Which Reading Strategies?" *Practically Primary* 4 (2): 17–18.

Luke, A., and P. Freebody. 1999. "A Map of Possible Practices: Further Notes on the Four Resources Model." *Practically Primary* 4 (2): 5–8.

Moustafa, M. 1997. *Beyond Traditional Phonics: Research Discoveries and Reading Instructions.* Portsmouth, NH: Heinemann.

"Reading the Signs and Following the Tracks." 1999. Editor's introduction. *Practically Primary* 4 (2): 3.

Scholes, R. 1998. "The Case Against Phonemic Awareness." *Journal of Research in Reading* 21 (3).

Smith, F. 1999. "Why Systematic Phonics and Phonemic Awareness Instruction Constitute an Education Hazard." *Language Arts* 77 (2): 153.

Children's Books

Reece, J. 1976. *Lester and Clyde*. Auckland, Ashton: Scholastic.

Chapter 4

TEXT PARTICIPANT: MAKING MEANING

In short the [child as] meaning maker metaphor puts the student at the center of the learning process. It makes both possible and acceptable a plurality of meanings, for the environment does not exist only to impose standardized meanings but rather to help students improve their unique meaning making capabilities.

> —NEIL POSTMAN AND CHARLES WEINGARTNER (1969, 99)

[An approach to literature] should not simply assert that there is one meaning (that of the author and the text) nor that there are limitless meanings, but that the world of the text and the world of the reader intersect in complex ways so that there are a set of contemporary and communal readings of text.

> —ALAN PURVES (1993, 360)

Readers as Meaning Makers

When the reader as code breaker enters the text, he becomes a text participant (Luke and Freebody 1999) and integrates these two reading practices until he reaches the end of the text. (Of course, the reader might also be reading as text user and text analyst, but my focus in this chapter is the reader as text participant.) With some books, we are actually participating before we begin code breaking. For example, when we read a title from a series of books from which we have read other titles, we often predict ahead what might have happened to the characters since we left them in the last book before we even open the new book. We might ponder their developing relationships, for example.

Because each one of us has different life experiences and different values, we bring different baggage with us when we participate in text. Think for a moment of a newspaper report that attacks literacy levels and lays the blame on new teaching methods. We of the teaching profession may bristle at such a report because our considerable expertise informs us that such reports are false. However, many parents of young children will not make this same meaning. They may become increasingly nervous about the potential of their local school to successfully bring their young children to literacy. On the other hand, the commercial publisher of a quick-fix literacy program will react with yet another interpretation. She may rub her hands with glee as she forsees increased sales and company profits.

Even readers of one-word texts do not make the same meanings. Think for a moment of the stop sign positioned on street corners. What does that mean to you? For some drivers, it means bring the car to a stationary position. For others, it means slow to a crawl but keep moving if no other vehicles are coming. Yet for other drivers, it means keep driving but be prepared to blast the horn or apply the brakes quickly!

How many more meanings must be possible for works of literature? A storybook has characters from different cultures, set in different countries, perhaps in other times. Any of these is the cause for multiple perspectives from a class of children, all with differing life experiences, and the addition of the plot and the actions taken by the characters creates even more possible interpretations.

Australian children's author Libby Gleeson (2000) talks of stories as places to play. She attributes this idea to Geoff Williams. He likened stories to "adventure playgrounds in which the nature of the game is strongly influenced but not wholly determined by the structures available. We can't just play any game around the structures, but there is also not just one game we are allowed to play" (Gleeson 2000, 5). I like this analogy; as there are many ways to play on an adventure playground, so are there many meanings to make once inside a good story.

Text Participation and Text Purpose

Text participation (Luke and Freebody 1999), or comprehension, or making meaning, occurs throughout a reading event. It is not something done at the end when the text is finished. Depending on the text type, the participation may vary. A chef reading a new recipe may be thinking of the ingredients she will need to purchase before making the recipe. Another reader, while reading a crime novel, may be predicting who the villain is. A child reading a Dr. Seuss story may be laughing as she reads.

The ways we make meaning or understand a text are linked directly with our reading purposes, which in turn are linked to the types of text we are reading. If a child is reading instructions to play an electronic game, the measure of success will be his ability to play the game without looking at the directions. There is no need to administer a multiple-choice reading test to discover if the child has understood!

It does sometimes occur that a reader's purposes are externally determined and this has the potential to inhibit and control the way the reader may participate. Think what happens when teachers give students novels to read for the purpose of answering literal or comprehension questions or writing an essay. Of course, enjoyment of the novel is ruined, for the reader's preferred way of participating by relaxing, or escaping, or imagining, or responding personally, is derailed.

A further anecdote about Nicholas: When he was three, we went to the zoo together. Each time we came to a signpost pointing the way to different displays, I read aloud the options and he chose where we would next proceed. One of his final choices was the reptile enclosure. The reptiles were housed in glass-fronted, sealed enclosures. The first enclosure housed a rather large snake that was sleeping. Nicholas tapped on the glass, trying to attract the snake's attention. I drew his attention to a sign attached to the glass. "The sign says, 'Do not tap the glass,'" I said as I pointed to the words. He silently observed the words.

We proceeded to work our way from reptile enclosure to reptile enclosure. Nicholas did not attempt to tap the glass again. However, when we got to the very last enclosure, which contained several small crocodiles, Nicholas noticed that there was no sign on the glass. He turned toward me and said, 'It doesn't say, 'Do not tap the glass.'" Without waiting for my response, he proceeded to tap the glass and talk to the crocodiles. Nicholas' actions revealed how well he had understood or participated with the signs on the glass of the reptile enclosures, and as well his willingness to comply with the direction. This was reading for living!

A Lifelong Love of Reading

All teaching of reading must be with the intent of developing lifelong readers. There is no point in anyone reading if the intent is not to understand or to make meaning. Meaning is central to all reading lessons. If children can see no point in learning to read, why should they even try?

Some class reading activities do little to contribute to a lifelong love of reading because they are without meaning. Where the reading lesson is exactly the same boring routine each day, where reading lessons focus on isolated bits of language and never on whole texts, and where children complete busywork on worksheets, sadly, learning to read will be the last thing on these children's wish lists. The activities just mentioned are pseudo reading activities. They provide no joy. They contribute nothing positive to the children's lives. They are not for living. They will never contribute to a lifelong love of reading. Imagine if all the hours spent doing worksheets were replaced by teachers who love literature, reading aloud to their students—what an impact this would have on children's reading! What an impact it would have on their lives.

Children's Questions

If children are meaning makers and bring their own understandings to text, *they* must formulate questions in response to *their* puzzles, uncertainties, and interests so their interpretation of the text can grow. "We must critically examine the egocentric notion that our teacher-posed questions and text interpretations will further students' understandings better than letting them discuss the questions they think should be considered" (Commeyras and Sumer 1996, 264).

It is important that from the earliest stages of learning to read, young learners are encouraged to interact with and to ask questions of text. This says to these young readers that the texts are there for them; they can have fun with them, they can learn from them, they can criticize them. This practice of having children ask questions of text puts each child at the center of his learning. The curriculum starts with the child, his needs, and his interests and not with a teaching manual that sets out the questions for the teacher to ask.

Of course, this does not mean that the teacher cannot ask questions. The teacher must ask questions that prod unexplored issues, deepen understanding, and seek alternate points of view. The teacher may also demonstrate types of questions not being asked by the children.

Strategies for Text Participation

Predict the Story

Rationale   Reading is not word naming. Having children predict what a text might be about develops the expectation that text is about something, that readers read to make meaning.

Purpose   The purpose of this activity is to have children predict what a story might be about from information conveyed in the title.

Strategy   Begin by reading the title of the story and showing the cover art. Ask individual children to say briefly what they think the story will be about. Record each child's prediction along with the child's name. Read the story and then refer to the earlier predictions and check whether any were true. Ask the successful predictors what made them predict as they did. You might also have the children discuss whether the title was appropriate for the story.

Children Ask Questions

Rationale   In the process of reading to make meaning, readers constantly answer puzzles and questions that come to mind. Sometimes they stop and reread to find answers to these puzzles. If our aim is to develop child readers who are meaning makers, we should value the children's questions and help them find answers to these questions, rather than always having them answer teacher-posed questions. Imagine as adults how we would feel if every time we finished a novel we had to answer questions posed by someone else.

Purpose   This activity encourages children to ask questions of texts.

Strategies   If using this strategy with the whole class, before reading a story or a factual text to the class, tell the children that at the end you will be listing all their questions, uncertainties, and puzzles about the text. Then read the text. After reading, list on a large chart the children's questions, noting the name of each questioner. Start with the more literal questions, and have someone from the whole group offer an answer. For the more interpretive questions, ask the questioners to move to different spots on the carpet. Have other classmates choose a question to discuss and then join the appropriate questioner. Usually, this means five or six small groups sitting around the classroom with group members discussing just one child's question. Have them share their individual interpretations and help the questioner reach an answer she is happy with.

When the whole class meets back together, ask each questioner to report on some of the solutions offered by classmates and share the answer he or she has now come to. I share an example of this strategy from a K–2 classroom. The text was an award-winning children's picture storybook, *John Brown, Rose and the Midnight Cat* by Jenny Wagner. It tells of an elderly lady, Rose, who lives alone with her dog, John Brown. One night Rose notices a cat outside her window. She asks the dog to let it in. The dog will not. John Brown keeps refusing further requests to let in the cat. One night Rose puts out a saucer of milk. When she is not looking, the dog tips it out. Then the old lady takes to staying in bed, day after day after day. In the end, John Brown lets the cat in and Rose is happy.

Following are some of the questions the children asked. I have included just some of the answers proffered by different children. There were no answers to these questions anywhere in the book.

> *How did her husband die?* (Nicola)
> They lived in the country so I think he was bitten.
> He might have been run over by a tractor.
>
> *How did the dog talk?* (Tim)
> The old lady understood dog language.
> It was a secret between the old lady and the dog that the dog could talk.

Why did the dog want the cat to stay outside? (Blossom)

He thought Granny wouldn't play with him.

He was frightened the cat would scratch him.

He didn't like cats.

How come the cat wanted to come inside? (Jack)

He was cold and lonely.

He wanted to sit in a warm chair.

He was a stray.

Why was the Granny sick? (Joska)

She was allergic to dog fur.

When the children ask the questions and all children work in small groups to help find answers, so much more thinking and learning occurs than when the teacher asks two or three questions and finds several children to guess her answers. The questions and answers listed previously are an insight into the children's minds.

When children read independently, they should be asking their own questions as they read. They should ask questions of both fiction and nonfiction texts. Sometimes the use of sticky notes helps. Children can write their questions on a sticky note and paste it on the page where the question is relevant. Then when it is time for children to discuss their questions in their small groups they are readily able to find the relevant page of text. (See also Chapter 8.)

What's on Your Mind?

Rationale   Responding personally to literature is a way of learning about ourselves and the world around us. Children read literature for their own purposes, not just those of the teacher. Teachers must ensure that literature activities do not strangle and repress individual interpretations. They must ensure that their teaching does not imply that there is only one interpretation of any piece of literature.

Purpose   This activity gives children some room to move in their response to literature; they may interpret the story or explain the author's theme or reflect on related life experiences or perhaps make comparisons with some other work of literature.

Strategy   After children have heard or read a story, a poem, or a news report, ask them to respond in writing to the following prompt: "Write what's on your mind after listening to/reading the poem/story." This is a wonderful stimulus for gaining personal responses from the children. It is open-ended enough to allow the children to discuss the text if they so wish or to reflect upon related life experiences if they prefer. I find it is in responding in this way that children reveal many of their fears and worries; they really do bring their lives into the classroom.

"New Baby Poem 2" by Eloise Greenfield   In one K–2 class, I read "New Baby Poem 2," which evokes gentle, warm, protective feelings about a baby falling asleep. I read the poem aloud to the children twice. The second time I had them close their eyes and let their bodies feel. I then gave the children copies of the poem and had them read it quietly with a friend. Following I gave them the prompt, "What's on your mind after listening to the poem?" For these younger learners, I added by way of clarification, "Write what the poem makes you think about." The responses shown in Figures 4–1 through 4–5 are all first-draft responses.

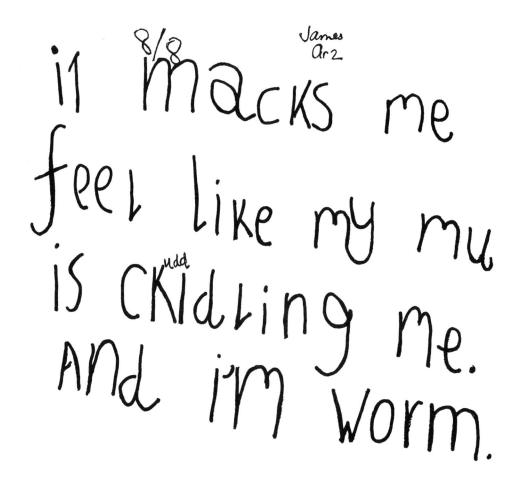

It makes me feel like my mom is cuddling me. And I'm warm.

Figure 4–1 James, Grade 2

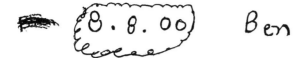

Ben

it makse me Felle
Like I am in aBaythe
With BuBols in it
An.D iam Flowting on
air
are AND with comfy comfy cushions
ens a rowend me Kosh
around

It makes me feel like I am in a bath with bubbles in it and I am floating on air, and with comfy cushions around me.

Figure 4–2 Ben, Grade 2

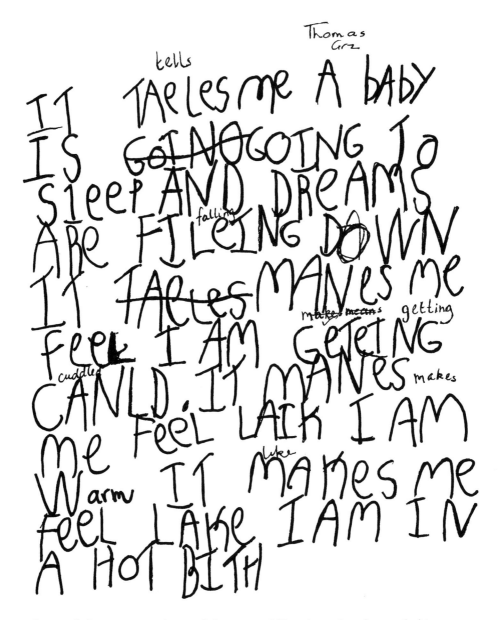

It tells me a baby is going to sleep and dreams are falling down. It makes me feel I am getting cuddled. It makes me feel like I am warm. It makes me feel like I am in a hot bath.

Figure 4–3 Thomas, Grade 2

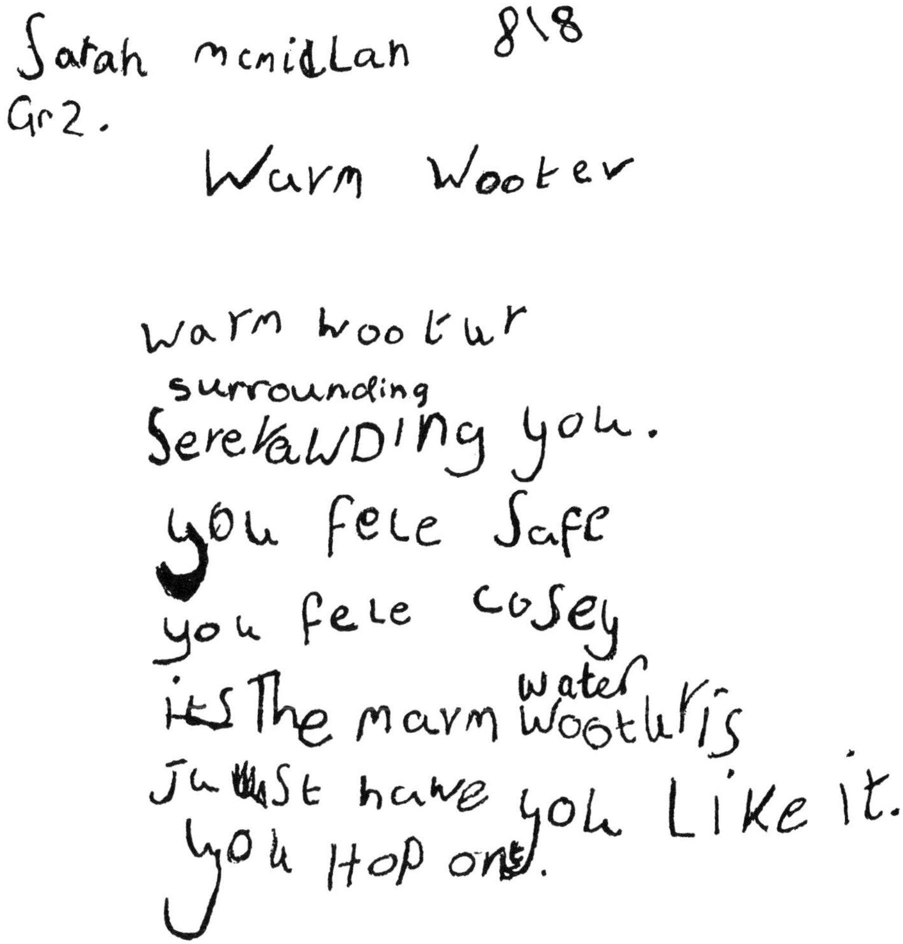

Sarah mcmillan   8\8
Gr2.
            Warm Wooter

warm wootur
  surrounding
SerekawDing you.
you fele Safe
you fele cosey
                    water
its The marm wooturis
Ju mst hawe you Like it.
  you Hop ond.

Warm Water

Warm, water
surrounding you.
You feel safe.
You feel cozy.
The warm water is
just how you like it.
You hop out.

Figure 4–4 Sarah, Grade 2

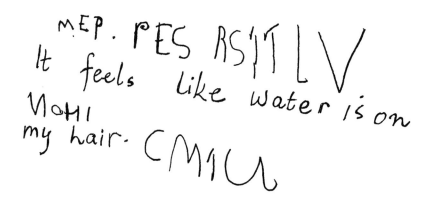

It feels like water is on my hair.

Figure 4–5 Tim, Kindergarten

***"It Is Grey Out"* by Karla Kuskin**   In another class, we looked at "It Is Grey Out," a nonrhyming poem of eight lines about a gray day and the grayness within the speaker.

The poem was written on a large chart for all these grades 2–3 children to see. I read the poem twice and asked them to respond to the following prompt: "What's on your mind after listening to the poem?" One child wrote this poem:

> Sleeping on the coch
> The phone ringing
> Mum answing it.
> Dad getting up
> Mum and dad siting
> Next to me
> Telling me my girtgat (grandma)
> Had died

> Trying to dig dip into
> the couch trying
> not to cry
> But I new there was
> nothing I cuod do

—Laura, grade 3

Note the depth of personal involvement in Laura's response. Sadly, machine-marked multiple-choice tests cannot process this level of reader participation and involvement with literature.

The Next Place by Warren Harrison   Open-ended teaching strategies are right for learners of all ages. This same strategy of responding to "What's on your mind after reading this story/poem?" is equally worth using with older as with the younger children. *The Next Place* is a picture storybook written in poetic language, with beautiful, ethereal artwork. The text does not tell a narrative but rather gives a description of what might be an afterlife. I read this aloud twice to a grades 5–6 class. The students were entranced. Then I asked them to repond to the prompt "Write what's on your mind after listening to the book." Figures 4–6 through 4–11 on pages 84–87 show several student's responses.

The responses to *The Next Place* illustrate the value of this strategy. The open-ended nature of the instruction allowed children to respond in very individual ways. Some reflected on related life experiences. For example, Hannah reflected on the grandparents she never met. (Text Participant)

Some took a critical literacy perspective. For example, Eugene acknowledged that there are many religions that believe in other lives and then suggested that the author is a member of one such religion. (Text Analyst) He also looked at his own beliefs about an afterlife. "No one knows if there is or there isn't a life after death. So many people believe in it. It's good listening to these things because we can only guess." One senses his inner struggle about what he believed. (Text User)

Some students, such as Adele and Jacqui, used writing to come to understand the ideas in the text. Sam identified an author message to him. "It told me to explore other areas." I wonder if he will heed this advice.

Still others, like Darcy, used this opportunity to play around with the style of writing. He also explains what he thought the author was saying. (Text Participant)

Give Advice to a Character

Rationale   Sometimes when stories are read aloud, some children daydream on the fringe of the group; they are not absolutely involved. When children are given a focus for their listening, it helps them participate more fully with the story.

Purpose   This activity encourages children to participate with the characters in a story by offering them advice.

the Next Place

22/3/00

Hannah

Towards the start of the book I felt like I was in a dreem I had when I was 4 or 5, I'm alone but I'm not londy, the places that I go to are femilier but I have never seen before. I felt like I was asleep and awake at the same times, I was in dreem land but in controll of w dremped

Towards the end I thaut about of my dead grand-perents Marie and brien of whom I've never met but of Youland impeticular who died in when I was in grade 3.

All throug I felt more relaxt than I have in a long time. I think others are relaxed to it has not been so quiet in here (when kids are in here) for 2 years.

It puts me in the mood to just sit and day dream

Towards the start of the book I felt like I was in a dream I had when I was 4 or 5. I'm alone but I'm not lonely, the places that I go to are familiar, but I have never seen them before. I felt like I was asleep and awake at the same time. I was in dreamland but in control of what I dreamed.

Towards the end I thought about my dead grandparents Marie and Brian of whom I've never met but of Yoland in particular, who died when I was in grade 3.

All through I felt more relaxed than I have in a long time. I think others are relaxed too. It has not been so quiet in here (when kids are in here) for 2 years.

It puts me in the mood to just sit and daydream.

Figure 4–6 Hannah, Grade 6

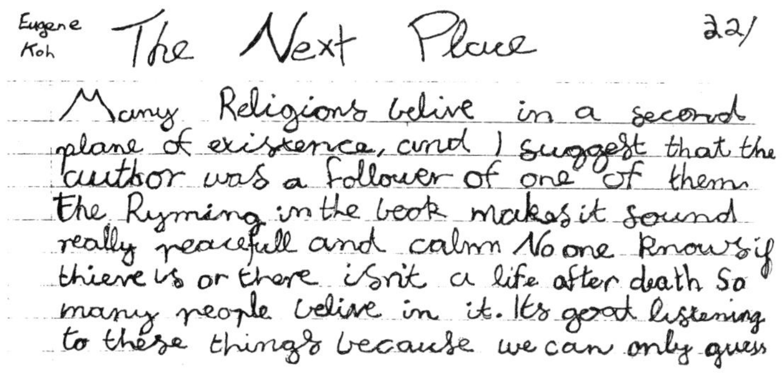

Eugene
Koh

The Next Place 22/

Many Religions belive in a second plane of existence, and I suggest that the author was a follower of one of them. The Ryming in the book makes it sound really peacefull and calm No one knows if thiere is or there isn't a life after death So many people belive in it. Its good listening to these things because we can only guess

Many religions believe in a second place of existence and I suggest that the author was a follower of one of them. The rhyming in the book makes it sound really peaceful and calm. No one knows if there is or there isn't a life after death. So many people believe in it. It's good listening to these things because we can only guess.

Figure 4–7 Eugene, Grade 6

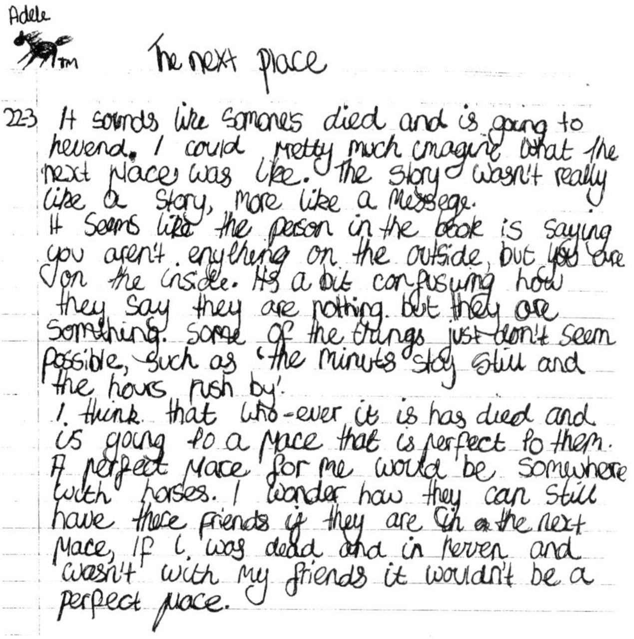

Adele

he next place

223 It sounds like somone's died and is going to hevend. I could pretty much imagine what the next place was like. The story wasn't really like a story, more like a message.
It seems like the person in the book is saying you aren't enything on the outside, but you are on the inside. Its a bit confusing how they say they are nothing. but they are something. some of the things just don't seem possible, such as 'the minuts stay still and the hours rush by'.
I think. that who-ever it is has died and. is going to a place that is perfect to them. A perfect place for me would be somewhere with horses. I wonder how they can still have there friends if they are in the next place, if i. was dead and in heven and wasn't with my friends it wouldn't be a perfect place.

It sounds like someone's died and is going to Heaven. I could pretty much imagine what the next place was like. The story wasn't really like a story, more like a message.
It seems like the person in the book is saying you aren't anything on the outside, but you are on the inside. It's a bit confusing how they say they are nothing but they are something. Some of the things just don't seem possible, such as "the minutes stay still and the hours rush by."
I think that whoever it is has died and is going to a place that is perfect for them. A perfect place for me would be somewhere with horses. I wonder how they can still have their friends if they are in the next place. If I were dead and in Heaven and wasn't with my friends it wouldn't be a perfect place.

Figure 4–8 Adele, Grade 6

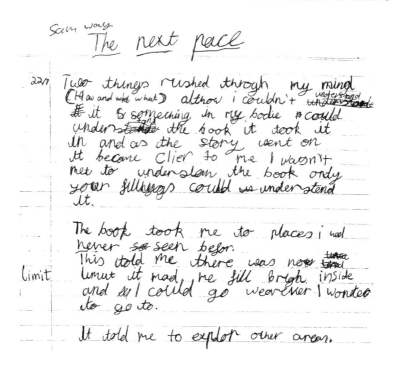

Two things rushed through my mind (how and what); although I couldn't understand it, something in my body could understand the book. It took it in and as the story went on it became clearer to me I wasn't meant to understand the book; only your feelings could understand it.

The book took me to places I had never seen before. This told me there was no limit. It made me feel bright inside and I could go wherever I wanted to go.

It told me to explore other areas.

Figure 4–9 Sam, Grade 5

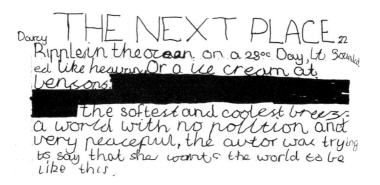

Ripple in the ocean on a 28-degree day. It seemed like Heaven or an ice cream at Bensons, the softest and coolest breeze, a world with no pollution and very peaceful. The author was trying to say that she wants the world to be like this.

Figure 4–10 Darcy, Grade 5

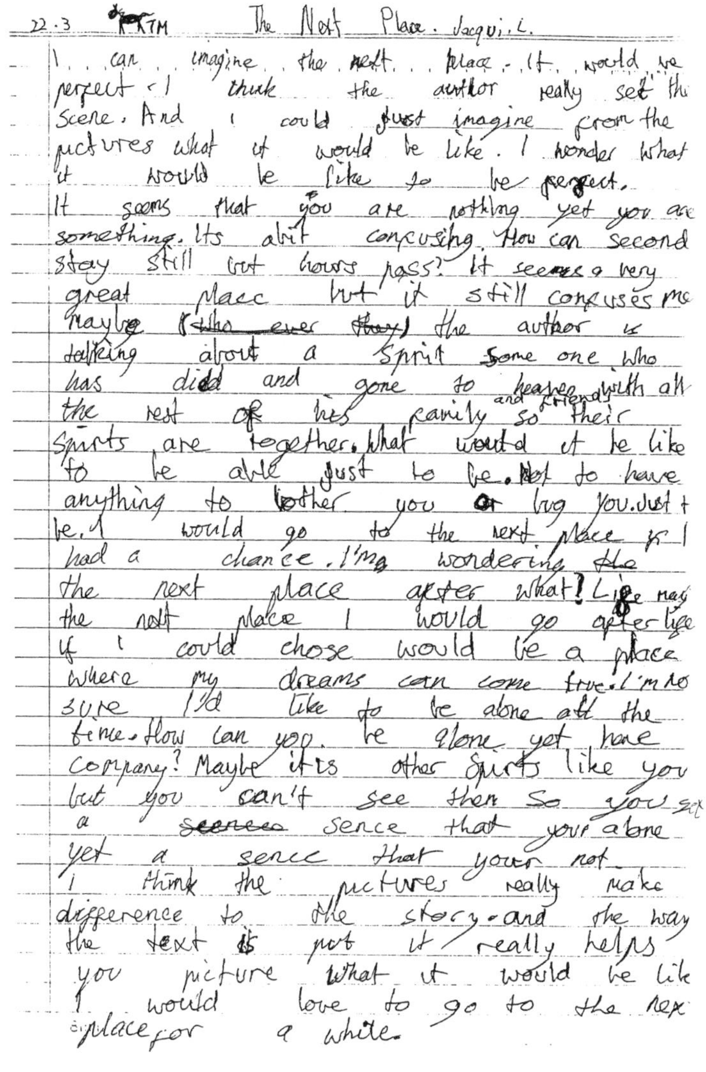
22·3 KTM The Next Place. Jacqui. L.

I can imagine the next place. It would be perfect. I think the author really set the scene. And I could just imagine from the pictures what it would be like. I wonder what it would be like to be perfect. It seems that you are nothing yet you are something. Its abit confusing. How can second stay still but hours pass? It seems a very great place but it still confuses me maybe (who ever they) the author is talking about a spirit some one who has died and gone to heaven with all the rest of his family and friends so their spirits are together. What would it be like to be able just to be. Not to have anything to bother you or bug you. Just be. I would go to the next place if I had a chance. I'm wondering the the next place after what! Life may the next place I would go after life if I could chose would be a place where my dreams can come true. I'm not sure I'd like to be alone all the time. How can you be alone yet have company? Maybe it is other spirits like you but you can't see them so you get a sence that your alone yet a sence that your not. I think the pictures really make difference to the story and the way the text is put it really helps you picture what it would be like I would love to go to the next place for a while.

I can imagine the next place. It would be perfect. I think the author really set the scene. And I could just imagine from the pictures what it would be like. I wonder what it would be like to be perfect. It seems that you are nothing yet you are something. It's a bit confusing. How can seconds stay still but hours pass? It seems a very great place but it still confuses me. Maybe the author is talking about a spirit, someone who has died and gone to Heaven with all the rest of his family and friends so their spirits are together. What would it be like to be able just to be? Not to have anything to bother you or bug you. Just be. I would go to the next place if I had a chance. I'm wondering, the next place after what? Life maybe. The next place I would go after life if I could choose would be a place where my dreams can come true. I'm not sure I'd like to be alone all the time. How can you be alone yet have company? Maybe it is other spirits like you but you can't see them so you get a sense that you're alone yet a sense that you're not. I think the pictures really make a difference to the story and the way the text is put really helps you picture what it would be like. I would love to go to the next place for a while.

Figure 4–11 Jacqui, Grade 5

Strategy Ask all children to sit on the carpet with a pencil and a notepad or a piece of paper resting on a chalkboard or a clipboard on their knees. Before commencing to read the story aloud, tell the children that at one or two places in the story you will ask them to write some advice for a character.

The Art Lesson **by Tomie dePaola** I did this activity with one class using the book *The Art Lesson. The Art Lesson* is an autobiographical account of Tomie dePaola's childhood. He wanted to draw from the moment he was born. He couldn't wait to go to school to have art lessons with the art teacher. Just after he started first grade, his family gave him a box of sixty-four Crayola crayons for his birthday. He was so excited! His first-grade teacher told the class that on the next Monday they would practice art in readiness for the commencement of the art teacher's lessons the next month. So on the following Monday, Tomie took his box of sixty-four Crayola crayons to school. His teacher was not pleased. She said everyone must use the same crayons. The school crayon packets contained only eight colors. She ordered Tomie to take his packet of sixty-four crayons home and to leave them there. This is a good point in the story to have the children give advice to Tomie. Figures 4–12 through 4–15 show some of my students' responses.

"Arithmetic" **by Gawin Ewart** This strategy of having children give advice to a character may be used with poetry as well as with stories. In the following example, the poem "Arithmetic" is used with a grades 4–6 class. "Arithmetic" is a nonrhyming poem written in the first person. It recounts the harshness of life for an eleven-year-old who is the eldest of five children. The father is away and the mother works long hours, so this eleven-year-old has much responsibility caring for four much younger siblings. In addition, the eleven-year-old is not doing well in school.

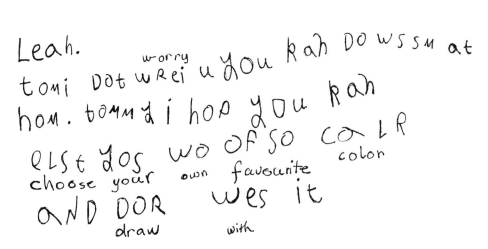

Tomie, don't worry. You can do some at home. Tomie, I hope you can choose your favorite color and draw with it.

Figure 4–12 Leah, Grade 1

Bonnie·S·   Age 7·

tommy you can play
with our coloured craons·
at Home· don't Be Sad
tommy·

Tommy, you can play with our colored crayons at home. Don't be sad, Tommy.

Figure 4–13 Bonnie, Grade 1

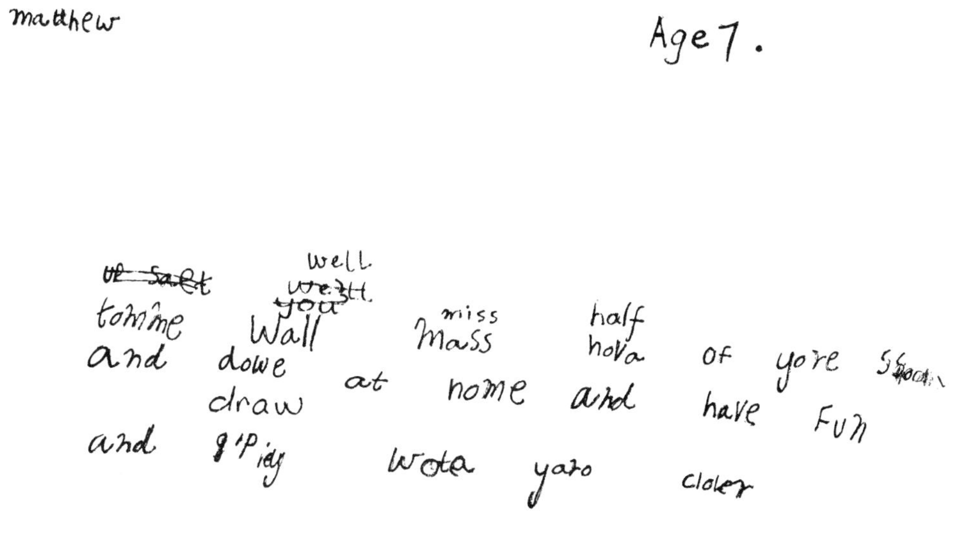

matthew   Age 7·

tommie Wall miss half
and dowe draw at home and have Fun
and play wota yaro cloler

Tomie, well, miss half of your school and draw at home and have fun and play with your colors.

Figure 4–14 Matthew, Grade 2

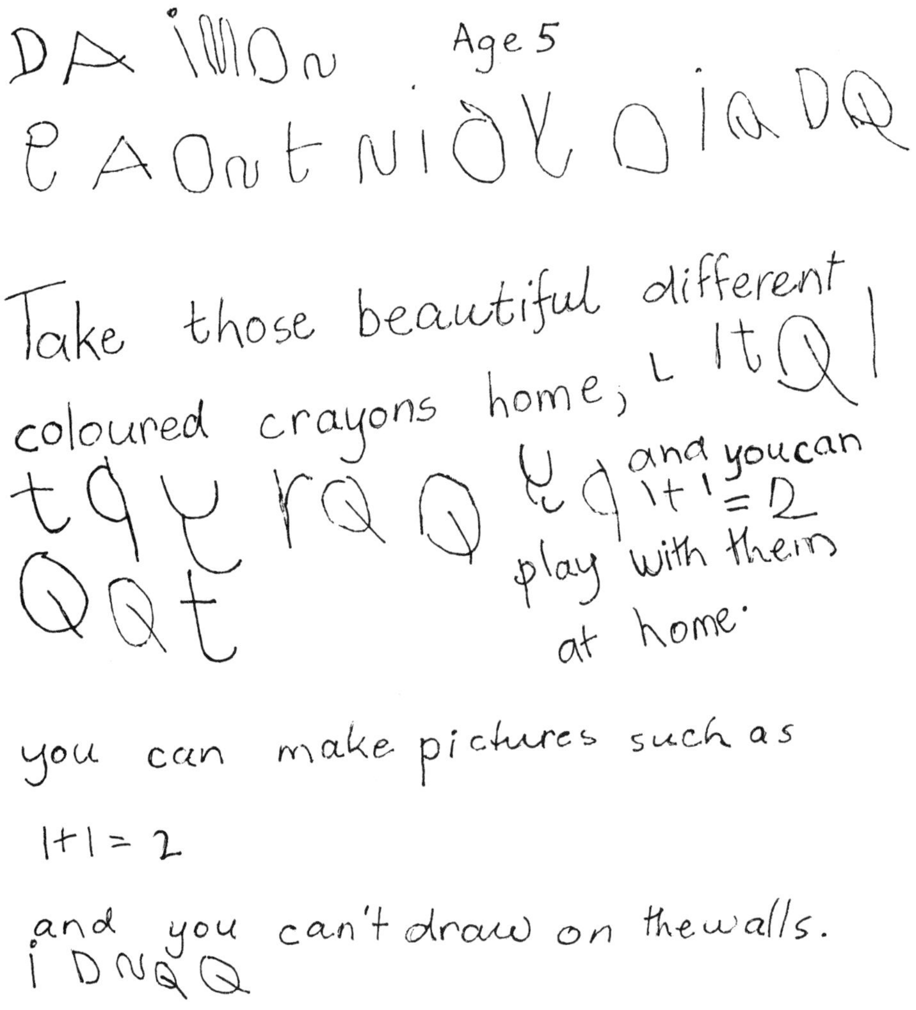

DA iMON   Age 5
E A On t NiÒℓ O iQ DQ

Take those beautiful different
coloured crayons home, L It Q I
t q ℓ r Q Q ℓ q and youcan it¹=2
Q Q t   play with them
                          at home.

you can make pictures such as

I+I= 2

and you can't draw on the walls.
i D NQ Q

Take those beautiful different-colored crayons home, and you can play with them at home.
You can make pictures such as as 1 + 1 + 2, and you can't draw on the walls.

Figure 4–15 Daimon, Age 5

The teacher displayed a large copy of the poem for all the children to see and then read it aloud. She checked for words the children did not understand. In this poem, children often ask about the meanings of *rec* and *larky*. Next, the children read the poem silently. They then wrote advice for the child speaking in the poem. Here's one girl's response:

> I've never been in your position before but I got most of the picture so I can help you. I see that Doreen Maloney is your enemy or else she would not be calling you a fool. Well the Recreation hall should be a fun time for you to relax and read a book thats my idea of fun or soak in warm bath water. I would like to have 5 brothers or sisters. Good ones not like my younger brother he is such a pain I have to tell him at least 10 times before he dose it. If you need to learn your to times tables then practies It dose not matter if your tired keep your self awake. Show your teacher and friends your not a Dunce. Your mum is only working for you children to have food in your mouths and a roof over your head so that shouldn't be a problem at all if you think about it. And your Dad will be back soon. And when your Mum comes back sit and talk to her talking won't hert And 1 more piece of advice dont try to be exzactly like the others be an individual
> good luck and best wishes
>
> —Cynthia, grade 5/6

The examples I have shared here are all from literature. However, this activity can also be used as a way of responding to a character in a history text or someone in a contemporary news report.

Listening, Speaking, and Writing in Role
This strategy is adapted from the work of Susan Close (1993).

Rationale When children listen, speak, and write in role, they participate more intensely and sensitively with the text. They also develop the ability to empathize with the characters' thoughts and feelings.

Purpose In this activity, children listen, speak, and write as a particular character in a story.

Strategy Divide the class into groups according to the number of characters in the story. Have each group sit together and listen as one particular character from the story. Ask each child to think and feel as the character might feel throughout the story. For example, in the book *The Ghost Eye Tree* by Bill Martin Jr. and John Archambault, there are two characters, so there woud be two listening groups. One would listen as the sister, Ellie, and the other as her younger brother.

After you have assigned the roles, read the story aloud as children listen in role. Stop after a while to interview the characters. Move among the children, stopping in front of several as if you are holding a microphone. Question the characters. They must reply in role. For example, if you were reading *The Ghost Eye Tree*, you could ask the brother, "What were you thinking when your mother asked you to accompany your sister to fetch a bucket of milk?" or "Why did you insist on wearing your hat?" You could ask Ellie, "What were your thoughts when your mother asked you to take your little brother and fetch some milk?" or "Why did you run back to retrieve your brother's hat?"

Continue reading the story aloud, while the children continue to listen in the same role. When you have finished the book, ask the children to write in role, responding to a prompt like "What was it like for you in that story?" The following is a response a student wrote in the role of the brother in *The Ghost Eye Tree*.

> I felt like its not very fere (fair) at all I was pretty sceade (scared) at the time and My Mum always ast (asked) me to get a bucket of milk. But I can't tall (tell) my mum about the ghost eye tree because I will be scede (scared) to. But I was felt tough relly tough every time I get my hat I wolld (would) always pot (put) my hat over one eye and walk of and I hated it when my sister says "you get that dame hat that dagey hat that shupered (stupid) hat that silly hat"
> 	I like this hat I love this hat

—STACEY, GRADE 3

Painting Images

Rationale Mankind's various symbol systems are all ways of making and expressing meaning. Understanding of verbal texts that describe may be enhanced by transforming these texts into paintings or drawings.

Purpose This activity enhances children's understanding of descriptive texts and brings children to understand the capacity of words to create strong visual images.

Strategy The strategy of children painting images from poetry is equally appropriate with five-year-olds and twelve-year-olds. For example, I used the following poem with a class of K–1 students.

Goldfish

In the goldfish bowl
round eyes stare.
Light reflects
orange, yellow, lemon
through the water.
The goldfish
vacuum cleans the fish feed
from the surface
dives
swims monotonously around
the glass cage.

—LORRAINE WILSON

To begin, write the poem on a large chart for all the children to see. Then read the poem aloud. Check whether there are any words the children don't understand. In this poem, the word *monotonously* sometimes needs explanation. Ask the children to close their eyes as you reread the poem. Tell them to let pictures from the poem fill their minds. Next, give children individual copies of the poem. Have them read it for themselves, focusing on the pictures in their minds. Have them underline the line or phrase or words that put the best and sharpest picture in their heads.

Next have children sketch this picture as large as they can and then color it using water-based coloring pencils, to which they will later add water for a painted effect. Paste the relevant text from the poem onto each painting, and mount the images in a beautiful big book.

Each class book will include several paintings of the same line or set of words. The paintings of the same line of text are often quite different. This is a very concrete way of demonstrating how each one of us brings our own meaning to the text.

Character Grid

Rationale   Developing characters in narrative requires the author to have each character behave and react consistently, in keeping with his character description. Having children write the thoughts and the feelings of different characters toward the same story event provides a focus for their participation within the text and also builds understanding of the need to have characters behave consistently throughout a story. Additionally, it develops their capacity to see an event from different points of view.

Purpose   The aim of this activity is to have the children identify the different thoughts and feelings of the characters in a story (in this case, *Cinderella*) at different points in the story.

Strategy   The story *Cinderella* could be used with any school-age group. Before the lesson, draw up a grid featuring several characters from the story and several story events. For example, see the grid on page 95.

With young children, read the story aloud to the whole class. Have older students read the story for themselves. After the reading of the story, have each child individually complete the grid, writing in what each character might have been thinking or feeling or saying at each of the story events. When a reader can see the same story event from several different perspectives, it is a good sign that the reader has comprehended the story very well. When discussing the children's responses, talk about the language used by each character. Did, for example, the children use the same language for the king as for the ugly sister? If not, why not? How might a king speak? This is a way of having the children think about the characters they write into their stories and the dialogue they attribute to them.

Summarize a Factual Text

Rationale   Factual texts are written to inform. Often we read factual texts to glean information for reports, books, or assignments we are writing, which necessitates taking notes from the original source. When information is read aloud to children and they

Character Grid

Story Event	Character	Character	Character	Character	Character

Cinderella (feelings/thoughts)

Story Event	King	Cinderella	Ugly Sister	Stepmother	Prince
The invitation to the first ball is sent out.	Relief; at last his son might settle down.	She wished she could go. Sad, lonely.	Arrogant, superior.	Eager for one of her girls to win the prince.	Mixed feelings— regret at loss of freedom but wouldn't mind a beautiful wife.
Cinderella arrives in the ballroom.	"There's another beautiful girl. Surely he will find a wife."	She feels shy. "I wish I knew someone to talk to."	"She looks a little familiar."		"Mmmm, now there's a possibility."
The prince dances with Cinderella.	Hopeful	Dreamy	Jealous	"Why is he dancing with *her?*"	Ecstatic
The page brings the glass slipper to Cinderella's house.		"I hope I get to try on the slipper."	"Drat!"	"It's going to end happily! I know the prince will choose one of my daughters."	"Baron, do you not have another daughter?"

are then required to make notes, they are unable to copy great chunks from the book because they cannot see the text. Thus, plagiarism is avoided. In keeping with a holistic theory of learning, demonstrations by experienced writers are important in the process of learning to write.

Purpose   This activity helps children develop the ability to summarize and take notes from factual texts.

Strategy   The following example comes from a class of K–2 students who were undertaking an integrated study of space. First, the teacher read aloud two paragraphs from a factual text about the planets. She then explicitly talked about the main ideas and the key words and listed these key words on the chalkboard. Next, she combined these into sentences in her own way. She demonstrated this process to the children on two further occasions.

In the fourth session, she read a paragraph about the sun aloud to the children and required them to list some of the key words and then rewrite the information in their own words. For example:

Sun ———————— star
No sun ———————— No Life

The sun is a star
If the sun was Not there, ther wod
be no life
                              —ANNABELLE, GRADE 2

Sun. big star ———————— Hot gas
No sun ———————— Life dies. Earth

The sun is the biggest Star.
The sun is made of hot gas & fire.
If the sun doesn't show any more light
every-thing that lives dies.

                              —SOPHIA, GRADE 2

Participating in a Procedural Text

Rationale   The purpose of a procedural text is to tell how to make or do something, such as how to make a dog kennel or how to perform mouth-to-mouth resuscitation. How well the finished product or procedure is executed is a measure of how well the reader understood the text or was able to participate with it.

Purpose   In our example, the purpose of this activity is to have children make skittles and then play a game of skittles with classmates. (Skittles is a children's version of ten-pin bowling.)

Strategy The following example occurred as part of an integrated unit on toys. Young children followed a procedural text to construct the skittles. They then followed the instructions in another procedural text to participate in a game of skittles.

SKITTLE PEOPLE

Materials

- plastic drink bottles with caps
- sand
- funnel
- paint and brushes
- decorations

Method

1. Use a funnel to fill the bottle half full with sand. Screw cap on firmly.
2. Paint a face on the skittle.
3. Decorate the skittle (e.g., with hair, clothes).

HOW TO PLAY SKITTLES

Materials

- 10 skittles
- 1 ball
- 2 to 4 players

Instructions

1. Set ten skittles up as shown. Four skittles in the back row, then three, then two, and one skittle in the front row.

   X X X X
    X X X
     X X
      X

2. Draw a line 5 big steps from the skittles.
3. Take turns rolling the ball. See how many skittles you can knock down.
4. A scorer writes down each player's score.
5. Each player has three turns.
6. The highest score wins.

The children's brightly colored skittles, which held together as they later played the game, and their enjoyment as they enthusiastically played skittles showed how well they had understood what they had read. Of course, the teacher's demonstration also helped!

Evaluation

When evaluating a child's meaning making, observe whether the child

predicts successfully

retells with understanding

recounts related experiences

expresses emotion about what he has read

challenges another's interpretation

empathizes with a character

asks questions of a text

makes sensible predictions as he reads

says, "That didn't make sense"

chooses to reread a favorite text

chooses to read books by the same author or from the same series

finds books to read around his interests

achieves the text purpose (e.g., reads a recipe and makes edible chocolate chip cookies)

reveals understanding in a journal entry

makes links to other texts he has read

Summary: Making Meaning

The practice of text participation or making meaning is central to reading. Central to reading instruction is the view of the child or the reader as meaning maker. Meaning is within each child. Children's interpretations must be respected. Children may be challenged and asked to justify their interpretations, but there is not just one interpretation of a text. Because of our differing backgrounds and differing value systems, we respond to the same texts in differing ways. Interpretations of text may change over time or after discussion. Through discussion of why we have different understandings and reactions to one text, we come to understand better our own and others' points of view; we learn more about ourselves and others, so we enhance the quality of our lives.

References

Close, S. 1993. *Thoughtful Interactions: Nurturing Quality Response*. Strategy outlined in Literacy for the New Millenium Conference, Australian Reading Association, Melbourne.

Commeyras, M. and G. Sumner. 1996. "Literature Discussions Based on Student Posed Questions." *The Reading Teacher* 50 (3): 262–65.

Gleeson, L. 2000. "Dreaming of the Great Bear." *Practically Primary* 5 (3): 5.

Luke, A., and P. Freebody. 1999. "A Map of Possible Practices: Further Notes on the Four Resources Model." *Practically Primary* 4 (2): 5.

Purves, A. 1993. "Toward a Reevaluation of Reader Response and School Literature." *Language Arts* 70 (5): 360.

Children's Books

dePaola, T. 1989. *The Art Lesson*. New York: G. P. Putnam's Sons.

Hanson, W. 1998. *The Next Place*. Sisterdale, TX: Mission Publishing.

Martin, B. Jr., and J. Archambault. 1985. *The Ghost Eye Tree*. London: Holt Rinehart Winston.

Wagner, J. 1979. *John Brown, Rose and the Midnight Cat*. Australia: Puffin Books.

Children's Poems

Ewart, G. 1988. "Arithmetic." In *Strictly Private: An Anthology of Poetry*, comp. R. Mc Gough, p. 19 London: Penguin Books.

Greenfield, E. 1988. "New Baby Poem 2." In *Night on Neighbourhood St.,* p. 11 New York: Dial Books for Young Readers.

Kuskin, K. 1980. "It Is Grey Out." In *Dogs and Dragons, Trees and Dreams,* p. 40. New York: Harper Trophy.

Chapter 5

USING TEXT: READING FOR A PURPOSE

*Effective literacy draws on a repertoire of practices that allow
learners, as they engage in reading and writing activities, to: . .
use texts functionally: traversing the social relations around texts;
knowing about and acting on the different cultural and social
functions that various texts perform both inside and outside
school and knowing that these functions shape the ways texts are
structured, their tone, their degree of formality and their sequence
of components.*

—PETER FREEBODY AND ALLAN LUKE (1999, 5)

Different Texts for Different Life Activities

Think for a moment. Do we ever complete a day in our lives without reading something? When did you last go a day without reading anything? Every day, each one of us reads for a wide range of purposes as we negotiate our family, our friends, our work, and the wider community. (We really do read to live!) I find I cannot make a cup of coffee in our school staffroom now without reading. Do I want caffeinated or decaffeinated coffee? Do I want soy milk, heavy cream, light cream, non-dairy creamer, or skim milk?

Reading purposes include those related to living and working in our particular community together with humanistic purposes. Such purposes include learning about and understanding ourselves and empathizing with the thoughts and the feelings of others. In any one day, we read to negotiate daily routines, such as driving to work, reading the bus schedule, and making purchases at the supermarket. Some of us subscribe to a local newspaper to keep informed of local happenings. Alternatively, we may turn to a particular section of that newspaper to satisfy some particular need. For example, if we are looking for a used car we may read the classifieds to get an approximate price on the vehicle we are looking for. A horse-racing enthusiast reads the racing form guide in the daily newspaper to better place his bets and hopefully collect. A politician browses the main daily newspapers each morning to read how he or she has been reported, to keep informed of what the opposition is saying, and to stay abreast of current issues so that he or she may be better prepared for interviews.

Of course, through the day we also read as part of our particular jobs. On return to our homes, we may read a letter from a friend who is experiencing hard times. We mull over the letter, wondering how best to help. At the end of the day, many of us turn to works of fiction, our aim being to relax, to switch off and unwind. Fictional works have the capacity to satisfy various reading needs: a reader may read to relax, unwind after a stressful day at work, or escape; to explore possible new ways of being; or to learn about other settings, other times, other lifestyles, and human behavior in general.

Because our life interests and needs differ, our reading purposes vary; because our reading purposes vary, the texts we read differ. "Since reading and writing are nothing if not social, then being a successful reader is being able to participate in those social activities in which written text plays a central part" (Freebody 1992, 6).

Text Purpose and Text Shape

As we read with purpose in mind, so too we write for a purpose. Writing is social. Over time different groups of people have created different texts to meet their different needs. Think for a moment of the route maps we see today in subway shelters. Such a text was not known in the days of horse-drawn vehicles. Think for a moment of those car advertisements that fill our weekend newspapers. They are short. The necessary elements are the brand name, the date of the model, the asking price, and the telephone number of the dealer. The prospective buyer must have this information before buying. The language is brief and technical, sometimes a little persuasive (e.g., "like new" or "one owner.") The advertiser wants to sell. No words are wasted, for each word costs money.

Our writing purpose impacts upon and helps determine the shape of the writing. The structure of a factual book about sea creatures differs from that of a story about a particular sea creature. The purpose of the factual book is to inform, hence the information contained within is grouped around topics. The first section might be about the many varieties of sea creatures, the second about their eating patterns. These sections or topics are listed in the table of contents for speedy retrieval and are signposted throughout the book with eye-catching headings. The purpose of the factual book is to inform, hence the reader dips into the book wherever the required information is to be found. A factual book such as this does not have to be read in its entirety; the reader does not have to start reading from the first page.

However, a storybook about a sea creature is structured differently because it serves a different purpose. A narrative about a sea creature is read from the start to the finish so one may follow the plot. The purpose of the narrative is to tell a story. One cannot read a story by reading one section only. The opening of a narrative introduces the characters, the setting, and the time period in which the story is set. The opening is very important, for it must hook the reader so he will keep reading.

Not only do the schematic organizing features differ between texts; so do the linguistic items used. A story has specific characters with names to enable the reader to follow their exploits through the plot. The characters may talk to one another, hence there will be direct speech. We rarely find direct speech or dialogue in factual texts. Factual information texts do not have specific characters but rather speak about classes of things. Factual texts are for the purpose of conveying information, so the language is precise, objective, and technical. Personal pronouns are out of place in a factual report.

In classrooms the structure of different genres and text types should be discussed as those text types are being read and constructed and used as part of a class study such as animals or habitats or machines. The language to describe the schematic features of texts should be used in the context of using and composing texts. Such teaching informs students not only about the structure of a text but how best to make use of it.

When discussing a particular text, the teacher might pose the following questions.

Factual Text

How does this text begin?

Is this the same way a story begins?

What is the table of contents for?

Look at the artwork in this book about sharks. What do you notice?

Is this artwork like or different from the artwork in a storybook about a shark?

Instructional Text

What are the different sections of this recipe?

Why are the ingredients listed before the method?

Why is the method placed last in the recipe?

Storybook

What did we learn in the first paragraph of this story?

What was the main problem or complication in this story?

How did the author resolve this problem?

Genre Teaching

In recent decades, the realization that purpose shapes a text and that particular text forms are recognizable, together with a belief that competence in the factual text genre is a necessary prerequisite for access to both tertiary education and the business world, has given rise to what has become known as genre teaching. Such teaching includes explicit instruction in the schematic and linguistic text features of particular genres. While different texts are shaped differently, it must never be forgotten that successful writing is that which achieves its purpose. Rigid adherence to particular formulae may stifle creativity in writing. In discussing this issue, Kress (1999) writes, "a literacy pedagogy based on this version of genre theory would ask young writers to fit their writing to pre-existing schemata, and turn their writing into the mechanical performance of acquired rigid competence. This would prove the antithesis of lively, dynamic writing and of course would encourage stability to the point of stasis" (464). Sometimes writers must break from what is expected—to surprise or shock—to attract the reader's attention and achieve the intended outcome.

Reader Purpose Versus Author Purpose

While the purposes of factual texts appear quite obvious, for example, to inform, instruct about how to do something, or explain how something works, the author purposes of fictional works are not quite so clear-cut. While I'm sure writers of fiction would all agree they set out to tell a story, it is true that sometimes they have other purposes in mind, such as to expose the exploitation of women in particular countries or to promote the cause of one side or the other in some past conflict. I know from attending writer festivals that writers get quite agitated when critics and interviewers attribute purposes to their writing that the authors say were never theirs. I heard one writer reply to one interviewer's interpretation with "I had a story to write and I wrote it." Of course when a reader endeavors to identify underlying author purposes, this reader is working as text analyst and is engaging with critical literacy.

Whatever the author's purpose might have been, I do believe that teachers use works of fiction for purposes not necessarily intended by the writers. Many children's book writers cringe when they see the uses made of their works in curriculum guides! I have seen well-loved children's stories cited as the texts to use for instruction in proper nouns or particular spelling patterns.

Apart from the instructional use, different readers do make different use of the same works of fiction. I think for example of *Death of a River Guide* by Richard Flanagan (1994). Reading this book, I took in huge gulps of the river, the vegetation, and the people and determined that one day I would see the Tasmanian wilderness. I can imagine that others who take part in white-water rafting would read it for an entirely different purpose, possibly to learn more about the safe negotiation of raging streams.

Children and Magazines

All of us react negatively when being asked to learn or remember information or procedures for which we fail to see the relevance or use. If children are to be committed readers who choose to read for a range of reasons outside of school hours, all as part of their daily lives, then early reading lessons must not only center on meaning but also seem relevant and necessary to the children.

In upper elementary classes, I find that many students are devotees of particular magazines to which they subscribe and read outside of school. Sometimes these magazines are part of the culture of childhood. I encourage the children to bring their magazines to school to share. Many boys who are not so keen on reading novels are quite passionate about particular magazines. Christian, a grade 4 boy, introduced me to the video game magazine N64. He loaned me several of his magazines to take home and read. However, I experienced great difficulty reading them. I did not know where to start. I did not understand the way the language was being used. For example, the magazine contained pages of "Cheats." I felt a little uncomfortable even looking at these pages. In my experience, cheating was something respectable people didn't do! As well, the fact that I had never played a video game made this reading activity extremely difficult for me.

Back in the classroom I told the children how difficult to read I found the magazine. I asked them about the Cheats. Were these magazines encouraging the young readers to be dishonest? The children soon put me right. They all knew about the Cheats and they proceeded to animatedly assure me that it was all right to read the Cheats. In fact, this was the first section of the magazine many of the children turned to. Cheats are clues, tips, and shortcuts for winning particular games.

As to how to read the magazine, Christian was very clear about this. "Well, you get your magazine. You turn on your game. You look down the table of contents and find the game you are playing and turn to that page. Then you read one step at a time and do that step on your game. Then you read the next step, and so on. That's how you learn to play the game." Christian's purpose in reading this magazine was crystal clear. In this situation, Christian was a text user. Christian's comments highlight how the text shape linked directly with the text purpose, which was completing a particular game successfully. There was a table of contents to help the reader find a particular game; there were sequential steps for the reader to complete.

When the students talk about the magazines they read, what comes through is the authentic purposes for which they are reading. Their reading of these texts is driven by real need. If only we could embed such need or perceived purpose into all classroom reading.

Currently, I am seeing groups of children (almost all boys) in the schoolyard poring over albums filled with Pokémon cards. At recess time, instead of playing football or tag they are choosing to share and swap and read these collectible cards. Yet again, they are reading as part of the school ground culture.

Levelled Reading Books

In parts of Australia currently there is a return to the use of levelled readers, the books children read as part of a dedicated two-hour literacy block. In the state of Victoria, all schools taking part in the Early Years Literacy Program use levelled readers in the early primary grades. Almost all schools are part of this program because in Victoria, literacy funding is currently tied to compliance with this program. Strangely, the levels being used are those of the Reading Recovery Program, which was a program designed to help the least proficient readers in any grade 1 class. Is it not worrying that all children in the state—even the most proficient—are reading on levels designed for the least proficient?

Children know the levels on which they are reading. When asked why they are reading a particular book, they reply, "I'm on level 7. This book is level 7." The reason for reading a particular book, therefore, is because it's on a particular level and the child is deemed to be reading on that level. Children perceive the purpose of classroom reading as progressing to higher and higher levels. At this very time in Victoria, wonderful junior novels, including some that have won awards, are being placed on broad bands (somewhat wider levels). It appears that in the near future, competent eight-, nine- and, ten-year-old readers will no longer be able to choose the novels they wish to read but will also read on levels.

When books are levelled, value is placed on progressing to higher and higher levels rather than on making meaning, using the text, or being a text analyst. How can children's diverse interests and purposes for reading match a predetermined sequence of books?

One wonders at what stage one no longer needs to be levelled in one's reading. Could this be at the end of elementary school, or is it at the end of high school, or it is perhaps at the end of college? After one comes off levels, does one's reading level continue to increase? Imagine a public library where the books were grouped according to adult levels! One wonders if as one ages, one starts backsliding to levels attained at an earlier age. If so, at what age does one's level start to slide backward? Is it at thirty or perhaps forty? If this hypothetical backsliding down reading levels did occur for adult readers, would one slide down the other side of the hill, meeting unseen titles, or would one go down the side one came up? If so, one would have to read the same books he or she read on the way up the levelled hill. Perhaps I should not advertise this idea; some entrepreneur might start packaging adult-levelled books for the unchartered downward slope of the hill of life!

First Levels

When one reads the books being written for the earliest levels, one wonders how such books could inspire any child to keep reading. They are about nothing. Many books being written and published today to teach reading are just as meaningless as the worst of the controlled vocabulary readers of the 1960s. The production may be glossier, but contentwise they are impoverished. Comparing levelled reading texts with books is like comparing processed white bread with sourdough, multigrain, and rye loaves.

Because of the drive to have children reading levelled books from the commencement of school, many children are reading books when they would be better engaged in exciting firsthand experiences (playing in sand, blowing bubbles, planting seeds, watching chickens hatch) and listening to stories read aloud.

Today, parents of newborn babies are encouraged to read to their infants from birth. Imagine if they read level 1 books. How insulting! "Welcome, Baby, to this wonderful world and now listen to this drivel." Seriously, imagine the unfortunate impact on the language development of babies if they were read levelled texts from birth.

If reading begins at birth, why aren't babies on level 1 books? Why are level 1 books delayed until the children are five years old? Does a level 1 book have one word per page or two words? Are the same words to be on each page? Does the text have to make sense? For the author of a level 1 book, what priority is given to meaning and purpose in the writing?

While there may be an occasional book by a skillful author with only one or two words per page, most of the books written to teach reading with few words per page are simply not worth reading. Many have one sentence pattern repeated page after page after page. I think a good question to ask when considering books for purchase is "Will any person (child or adult) want to read this book a second time?" Taking into account the limited book budgets most schools have, if the aim is to develop children who are passionate about books, perhaps it would be wiser to stop buying the thin, uninteresting levelled early readers and instead use this money to buy well-loved children's favorites. The book stock may be reduced in quantity but certainly increased in quality. Just this week I was speaking to undergraduates about predictable texts and held up as an example *The Very Hungry Caterpillar* by Eric Carle. The students broke into smiles. They remembered fondly this book from their childhood. They remembered the holes in the pages and they remembered the story, for when I commenced reading the text, they immediately joined in. There is something very right about a children's book that stays with us into our adult lives. It is this type of book children should be encountering at reading time in their classrooms.

I think again of Nicholas, my great-nephew, and his passion for books. He now helps his parents and I read some of his books to him. How humiliating it will be for him—and many other children—to be offered early levelled books when he enters school. Nicholas expects books to be about something. He expects to learn something when he reads a book. He expects books to be worth reading and rereading.

A friend's five-year-old niece started school last year. She could read when she entered school. In the first week her teacher gave her a levelled reader as a take-home book. "I don't do those," spoke up the five-year-old. "I do novels." To the teacher's credit, she allowed this little girl to borrow the books she wanted, which she could read.

Of course, having children read on levels makes measurement and comparison easier. If schools have all five-year-olds reading particular books on level 1 before they progress to level 2, this makes for easier collection of comparative data than when schools buy their book stock around their children's interests and individual children have choices over what they read.

While politicians flaunt the comparative data, is it not relevant that levelled books might be deterring children from learning to read; that reading is associated with boring, trivial texts, that there is no purpose in reading and, hence, no relevance to the children's lives?

If children are not reading, it seems pointless to try to write books for them to read by themselves. Rather, their language and literacy curriculum should focus on expanding their life experiences, developing their oral language, expanding their understandings of written language, and reading aloud to them quality, authentic texts.

Matching Books to Children

When promoters of levelled texts speak of matching books to children, what in fact are they matching? They cannot match the many diverse interests and purposes of a multitude of young learners. They cannot match the diverse vocabulary or syntactic patterns of these wide-ranging students, for their high-frequency words such as first names, hometowns, and cultural practices will be different, as will their particular dialects and first languages. What then are the books matching?

Many young pupils have strong interests, often of a scientific nature, when they enter school. They know much already about lightbulbs and batteries or sharks or orchids and they want to learn more. I think immediately of three young boys each with a passion for one of these topics. What does a school do to their interest in and purpose for reading when it denies them the opportunity to borrow and read books about these personal interests?

Integrated Curriculum

For reading to serve real purposes in school it follows that reading should be integrated with the rest of the curriculum. Learning to read factual texts such as informational reports should occur at the same time as the children are learning about social and scientific issues such as habitats or the clothes we wear or food chains. Learning to read procedural texts may occur at the same time children are learning how to cook particular dishes or carry out first-aid procedures such as CPR. Sadly, all too often, literacy learning is taught apart from the rest of the curriculum as if it is serving some purpose of its own and is not related to the children's lives. "In school literacy is treated as a neutral object to be studied and mastered. Literacy itself is treated as an autonomous object, one that has a life world of its own unconnected to the ways in which it is actually used by people in their lives . . . the children's role is to learn it rather than to use it" (Hall 1998, 9).

In all our planning for literacy in schools, we must remember that we do not learn to read to read; we learn to read to do other things.

Classroom Strategies for Reading for Real Purposes: Everyday Texts

Class News Board

Rationale A class news board displayed near the door with relevant daily news is one way of building a classroom community inclusive of parents, students, and teachers. Announcements and notices can be about classroom events, the children, or their families.

Purpose Class news boards develop children's reading abilities as they read daily news relating to their classroom and classmates.

Strategy Each morning before the children and their parents enter the classroom, display a news sentence on an easel by the door. Most of the sentences should give some news regarding a class member. For example:

> It is Jessica's birthday today.
> Welcome back, Jamie.
> Maurice has a new baby sister, Holly Jane.
> Aiden is in the hospital. Get well soon, Aiden.

As the children enter the classroom, encourage them to read the news sentence and respond to it in appropriate ways, for example, wish Jessica a happy birthday or congratulate Maurice on his new baby sister.

Reading School Signs

Rationale There are many signs around school buildings that some adults take for granted. However, these signs are contextually placed and offer opportunities for authentic reading.

Purpose As part of the school orientation program, children learn where particular facilities are, as well as the purposes for other printed signs in the school environment, by referring to all these signs.

Strategy Early in the school year, take a class of new enrollees on a walk about the school. Stop and point to different signs and ask the children to read them or try to predict what they say. Discuss the first letters of some signs. On subsequent walks, ask children to read the signs. Signs could include Office, Staff Room, Library Open 1:30–2:00 P.M., Art Room, Boys Bathroom, Girls Bathroom, No Running Inside, No Dogs Allowed.

Reading Clothing as Part of Integrated Unit on Clothing

Rationale When we buy clothing there is print to read. T-shirts, jeans, sneakers are all texts to be read by children.

Purpose The purpose of this activity is to establish the reasons for the writing found on clothing.

Strategies Have children read the labels on the clothing they wear to school. Ask them to list what the labels say. Then have them try to group the types of information found on clothing labels, such as size, fabric, laundering instructions, flammability, and place of manufacture. Discuss why this information is given. Then have them ask their parents what use they make of clothing labels. Invite some parents into the classroom to tell how and why they read clothing labels. Back at school, make a class list of the reasons we read clothing labels.

Or, do the following activity to establish the reasons for the writing found on T-shirts. Set aside a particular day for all class members to wear a T-shirt that has writing on it. To begin, have the children move around, reading one another's T-shirts. Then ask them to get into small groups to copy the writing from each T-shirt and then note the purpose for the writing. For example:

Star Wars	to make us go to the movie
New York; Melbourne	to tell everyone where we've been
My Mommy loves me; I am Grandma's darling	to make us feel special

Reading Zoo Labels

Rationale At the zoo, print is used to point the way to different animal displays and different facilities. It is used to name the species of animals and to tell about their places of origin. By reading the print at the zoo, our visit is better managed and we are better informed.

Purpose Through this activity children help navigate the way around the zoo and learn about the animals by reading the signs.

Strategy You can do this activity when your early primary class is on a school excursion to the zoo as part of an integrated study of animals. While at the zoo, refer to a large map of the grounds near the entrance and to various signposts throughout the visit. Encourage the children to make use of these authentic texts in determining where the class should go next. As children move around the zoo and ask questions about particular animals, encourage them to read the labels by the enclosures. The labels generally tell the name of the animal and its country of origin.

When you return to school, have the children jointly construct a zoo. When the models are complete, ask the children to write and position their labels. Erect signposts to point the way to different animal enclosures. Affix labels to animal enclosures.

Road Signs

Rationale Road signs are intended to make traffic operate smoothly and keep all travellers safe. Those using the roads should observe the road signs. Young children coming to school need instruction in safe road behavior.

Purpose Through this activity, children read and observe local road signs.

Strategy On a neighborhood walk, take the opportunity to stop at road signs and have children read them and discuss their meanings. Of course, all participants should also observe the road signs' instructions while on the walk.

Back at school, have the children make some signs of their own to be observed in the transport area of their classroom. The signs could be used with blocks, cars, trucks, trains, traffic lights, people, garages, and so on.

Community Maps

Rationale Community maps are necessary texts in finding particular localities.

Purpose This activity introduces children to their community map and has them use it to show the best ways of reaching certain destinations.

Strategy You can use this activity within the context of an integrated study of your Community with grades 3–4 children. Begin by having the children draw maps showing how to reach their homes from the school. Make copies of one or two of the maps made by children living close to the school. Then, as a class, use the child's map on a class walk to find his or her home. Back at school, display an enlarged copy of the street directory and have the children compare the child's map with the official street directory. Note here that young children's maps will be approximations of conventional maps. The sophistication of the children's maps will depend on both their experience with conventional maps and their knowledge of the area they are mapping.

Next, give each child a copy of the community map. Ask them to work with partners to plot the most direct route to particular destinations such as a park. Have the children read from their maps the routes they have chosen.

After using several maps, ask the children to list the features that are necessary on maps, why these features are important, and what the purpose of a map is.

Book Launch Invitation

Rationale   In the real world, publishing companies hold book launches to celebrate the publication of new titles. To these launches, authors invite family members, friends, and colleagues. In the classroom we can also celebrate the publication of books. Here the books are written by the children, and they invite their family members and siblings within the school to join in the celebration. Such a celebration builds positive images in the children of themselves as writers.

Purpose   The purpose of this activity is write invitations for guests to a class book launch.

Strategy   If the children have published books in class time, plan a book launch, where light refreshments will be served, to celebrate and inform parents about the classroom publishing program. First, discuss with the children the idea of holding a book launch to celebrate the publication of their class books. Ask them what a book launch is. Discuss what happens at a book launch.

Tell them invitations will need to be written to the guests. Let the children read some old invitations to determine the necessary features of invitations. Then elicit from the children the information that must be included in their invitations and list these features on the board or a chart for all to see. Features should include who the invitation is for, what the event is, the time and the place of the event, and the reply date. Discuss the best sequence for these items.

Next, draft the invitation together. Check that all necessary information is included. Check spelling, capital letters, and punctuation. This is a good opportunity for some teaching of these features (e.g., capital letters for the name of school and the name of month). You can also discuss the spelling and the sound-letter patterns of some words such as *author* and *launch*. Do the children know other words with similar sound-letter patterns? Start a list.

author	launch
launch	lunch
laundry	bunch
Paul	

Then have the children hand letter the invitations. Each child should write in the names of his or her guests and sign each invitation with his or her name.

Classroom Strategies for Reading for Real Purposes: Nonfiction Texts

Reading a Recipe (Procedural Text)

Rationale   We learn about the structure of different texts as we use them in our lives. It is as young readers follow a recipe to make a particular dish that they learn how to make that dish at the same time as they learn to read and learn about procedural texts.

Purpose   In this activity, students follow a recipe to make salad sandwiches and learn about the schematic structure of a recipe.

Strategy   You can use this activity with first and second graders as part of an integrated study on healthy foods. To begin, display a large recipe for salad sandwiches in the classroom. Read the recipe with the children. Tell the children that on the following day they will make salad sandwiches in their classroom for lunch.

Next, write a shopping list together. Depending on the ages of the children, they might work in small groups to draw up the shopping list and later meet as a whole class to compare and check that all ingredients are on the lists in sufficient quantities. Type the shopping list and distribute one to each child. Go shopping as a class, with all children checking off their shopping lists.

The next morning (with parents to help with supervision), have small groups of children cluster around tables with all ingredients on each cluster of tables. Each small group is responsible for making their group's sandwiches. Ask the supervising adults to refer children to the recipe when needed.

SALAD SANDWICHES

Ingredients

sliced brown bread

sliced cheese

carrot

celery

lettuce

tomato

Method

1. Wash all the vegetables.
2. Scrape and grate the carrots.
3. Slice the celery.
4. Break the lettuce into pieces.
5. Wash and slice the tomatoes.

6. Butter the bread.

7. On the bread, place layers of cheese, lettuce, tomato, carrot, and celery.

8. Cut each sandwich into quarters.

9. Eat and enjoy!

Note: The supervising adult will discuss necessary safety precautions when using sharp knives.

When they are done, have the children clean up their tables. At lunch time children eat their sandwiches.

After lunch, revisit the recipe, encouraging the children to look at the shape and the schematic features of the recipe. Ask the following questions:

What were we making? Where are we told that? Why does that come first?

How did we know what to buy? Where was this positioned in the text? Why?

Where are we told how to make the sandwiches?

How did we know what to do first?

Why are the steps numbered?

Reading Information Report Texts

Rationale   Not all texts are read in the same way. An information report provides factual information about a class of things. One does not necessarily need to read the whole report to find the information one needs. Retrieval-organizing features such as the table of contents and the index are part of this genre, enabling readers to find the information they need expeditiously.

Purpose   In the context of finding answers to their questions, the children learn how to retrieve information from information reports by using the table of contents and the index.

Strategy   At the start of an integrated learning unit, such as one on insects, read the questions the children have about the topic. This is often called the Things We Want to Find Out chart.

Borrow factual texts about insects from libraries. With younger children, first demonstrate how to use the table of contents and the glossary to find the relevant section. Select one of the questions from the children's list, turn to the table of contents, read the book sections, and ponder out loud which section to turn to find an answer to the question. Have the children give suggestions. Sometimes they may need to use the index to retrieve particular items of information.

Then have the children work alone or with friends to find answers to their questions. Sometimes you may need to mark pertinent sections in some of the thicker or more complex books. Some answers to the children's questions may be found in diagrams.

Finally, ask the children to write and illustrate what they have learned.

Writing Information Reports

Rationale   We learn to write different text types when we have authentic opportunity to do so, that is, in the context of learning about the physical or social world. Jointly constructing an information report with the whole class is a demonstration of how to go about writing such a text.

Purpose   To write an information report book about a topic under study.

Strategies   In this section I discuss two strategies. The first is constructing a whole-class big book with K–2 students. Begin this activity three or four weeks into an integrated unit when children have acquired new understandings about the topic.

First, have each child write a true statement about the agreed-upon topic (e.g., butterflies). Ask them to write their statements on large strips of paper with dark-colored felt pens. This is to ensure that when it comes to sharing the statements, all children will be able to see them.

Next, have the children sit in a whole-class circle and individually read aloud their statements. Ask the other children to listen for two things: (1) that the statement is true and (2) that the statement is in book language. If one child challenges another's statement, ask the two students to retire to a class table to jointly rewrite the statement.

Now, have children get in small groups and proofread and correct the spelling and the punctuation in their own and other group members' statements. Use some of these corrections for whole-class teaching.

Then gather the whole class in a circle again and have students spread all the statements in the middle. As a class, group to form the book sections. Have children suggest names for the book sections. Write the name of each section on a strip of paper and keep it with that section.

Separate the children into small groups so they can sequence the statements within each book section. Assign one book section to each group. Much discussion will occur here. Having only one statement per paper strip enables alternate sequences to be tried.

Gather the whole class once again to sequence the book sections. Then create the table of contents. Have children suggest possible book titles and vote for their preferred title. Discuss book design and publishing strategies. Have everybody help publish. Some can hand letter, some can complete artwork, some can do borders, and some can design and complete the table of contents, the cover, and the title pages. Finally, make individual copies of the text in small book format for individual children to read and illustrate.

The next strategy is called bundling and can be used with grades 3–6 students. This strategy is carried out in small cooperative groups of four children and should begin three to four weeks into an integrated unit. The children are to write and publish a book to inform about the topic. The children know the purpose for this writing, and therefore, as they work through to completion, they are text users, creating and shaping a text to achieve their purpose.

First have each group member write six statements of truth about the topic. Have them write the statements on a piece of notebook paper divided into six equal-sized pieces of paper. Later, each statement will be cut out and sorted along with all the other statements, so the pieces of paper should not be too small.

Next, have the children cut out their six statements. Each child reads aloud his statements while other group members listen for accuracy and book language. Next, the statements are pooled in the middle and sorted into groups that belong together. This is how the book section are formed. Then they can label each section of the book, sequence the statements in each section, and sequence the book sections.

Now they can make a strip draft. Tell them to paste each statement in correct sequence on a long, narrow strip of paper. This prevents the small statements from becoming lost. Now the children have a draft of their book. (See Figure 5–1.)

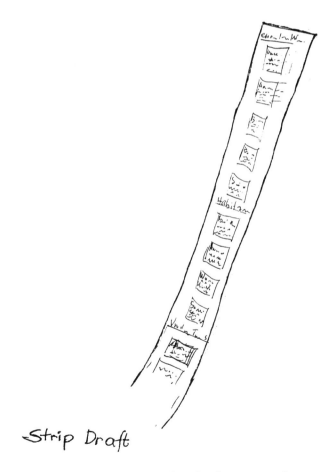

Strip Draft

Figure 5–1 Sketch of Strip Draft

Have them look at their draft and address the following:

Does it make sense? (Text Participant)

Is the information true? (Text Analyst)

Is there enough information in each section? (Text User)

Are there other sections we should include? (Text User)

Have we represented different perspectives (e.g., in a book about the environment)? Should we present other perspectives? (Text Analyst)

After answering these questions, children should proofread and edit accordingly. (Code Breaker) Next they can add other book features to the strip draft, such as a table of contents and an About the Authors page.

Now the group can discuss book design: what type of artwork should be used, whether it should be hand lettered or typed, where the text and borders should be placed, and so on. Finally, have the children publish their books.

Classroom Strategies for Reading for Real Purposes: Fiction Texts

Reading Aloud Before Going Home

Rationale   Reading aloud is invaluable in the process of developing lifelong readers. (Refer to Chapter 2 for an elaboration of the reasons.) You should plan to read aloud each day in the classroom. Reading aloud before leaving ensures the day ends with the class sitting together, content and at peace.

Purposes   One purpose of this activity is to develop a happy classroom climate. Story time is a calm time: cross words and frustrations experienced earlier in the day are forgotten. The class comes together as a whole on the mat. The children go home happy. Additional purposes include immersing the children in narrative; demonstrating how to read; introducing different writers and illustrators; and providing an opportunity for the children to identify with book characters, reflect on related experiences, and imagine and fantasize.

Strategy   Each classroom day, after the children have packed up their work and tidied their room, gather them on the mat in front of you and read a story book.

Reading a Picture Book to Prepare for Related Experiences

Rationale   It is through literature that we learn about ourselves and our life experiences. Literature can help prepare us for forthcoming events.

Purpose   This activity can help to prepare students for forthcoming experiences at school, in the following example, a doctor's visit. By way of explanation, in Australian schools, medical staff attend to vaccinate kindergarten children against childhood diseases such as measles, mumps, and rubella. As parents are not present, this can be quite traumatic for some children. The following strategy is relevant in this context.

Strategy   A doctor is to attend the school to administer injections to the children.

- Read aloud "Injections" by L. Wilson. At the end, encourage discussion by asking, "Who has had an injection?" "Tell us all what happened." "How did you feel?"
- Repeated readings might be taken with this book.
- Children play out doctor/injection situation in the classroom home corner where there is a white doctor's coat and plastic sticks that may serve as needles.
- Some children may write or draw about their previous experiences of having injections.

Reading a Narrative for Private Reflection

Rationale   There is no one right interpretation of literature. Sometimes the teacher's interpretation or the opinions of dominant children quash quieter children's thoughts and meanings. Hence, occasionally there are benefits in having no discussion after sharing a story. The children are left absolutely free with their thoughts, untainted by the opinions of others.

Purpose   This activity leaves all children able to reflect privately and imagine freely after listening to a story. Irene Rosenthal (1995) says, "I would like to posit the hypotheses, that literature, like fairy dust, gives readers the ability to fly" (113). We must carefully select poems and stories that will let readers fly like fairy dust.

Strategy   Read a title such as *Where the Wild Things Are* by Maurice Sendak. At the conclusion of the story, leave the children with their private interpretations. Children must not believe that every time a story is read an activity must be done.

Joint Construction of a Narrative

Rationale   Joint construction, with children and teacher all contributing, is a demonstration of how writing is done. Through jointly constructing a narrative, children learn about the selection of characters and matching characters to the setting and the time. They learn about developing plots and keeping readers interested and the importance of complications and satisfactory resolutions.

Purpose   The purpose of this activity is to jointly construct a narrative and hence inform children's understanding about the writing of narrative.

Strategy   As you plan the narrative, explicitly talk about the structure.

Who might our characters be?
If these are our characters, where might the setting be?

When will the story take place—now, in the future, or sometime in the past?

What would be an appropriate problem(s) for these characters in this setting in this time period?

What are the different ways this problem might be solved?

Will we have a happy or unhappy resolution to the problem?

Are we trying to get across some message in this story?

When you begin writing, address other issues.

How will the story start?

Could we start with dialogue?

Could we start with a dramatic event?

As the story develops, monitor the logic and the consistency of the characters with the setting and the time period. When the first draft is complete, reread the story for sense. Give consideration to the audience.

What age audience is this appropriate for?

Will the audience understand this?

Should we add more detail?

Are our descriptions clear and filled out?

Will the audience stay interested?

Is there enough action?

Should we take out this paragraph? Does it add anything to the story?

Choose the language carefully.

Have we used book language?

Have we repeated words unnecessarily?

Have we used the best/most appropriate words?

Analysis of Narrative Events

Rationale Narrative, or story, is written in a particular way. The characters are introduced at the beginning, as are the setting and the time period. Throughout the story the characters encounter complications, sometimes just one major one, sometimes minor ones as well. The story ends with resolution of the complications, sometimes happily, sometimes unhappily.

Purpose By examining the structure of a familiar narrative, children develop further their capacities to write narrative and specifically learn about appropriate story structure.

Strategy Read a story aloud. Ask the children to individually note what came at the beginning, the middle, and the end of the story. As can be seen from the following examples after the reading of *Hansel and Gretel*, not all narrative is strictly orientation, complication, and resolution. For example, Chris saw the fact that the stepmother did not want the children as a problem at the very beginning of the story.

Hansel and Gretel by Tony Ross			
Student/Grade	What do we learn at the start?	In the middle?	At the end?
Chris, grade 2	Problem: The wife did not want the children there.	Problem: The father tried to lose them.	They solved it.
Cameron, grade 2	The characters: They had a nasty stepmother.	Problems are: The stepmother sent them in the woods. They got lost and went to the wrong house.	All the problems were solved and they lived happily every after.

Creating Narratives for Puppet Plays

Rationale Narrative can inform while telling a story. Narrative involves characters in particular settings in particular time periods who encounter problems or complications that are resolved in various ways.

Purposes The purposes of this activity include the following:

- in a small cooperative group, using language to plan, persuade, and compromise on a joint project
- jointly constructing a narrative suitable for a puppet play that will inform, in this case, about the relationship between animals and their environments
- constructing puppets
- presenting the puppet play before the full class group

Strategy As part of a study of native animals and their environments, have children work in small groups to make a narrative for a puppet play. The characters should be native animals and the problem should have something do with the animals' environment. Provide the following materials: paper plates, collage materials, glue, felt pens, and rods for puppet sticks.

Session 1 Outline the project: discuss the writing of a puppet play, the construction of puppets, and the performance for classmates and parents. Model how to get started, leading a discussion with three students. Ask questions such as "Who might our animal characters be?" and "Where will the play be set? What is their environment?" Keep rough notes of decisions on the board. Have group members choose the puppet they would like to make and to control in he play.

Next, have the children form groups and plan as you demonstrate. Make sure they keep notes of their decisions. When they're ready, they can commence constructing puppets.

For the last ten minutes, have the children think about how their play might begin. Remind them that most, if not all, of a puppet play is dialogue. They might write the first introductory lines of their play. They should start thinking about the problem for their narrative, which must be linked to the animals' environment.

Session 2 Begin the next session by demonstrating with your group. Revise who your puppets are, the setting, and how your story will begin. Let your puppets speak the beginning of your play. Then brainstorm possible problems and choose which one you will develop.

Now have children work in small groups to revise the previous session's decisions and suggest possible problems or complications for their stories. They can continue to work on their puppets as well.

For the last ten to fifteen minutes, let the children practice their plays so far, that is, the beginning and the middle. Some groups can try out in front of the class. The audience should listen, keeping the following questions in mind:

Does it make sense?

Does the beginning grab our attention and make us want to listen for more?

Is the problem appropriate for the characters and the setting?

Is there enough dialogue to tell the audience what is happening?

Are any sound effects being used? Would sound effects contribute to the development of the plot?

Session 3 Begin again by demonstrating with your group. Rehearse your play so far, encouraging the puppeteers to fill out their conversations. Next, plan the solution to the problem, that is, how the play will end.

Then have the children get in small groups and rehearse their plays as they are so far developed. All work on puppets should be completed by now. If not, children should finish constructing the puppets. Children can then plan the resolution of the problem in their stories and rehearse some more. Ask some groups to rehearse in front of the whole class. Tell the audience to provide feedback about the narrative and about the performance, keeping these questions in mind:

Is there an internal logic to the narrative?

Are the problem and the resolution possible for these characters in this setting and this time period?

Is the ending satisfying?

Is the character development consistent?

If possible, videotape these performances, so each group can watch and learn from this rehearsal.

Session 4 After several more rehearsals, have the children perform for their classmates and family members. Videotape the performances for the children so small groups can watch and review their own plays. They may want to do further redrafting.

Reading Fiction to Learn

Rationale Fiction serves many purposes, one of which is to inform about lifestyles in different ages.

Purpose Through this activity, children learn about the lifestyle of some other culture, in this case, early European settlers in Australia.

Strategy The context of this example is an integrated study of early European settlement in Australia. Begin by reading aloud the short stories "The Drover's Wife" by Henry Lawson and "The Night We Watched for Wallabies" by Steele Rudd, or have the children read them individually. However, before reading, tell the children that while listening to or reading the stories, they should focus particularly on one of the following:

- the life of the women, e.g., their work, entertainment, companionship, medical facilities, how housework was done, menus, stresses, and so on
- the life of the men, e.g., their work, their role in the house, entertainment, companionship, transport, communication, stresses, and so on.

After reading the stories, have the children make notes individually or in small groups about the lifestyle of the people of the time.

Next, have some of the children assume the roles of the characters: e.g., the drover's wife and her son, from "The Drover's Wife," and Joe, the father, and Mrs. Brown from "The Night We Watched for Wallabies." Classmates can then interview them about their lifestyles.

See also Chapters 4 and 7 for strategies for responding personally to literature.

Classroom Strategies for Reading for Real Purposes: Any Text

Brainstorming About a Text Type

Rationale   As stated earlier, children learn language as they use language to learn. Children learn about particular text types as they learn about something else. It is important to find out children's existing understandings in order to plan for future learning.

Purpose   Through this activity, you will learn about the children's existing knowledge of a particular text type.

Strategy   The context of this strategy is the start of the study of a particular genre or text type. (Note that poetry is not considered a genre in the genrists' model, as it serves many different purposes. Hence I use the term *text type*.) The text type may be one the children will read and write as part of an integrated class study.

To begin, compile a list of individual children's statements about what they know about the text type or genre on a large chart. Write the children's names by their statements so that at any time throughout the study, individual children can revise, add to, or delete their statements. Refer to the chart at the start of each new teaching session and make necessary revisions and additions. The following example lists young children's understandings about poetry.

What Is Poetry?

it rhymes (Sam)	it can be happy (Kelly)
the words sound the same (Helen)	it's like a song, but it rhymes (Duc)
it's like a song (Frances)	it's a book (Brad)
it has pictures (Bill)	the words rhyme (Holly)

This chart was compiled in a K–1 classroom at the very start of the teaching unit. It indicates that generally, the children's knowledge of poetry was very much limited to rhyming poetry. It shows also young children's ignorance of the significance of shape in poetry. The children's understandings informed me that I should try to introduce poetry that did not rhyme, fill out their knowledge about the multiple purposes of poetry, and develop their awareness of the importance of shape to poetry.

Compare Genres

Rationale   Different genres have different organizing and linguistic features, which are determined by the purposes the texts serve. Comparing the features of two different genres heightens children's awareness to those particular organizing and linguistic features and to their links with text purpose and text audience.

Purpose This activity will help you determine children's existing knowledge about genres, in this case, the informational report genre and narrative, to inform future teaching.

Strategy You can use this strategy in the context of an integrated study of animals. For example, you can set a language goal for the children to learn about information report writing at the same time as using information report books to learn about animals.

Begin by having the children sit in small groups of three or four. Place a collection of books about animals in the middle of each group. The books can be narratives and factual books of the information report genre. The children can be familiar with some but not all of the books. Ask them to sort the books into two piles: storybooks and factual books. Then ask them to think about how they knew which pile to put each book in. What told them a book was a storybook or a factual book? Have a volunteer for each group list on a large chart the reasons the children give for making their decisions. When the class meets as a whole, compile a class list. For example:

Storybooks	**Information Books**
not true	has facts
tells information in a different way	shows serious photos
	doesn't matter where you start reading
not real pictures	titles are different
animals wear clothes, write, act like humans	tells real things
	index
fantasy	table of contents
imaginative writing	are true

Have children discuss the differences they have discovered. In further sessions, children can add other differences and similarities to their chart.

Evaluation

When evaluating children as text users, observe

> the different text types and genres the children choose to read
>
> whether the children's reading choices affect their writing
>
> the types of genres the children choose to write
>
> how well children achieve the purpose of a factual text (if reading procedural instructions to make a go-cart, for example, whether they complete the cart and are able to ride in it)

children's awareness of and use of different schematic features of different texts as they read (e.g., whether the children use the table of contents, index, and the glossary of an information report; whether children check and gather the necessary equipment for particular recipes or games when reading instructional texts)

whether children read magazines related to their hobbies and interests

whether children subscribe to magazines related to their interests

whether children choose to research via the Internet

how effectively the children shape their texts and choose linguistic items appropriate to audience and purpose when writing

Also, when children are reading literature, observe whether they

choose to reread favorite books

choose a particular type of narrative or a particular author (e.g., humorous, science fiction)

choose to borrow from the school library

relax and enjoy their books

refer to literature books they have read in classroom discussions of life issues

model their own fictional writing upon something they have read

Summary: Reading for a Purpose

In the big, wide world, people read for a wide range of purposes. Different social practices give rise to different literacies. Each one of us engages with different literacies, be they sports literacies or religious literacies or work literacies. Each one of us is a text user numerous times throughout each day. We've learned these literacies as we have engaged with the related social practices. So too with children: They learn language and literacies as they use them to live. They are text users as they get on with their lives, engaging in activities with their families and friends. "Children make sense of print in the environment because they encounter it as an integral part of interesting and important life activities in which they are engaged with others, such as having a hamburger or purchasing food" (Hudelson, 138).

School literacy programs must provide authentic purposes for reading of a humanistic nature and to do with organizing and surviving in the wider world. School literacy practices should also be accepting of and build upon the children's out-of-school literacy practices. Individual children must be helped to find texts to satisfy their life purposes. Their out-of-school hobbies may provide an inroad for them to reading with purpose. If children are to be lifelong readers, they must value reading because of the purposes reading can fulfill in their lives.

I return again to Nicholas: It was late September and we were gathered together, celebrating the birthday of Nicholas' mother, Jaqueline. Nicholas was five years and four months old and not yet at school. Prior to the evening meal, Jaqueline placed a container of four different dips together with crackers on a small table for people to help themselves to a snack. Nicholas' grandmother was sitting at a table sewing a bridesmaid's dress for another family member, so I suggested to Nicholas that he ask his grandma if she would like some dip. He walked over to her, and said, "Grandma, would you like some dip?"

She replied, "Yes, please, darling, but not a fishy one."

Nicholas walked back to the table. He picked up the lid of the commercial container, examined the four varieties listed on the lid, and reading from the lid, called, "There's a smoked salmon dip."

His grandmother replied, "Well, don't give me that one."

He proceeded to put some avocado dip on a cracker for her.

References

Flanagan, R. 1994. *Death of a River Guide*. Australia: McPhee Gribble.

Freebody, P. 1992. "A Socio-Cultural Approach: Resourcing Four Roles as a Literacy Learner." In *Prevention of Reading Failure*, ed. A. J. Watson and M. Badenhop, 48–60. Sydney: Ashton Scholastic.

Freebody, P., and A. Luke. 1999. "A Map of Possible Practices: Further Notes on the Four Resources Model." *Practically Primary* 4 (2): 5.

Hall, N. 1998. "Real Literacy in a School Setting: Five-Year-Olds Take on the World." *The Reading Teacher* 52 (1): 8–17.

Hudelson, S. "Literacy Development in Second Language Children." In *Educating Second Language Children: The Whole Child, the Whole Curriculum, the Whole Community*, ed. F. Genesee, 137–58. Cambridge: Cambridge University Press.

Kress, G. 1999. "Genre and Changing Contexts for English Language Arts." *Language Arts* 76 (6): 461–69.

Rosenthal, I. 1995. "Educating Through Literature: Flying Lessons with Maniac Magee." *Language Arts* 72 (2): 113–19.

Smith, F. 1988. *Joining the Literacy Club: Further Essays into Education*. Protsmouth, NH: Heinemann.

Children's Books

Carle, E. 1974. *The Very Hungry Caterpillar*. Great Britain: Puffin Books.

Lawson, H. 1963. "The Drover's Wife." In *Favourite Australian Stories*, comp. C. Thiele, 1–10. Adelaide: Rigby.

Rudd, S. 1963. "The Night We Watched for Wallabies." In *Favourite Australian Stories*, comp. C. Thiele, 111–14. Adelaide: Rigby.

Sendak, M. 1967. *Where the Wild Things Are*. England: Picture Puffin.

Wilson, L. 1987. *And the Teacher Got Mad*. Melbourne: Rigby.

Chapter 6

CRITICAL LITERACY: READING AS TEXT ANALYST

Critical literacy comes from a critical view of reality. This view is based on the premise that the social negotiations of the rules of proper behaviour, laws and social institutions are not conducted between equals because social, economic and political circumstances have given certain groups licence to assert undue influence over the outcomes.

Consequently, these outcomes benefit the negotiators unequally and the less dominant groups begin to doubt their self-worth and become dependent on the dominant group's values.

. . . However, a critical view of reality challenges the injuries and inequalities of the status quo by asking the question "Why are things the way they are?"

—PATRICK SHANNON IN QUESTIONS AND ANSWERS: CRITICAL LITERACY
BY K. STUMPF JONGSMA (1991, 518–19)

Developing Socially Aware Students

As outlined in Chapter 2, reading is more than reflecting back the words on the page. Reading is not soaking up the text without question or caution. Luke and Freebody's Four Resources Model better helps us see what is possible for readers. It enables teachers to ask, "Which of the practices possible for readers are developed and nurtured by my class program?"

As teachers, we work toward making our children literate, able to read and write. But how do we want them to read and write? For what purposes? What type of society do we envisage for our students? If we aim to develop students who are socially aware and able and willing to engage in democratic ways of doing things, what are the implications for curriculum and teaching practice?

Perhaps one way of ensuring students go into the world with a capacity and desire to work for a better society for all is to nurture them in classroom societies where they each feel valued, regardless of class, culture, race, or gender, and where the curriculum they live helps them better know and understand one another. I like Harste's (1996, xi) view of curriculum "as a metaphor for the lives we live and the people we want to be." Think for a moment of the curriculum we teach. What quality of life does it provide for each individual in our classrooms? How inclusive is this curriculum of children from other lands, other cultures, other economic classes? What is the impact of the curriculum we teach on the children's self-images and, hence, the people they will be? To what extent does it strengthen children to question and challenge existing power arrangements? On the other hand, what happens to children if the curriculum has one size for all—if the starting point for all is the same, if there is the same sequential path of learning for all, and if all children, despite differing strengths and interests, are herded toward the same narrow outcomes?

Reader as Text Analyst

Of course, if we wish to develop socially aware students, we must engage them in critical literacy practices where they assume the role of text analyst. The role of text analyst is crucial in the information age in which we live, with so much information generated so speedily via both electronic and print media, much of which is being controlled by fewer and fewer wealthy media barons. More than at any other time, readers need to be critically literate. Of course, individuals need to be critically literate to look out for their own interests, but for a more just and equitable society, we must read critically for others. Critical literacy involves knowing the following:

- All writing is a human construct.
- Writers have values.
- Writing involves writers making decisions.

- Writers' values affect the decisions they make.
- Although readers make their own meanings, writers aim to shape readers' meanings.
- Not all groups in our society have equal power.
- Not all groups in our society have equal opportunity to express their views through written texts; some voices are silent.
- Readers can reject particular stereotypes and points of view.

People reading critically ask questions like the ones in the following list. Questions are included for students of differing ages.

Some Questions to Ask of a Text

Who wrote this?

What was the author's motive for writing this?

What is the author's experience and expertise in the subject?

What has the author to gain from writing this?

Is this true?

What research evidence supports the author's claims?

What do other experts in this field say?

What are we not told?

Which questions are not asked?

Whose opinions are we not hearing?

Is this fair?

Is there another point of view?

How is the grandmother/grandfather portrayed in this book? Are all grandparents like this?

What is this saying about boys and girls/men and women/the elderly/people of different cultures/disabled people? Is this true for all members of this group?

Why is the main character a boy/girl?

What difference would it have made if the main character were a boy/girl/person of a different culture/person with a disability?

How else might the character have responded?

If you were the character, how might you have responded?

Why did the author choose to have the character respond in the way she did?

In this writing, who is powerful? Which people have no power?

In this story, violence was used to solve the problem. How else might the problem have been solved?

What is the author's underlying message?

How has the author used language to position the reader?

Which strategies is the author using to shape our meanings?

What are the design features of this magazine? Why are they included?

Classroom Practice for Developing Critical Literacy

In classrooms, both fiction and nonfiction texts may be interrogated by children. Classroom texts may be analyzed to see how different groups within our society are represented, for example, the disabled, the elderly, grandmothers, girls, boys, indigenous peoples, different racial groups, the unemployed, and so on. Author decisions made in the writing of fiction texts can be analyzed and related to the author's values and/or message. The credentials of authors can be challenged regarding their authority to write as they do. Texts are examined to see the ways authors try to influence reader interpretations, and the design features of texts such as magazines can be studied for the same reason.

Critical literacy does not start with older students or when children are independent readers. It begins from the earliest days of reading. Children learn to be critically literate at the same time that they become code breakers, text participants, and text users.

In this chapter, the strategies are embedded in the fully detailed critical study of particular texts, taken with children from five to twelve years of age. Examples 1–4 use picture storybooks and are done with emergent readers. The rationale for each of these is the same, but purposes vary slightly. Examples 5 and 6 are done with upper elementary children. Example 5 concerns the popular magazine "Smash Hits." In examples 1–4, note how emergent readers are engaged in critical literacy while the teacher is the code breaker.

Example 1: **Princess Smarty Pants** *by Babette Cole*

In this picture storybook, Babette Cole's princess is not the traditional stereotype. Princess Smarty Pants, while rich and pretty, does not want to get married. She does not dress in glamorous gowns and engages in some vigorous outdoor pursuits.

Rationale Picture storybooks are not value-free. They have been written by people who are not neutral but who think, feel, and value. Writers' values impact the way they shape their stories. Readers, as well as engaging with a story, need to identify the author's values and message and ask, "How do I feel on this issue?"

Purposes One purpose of this activity is to help children understand the following:

- Authors make decisions as they write.
- Authors' values influence the decisions they make.
- Authors try to shape reader meanings about groups within our society (e.g., princesses) by developing characters in particular ways.

Another purpose is to develop readers who are able to interrogate text.

Strategy   Before reading the story, the teacher told her K–2 children that the book was about a princess. She asked them to draw a princess and label what she was wearing. The children all drew princesses in full gowns in materials such as silk. Their labels included the following: "necklace," "ring," "crown," "pretty dress," "frills," and "silver shoes."

After hearing the story read aloud, the children then drew the princess from Cole's story and labelled what she wore. These labels did not include any jewelery, but rather "crown," "jeans," "daggy (tattered) shoes," "messy hair," and so on.

Next, the teacher asked the children to write why the author portrayed the princess in the way she did. Here are some of the children's responses (spelling has been corrected):

> Because she wanted her character to be smart and she changed it not like the other books, so it was not like the other books.

> Because if she married the prince, the prince would get all the money and she wouldn't get any.

> You can't have a good one always.

> She wanted to do something different—not copy anyone else. Girls don't have to be weak. They can be strong and do good stuff in stories.

Example 2: Rose Meets Mr. Wintergarten by Bob Graham

In this story, Rose's family moves in next door to elderly Mr. Wintergarten. Throughout the book, the illustrations show Rose's house to be brightly colored and the scene of much happy activity. Mr. Wintergarten's house is shown in gray with no sign of life. The local children tell frightening stories about Mr. Wintergarten. However, all this changes when Rose goes to retrieve her ball from Mr. Wintergarten's property.

Purpose   The same purposes listed in Example 1 apply here. In addition the story helps children understand that:

- Not all groups within our society have equal power.
- Readers can reject particular stereotypes and points of view.

Strategy   All the children in this P–1 class were seated on the carpet in front of the teacher. Children had writing paper and pencils supported on small chalkboards on their knees. The teacher began by reading the story aloud to the children. The children then responded in writing to the question "In this story, what was life like for Mr. Wintergarten?" Some of these young children wrote in their own codes, which the teacher transcribed after they had finished. (See Figures 6–1 through 6–3.)

He was mean. Then he was good.

Figure 6–1 Jackson, Age 5

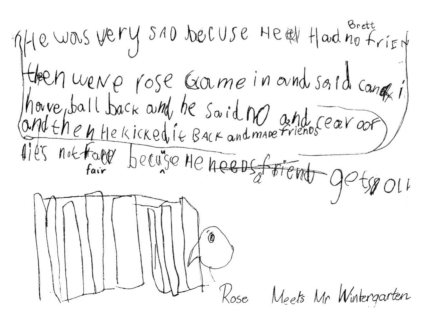

He was very sad because he had no friends.

Figure 6–2 Brett, Age 6

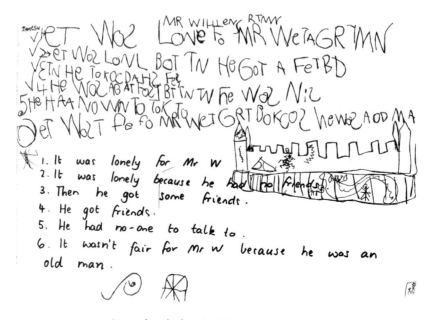

It was lonely for Mr. Wintergarten.

Figure 6–3 James, Age 6

Next, the teacher read the story aloud a second time and asked the children to respond to the question "Was it fair that Mr. Wintergarten lived as he did?" (See Figures 6–4 through 6–8.)

Finally, the children discussed the elderly people they knew. Did they live alone in dark houses? Is it true that all old people live alone and are grouchy?

Example 3: Playing Marbles *by Julie Brinkloe*

In this picture book, a young girl draws a circle in the dirt so she can play marbles. Two boys try to take over the circle. The girl stands her ground and the three children play a game together. The three players each win the same number of marbles.

Purpose   The same purposes listed in Example 1 apply here. In addition, the story helps children understand that: a changed author decision changes the course of a story.

Strategies

Session 1   The teaching focus of the following session was to develop an understanding that authors make decisions as they write. All the children in this P–2 class were seated on the carpet in front of the teacher. Children had pieces of writing paper supported on small chalkboards on their knees. The teacher began by reading the story aloud, stopping after the boys challenged the girl for her marble circle: "'We're playing here,' said the boy with freckles." The teacher asked the children to write their predictions of how the girl would respond. Then the teacher finished reading the story.

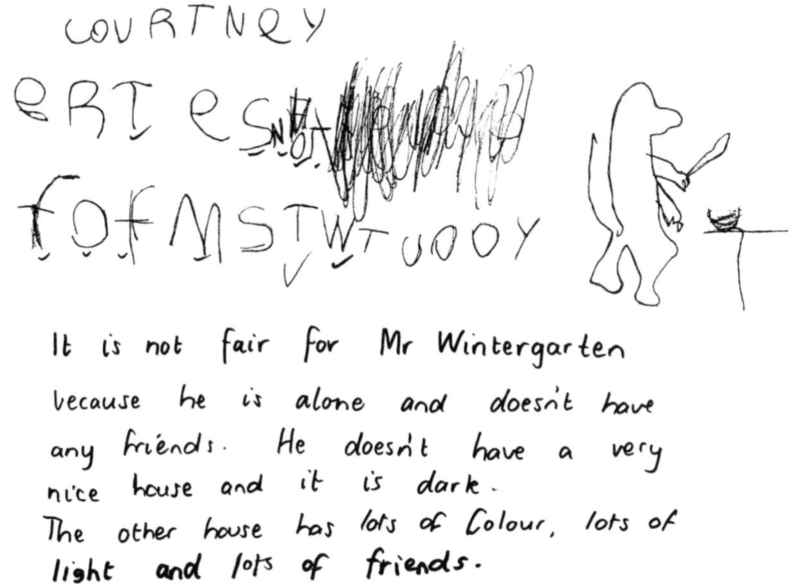

COURTNEY

ERI eS NoTfAIr

foFMSTWTuooY

It is not fair for Mr Wintergarten
because he is alone and doesn't have
any friends. He doesn't have a very
nice house and it is dark.
The other house has lots of Colour, lots of
light and lots of friends.

It is not fair for Mr. Wintergarten because he is alone and doesn't have any friends. He doesn't have a very nice house and it is dark. The other house has lots of color, lots of light, and lots of friends.

Figure 6–4 Courtney, Age 5

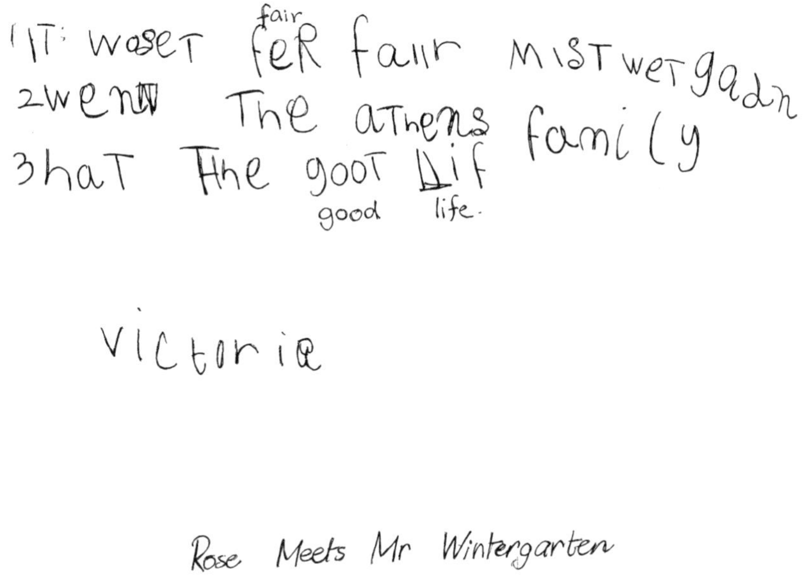

'IT' waseT feR fair faiir MISTweTgadn
2wenw The aThens family
3haT The gooT Lif good life.

ViCtorie

Rose Meets Mr Wintergarten

It wasn't fair for Mr. Wintergarten when the other family had the good life.

Figure 6–5 Victoria, Age 6

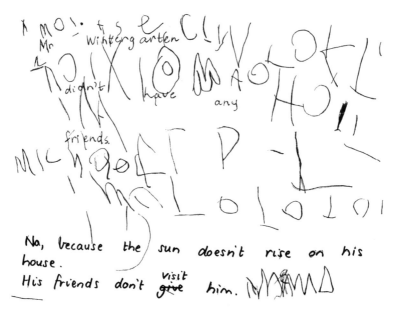

No, because the sun doesn't rise on his house. His friends don't visit him.

Figure 6–6 Michael, Age 4

Everyone should have more food to get more life into their heart.

Figure 6–7 Shannon, Age 5

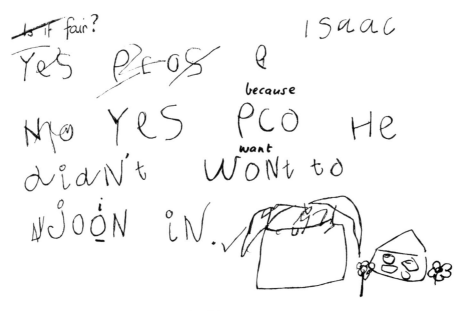

Yes, because he didn't want to join in.

Figure 6–8 Issac, Age 6

(Note: A second prediction could be made at the point in the story where the children decide to put in three marbles each, that is, nine altogether. Children could predict who will win the game or how many marbles each child will have at the end of the game.)

Next, the children shared their predictions and grouped them. These children's predictions of the girl's response to the boys' challenge fell into three groups:

1. Girl gives in to boys: *Wol I dot no.* (Well, I didn't know.)
2. Girl stands her ground: *I got he fost gos git a rit as wal!* (I got here first. Girls have got a right as well!)
3. Girl invites boys to play with her: *Do you want to play with me?*

In this classroom, three children predicted the girl would give in to the boys, nine predicted the girl would invite the boys to join her, and fifteen predicted the girl would stand her ground and keep claim on her territory.

Session 2 In this session, the teaching focus was to develop an understanding that a changed author decision changes the course of the story. The teacher began by reading the story aloud to the children. She referred to the three categories of responses the children had predicted. She chose a response from category 1 (girl gives in to boys): "Well, I didn't know." In small groups, the children retold the story using this alternate response. Then groups shared their stories and discussed how the changed response changed the course of the story. Here is one group's version:

> She gives up her ground because she doesn't want to play with the bullies. The girl goes far away to another area and plays marbles by herself. When the sun goes down, she goes home.
>   The girl is feeling not happy. She's feeling like a loser because she gave in to the boys.
>   After they scared her off, the boys play marbles in the girl's circle. When the sun starts to go down, they go home. They would be feeling happy because they've scared the girl off. They feel that they've won: that they're stronger than the girl.

Some individual children wrote their own versions of how the story might have changed with a different response, for example, "'Sorry, you can't play here,' said the girl."

> The boys trid to bolle (bully) her but she stood her grand (ground) and Sade (said) I got hea fost (first), and the boys went home in two diffrnt drakshns (directions).

> —ALEXANDRA, AGE 6

Session 3   The teaching focus of this session was to develop an understanding that authors' values affect the decisions they make and that authors try to influence the meanings we make. The teacher began by rereading the story. She drew attention to the ending, where each child won three marbles. In small groups, the children discussed Julie Brinkloe's decisions to (1) have the children play together and (2) have each child win an equal number of marbles. Why did she make these choices? Here, the students were identifying her purpose for writing the book.

Example 4: Tusk Tusk by David McKee

In this picture book, all the elephants in the world were once black or white. They hated each other. One day a terrible battle started. The peace-loving elephants hid deep in the jungle. Years later, they emerged and were now all gray. They lived peacefully until they noticed their different-sized ears.

Strategies

Session 1   Here, the teaching focus was to develop an understanding that authors make choices as they write. The grades 2–3 students sat in front of the teacher with notepads or paper on chalkboards on their knees. The teacher read aloud until the place in the story where the peace-loving elephants retire to the center of the jungle. The children wrote predictions of what would happen next. The teacher finished reading the story. The children shared their predictions and grouped them. This was done with the children sitting in a circle, each reading aloud and then placing his or her prediction in the appropriate pile.

Session 2   The teaching focus of this session was to develop an understanding that authors have values and that their values influence the decisions they make. In a sense, this book is a never-ending story, for when the gray peace-loving elephants come out of the jungle they live in peace until the little-eared elephants start giving the big-eared elephants strange looks.

The teacher began by reading the story aloud right to the end. Then she asked, "What might happen next?" She reread the story, substituting "big-eared" and "little-eared" for "black" and "white." When the peace-loving elephants, all with medium-sized ears, came out of the jungle, she asked the children to give possible differences for the next story. For example, now the long-toed elephant and the short-toed elephants start giving each other strange looks. Throughout this discussion the children came to see that the characters chosen by the author were different in relation to some body characteristic, e.g., color of skin, size of ears. Then children individually listed other possible body characteristics that might cause friction. For example:

thick trunks and thin trunks

sharp tusks and blunt tusks

big feet and little feet

Next, the teacher reread the book using some of the children's characteristics. Finally, as an optional activity, some individual children chose to innovate on McKee's text and write their own versions.

> Once all the elephants in the world were short tailed or long tailed. They loved all creatures but hated each other, and each kept to his own side of the jungle. One day the short tailed elephants decided to kill all the long tailed elephants and the long tailed elephants decided to kill all the short tailed elephants. The peace loving elephants from each side went to live in the darkest jungle and were never seen again. A battle began. It went on and on and on . . . until all the elephants were dead. For years no elephants were seen in the world. Then, one day, the grandchildren of the peace loving elephants came out of the jungle. They all had middle sized tails. Since then the elephants have lived in peace. But recently the big toed elephants have been giving each other strange looks.
>
> —Lexie, grade 2

Session 3 The teaching focus of the next lesson was to develop an understanding that authors try to shape reader meanings. The teacher began by rereading the story. She then asked, "Why did David Mckee write this story the way he did? What was his message?" Children individually wrote their answers.

> STOP RACISM
> Because otherwise you'll
> START A WAR!
> Pauline Hanson IS SAYING Too Many BROWN/BLACK people are MIGRATING into AUSTRALIA & aborinals ShoLD Migrate
>
> —Jesse, grade 3

Example 5: Using Mass Media Texts

Rationale Mass media texts are written to sell in large quantities to make profits for commercial publishing companies. However, they are not value-free. They, too, have been written by people who are not neutral but who think, feel, and value. Writers' values impact on the ways they shape their articles. As well as engaging with text, readers need to identify the writer's values and message and ask, "Is this true?" Readers should be alert to strategies used by publishers to increase sales.

Purposes One aim of this activity is to help children understand the following:

- Authors make decisions as they write.
- Authors' values influence the decisions they make.
- Authors try to shape reader meanings about groups within our society (e.g., pop stars) by writing about them in particular ways.
- Not all groups within our society have equal power and access to the media.
- Publishers use particular strategies to boost sales.

Another aim is to develop readers who are able to interrogate text and who will challenge the status quo.

Strategy

Sessions 1 and 2 Through a survey of children's reading habits (Wilson 1998), it was learned that of the texts read voluntarily by children outside school hours, the most popular was *Smash Hits*, which was closely followed by *TV Hits*. In the following example, a grade 3–5 class was working on an integrated unit of study on music. To commence the unit, children completed an interview sheet that included questions about their favorite groups and solo performers.

Next, the teacher photocopied interviews with Hansen and Cleopatra, two of the children's favorite groups, from *Smash Hits*. The children read the interviews and were asked to write in their own words what they learned from each article about the group and what each article did not tell them about the performers' lives. Not all the children found it easy to list what the articles did not tell, such as information about schooling, friends, hours spent in rehearsal, problems of being stars, and so on.

Session 3 Because in the two previous sessions, most children had had difficulty identifying what the interviewers were not asking about, in this third session, the children were given just the questions from a Smash Hits interview with members of Bachelor Girl, another group popular with the children. The article was titled "Rock Star or Pussycat?" and the interview was intended . . . to find out if they have what it takes to cut it in the biz!" The entertainers' answers to the questions were deleted from the sheet, as the purpose of the activity was to have the children focus only on the questions asked by the interviewer.

Rock Star or Pussycat?

Questions asked of Melbourne duo Bachelor Girl "to find out if they have what it takes to cut it in the biz!"

1. When was the last time you stayed up all night?
2. When was the last time you got into a brawl?
3. When was the last time you lost your voice?
4. When was the last time you got kicked out of a club?
5. Have you ever travelled in a limousine?
6. Has anyone famous ever asked you for an autograph?
7. Do you have a tattoo?
8. Would you get your tongue pierced?
9. Have you ever smashed up an instrument on stage?
10. When was the last time you stage dived?

The teacher asked the children to read the questions and respond to these prompts: Why did the interviewer ask these questions? Why not other questions? Only a few children had insight into the motives for these types of questions.

> These Q's are a bit unfair and personal for the person who is doing the A's. The journalist is asking these Q's to find out from the A's if the person who is doing the A's is weak or the opposite.
>
> —HARRISON, GRADE 5

> I think that the reporter is asking stupid questions to see how they react. I think he is trying to see how they handle it.
>
> —EUGENE, GRADE 5

Others felt the journalist was trying to ask different questions to those generally asked.

> I think they asked these questions because they're different. Usually they ask questions like what are your favourite hobbies, and so people don't get bored.
>
> —BRIDGET, GRADE 5

> To ask questions that people would not ask.
>
> —TOM, GRADE 4

Session 4 The teaching focus in this session was to reveal how writers try to shape reader meanings and, more specifically, to show how interviewers' questions can create the image they wish to portray. Because in the previous session few children had made a connection between the questions asked by the interviewers and the image they were trying to create, the focus was moved in this lesson from the pop stars to the children themselves. The teacher asked the children to complete two questionnaires about themselves.

Questionnaire 1

1. What is your grandmother like?
2. What is the kindest thing you have ever done?
3. Which is your favorite ice cream flavor?
4. How do you help your mother and father at home?
5. What do you read in bed?
6. What do you want to be when you grow up?

Questionnaire 2

1. When did you last have a fight?
2. What's the worst thing you have ever done?
3. Have you ever shoplifted?
4. When are you mean to your brothers and sisters?
5. When you are really angry, what do you do?
6. How loud do you like to play your music?

Many of the children were quite angry that they were asked to answer some of these questions.

> But it is none of your business. I think some of these questions are a bit privet and pear-sonell like what is the wost thing you have ever done or have you ever shoplifted. Sorry. I don't think this should be you're business but I filled it out anyway.
>
> —BRIDGET, GRADE 4

Next, the teacher read a child's answers to questionnaire 1 and asked the whole group to tell about that child. The children were unanimous that this was a good, kind, helpful person. Shuffling the papers, the teacher pretended to withdraw a second child's questionnaire but in fact read aloud the first child's responses to questionnaire 2. The children described this child as selfish, cruel, and unkind. The teacher then revealed that these two questionnaires had been completed by the same child. The children were amazed!

The teacher then asked her students to read each of their questionnaire responses and write some notes about the link between the questions and the image created.

> Questionaire 1: This page can make a person look like he's made of gold. It does this by focusing on all the good things.
>
> Questionaire 2: This page can destroy some one. It does this by focusing on all the bad things.
>
> —HARRISON, GRADE 5

> Questionnaire 1: I think these questions make me look like the nicest person on the planet.
>
> Questionnaire 2: These questions make me look like a person you wouldn't like to meet in a dark alley.

—Brad, grade 4

Having to answer these two sets of questions about themselves certainly alerted the children to the ways particular questions create particular images.

Further Sessions The study returned to articles found in the pop magazines, carefully examining the questions being posed to the pop stars and the possible reasons for the questions. The children wrote the questions they would like to ask their favorite pop stars.

Finally, in small groups, they identified the design features of these magazines and tried to give reasons for the inclusion of such features. Features identified included free gifts, short blocks of print, lots of color, many photographs, and the full texts of the latest songs. Then the class produced their own pop music magazine called *Sixteen's Super Cool Music Magazine.*

Example 6: The Rabbits *by John Marsden and Shaun Tan*

This picture book featuring rabbits attired in colonial military uniforms is a thought-provoking, haunting allegory of European settlement of Australia. The characters throughout are rabbits and Australian native animals, while the artwork shows much evidence of developing Western civilization with multistory buildings and heavy machinery. The book is suitable for upper-elementary children (grades 3–6).

Strategy Before showing the children *The Rabbits*, the teacher asked them to think for a moment about how rabbits are generally portrayed in picture books. The children then sketched rabbits as they are generally drawn in children's books. They wrote three words by their sketches to describe how rabbits are generally portrayed. All children drew realistic rabbits and their descriptive words were of the soft, cute, and cuddly type. (See Figure 6–9.)

Next, the teacher read the story aloud, showing the pictures to the children. She read the story again and asked the children to focus on the following question: "Why did John Marsden and Shaun Tan combine to develop this book in this way?" The children wrote possible reasons the author and the illustrator created this particular book.

> I think John Marsden wrote 'The Rabbits' because he wonted to expres his feelings about how white people came to Australia and kind of took over from the aborgenis the Rabits were the white people and the native animals were the black people.
>
> He was trying to say it like he were one of the black people.
>
> He is saying how he would have felt if he was a black person and his child got take away.

—Erica, grade 5

Figure 6–9 Anna's Sketch

John Marsden wants us to think that all rabbits are cut (cute) and about the white people invading the Black and taking over because it's just like when you introduce another species it killes native animals and it destroys the food chain exactly like the white invading the Black.

—DAISY, GRADE 4

The Rabbits represent the English because they are indiginus to England and the possums are indigenes to Australia.

  Also because possums are brown like the aboriginals and rabbits are white like the English. John Marsden and Shaun Tan were trying to say, "Look how much pain and suffering we have caused them." "And we are sorry."

—ERIC, GRADE 6

The author wanted us to think about the possums (aboriginals) and how the Rabbits (white people) took over the land. And how the land will never be the same. And that the Aborigines didn't need all the houses and clothes they just needed to have there real land & their own cultural ways of doing things.

—ANNA, GRADE 6

Evaluation

When evaluating children's abilities in critical literacy, observe whether the children do the following in discussion or in written responses to literature:

ask questions about the author's credentials/purposes

query choices made by the author in the construction of a text

attempt to identify some underlying author message

challenge how a particular social group was portrayed in a text

check several texts on the same subject to verify facts

make comments about the fairness or the injustice of events

wonder about the views of those not represented in the text

question particular character development

question the way conflict was solved by the author

discuss the power arrangements between characters

refer to alternate views of other writers on the same subject

note how particular linguistic items are used to refer to particular groups (e.g., *assertive/aggressive, colonials/invaders*)

take action and express their concerns to writers and publishers

Summary: Critical Literacy and a Socially Just Society

The strategies and children's responses included in this chapter are examples of young children engaging with critical literacy. These strategies aim to bring children to question how texts position them and challenge the printed word. For these children, reading is more than learning letters or words or answering teacher questions about books. It includes interrogating texts and studying author motives.

Such strategies are necessary for all people living in today's world. With control of the media in such few hands, the old adage "Do not believe all you read" has new relevance. Of course, critical literacy has applications across all texts—not only print but visual and oral ones as well—of any medium.

Critical literacy is particularly relevant for the members of the teaching profession because curriculum decisions are now being made by politicians, wealthy publishing companies, and others who may have no reputable insights into how children become literate and who have vested interests in the maintenance of existing power arrangements. We of the teaching profession must spot the inaccuracies and distortions that are promoted about the teaching of literacy so that we can work together with parents and children to achieve high levels of literacy necessary for life in this current time.

To work toward a more socially just society, students need practice in interrogating all sorts of texts, in examining how minority groups within our society are portrayed, and in challenging existing power arrangements. "Beyond the classroom, critical literacy is a call to read and write in ways that enable us as readers and writers to sort out the inaccuracies within our ideological investments. In the grip of ideological distortions, social groups misunderstand their true situations and accept representations of reality that impede recognition and pursuit of the interests and goals they have in common" (Lankshear 1991, 223) The focus of this book is the teaching of reading, but, of course, critical literacy involves both reading and writing. When children read critically, they can be encouraged to take action and respond to texts by writing critically. Their writing could include letters to newspapers, media outlets, local governmental bodies, and politicians. Such letters would describe and question inequalities and injustices the children perceive.

MISS N. VIRONMENT

Slogans on her T-shirt
Slogans on her car
Stickers on the windscreen
And on the bumper bar.

STOP ALL MINING
STOP THE DAMS
SAVE THE WHALE
RECYCLE CANS

We're always writing letters
To the radio or the press
Voicing our objections
To environmental mess.

BAN ALL LOGGING
SAVE THE TREES
RECYCLE PAPER
COMPOST LEAVES

She says it is our world to save
(She's facing her retirement)
If long lives we are to lead,
WE MUST SAVE OUR ENVIRONMENT.

—LORRAINE WILSON

References

Hartse, J. 1996. Foreword to *Sketching Stories, Stretching Minds*. By P. Whitin. Portsmouth, NH: Heinemann.

Lankshear, C. 1991. Getting It Right Is Hard: Redressing the Politics of Literarcy in the 1990's. In Selected Papers, 16th Australian Reading Association Conference, ALEA, Adelaide.

Stumpf Jongsma, K. 1991. "Questions and Answers: Critical Literacy." *The Reading Teacher* 44 (7): 518–19.

Wilson, L. 1998. *Reading Survey of Grades 5/6 Children*. Melbourne. Unpublished.

Children's Books

Brinckloe, J. 1988. *Playing Marbles*. New York: Morrow Junior Books.

Cole, B. 1986. *Princess Smarty Pants*. Great Britain: Picture Lions.

Graham, B. 1994. *Rose Meets Mr. Wintergarten*. Ringwood, Victoria: Puffin Books.

Marsden, J., and S. Tan. 1998. *The Rabbits*. Port Melbourne, Australia: Lothian.

McKee, D. 1987. *Tusk Tusk*. London: Beaver Books.

Chapter 7

LITERATURE TEACHING

The thought provoking literature class is an environment where students are encouraged to negotiate their own meanings by exploring possibilities, considering understandings from multiple perspectives, sharpening their own interpretations, and learning about features of literary style and analysis through the insights of their own responses. Responses are based as much on readers' own personal and cultural experiences as on the particular text and its author.

—JUDITH LANGER (1994, 207)

In this chapter I focus particularly on classroom organization for literature teaching. Literature teaching includes the whole class enjoying one book read aloud by the teacher, small-group study of a book, and individual literature choices. Literature teaching incorporates all four reading practices (Freebody and Luke 1999), as readers are code breakers, text participants, text users, and text analysts.

The literature books read aloud by the teacher must be carefully chosen. They should include demonstrations of different styles of writing and introduce children to authors they haven't read yet. When the teacher reads a book aloud to the whole class, it is an excellent opportunity for him or her to demonstrate the four practices. For example, the teacher can reread to make meaning, respond personally, encourage and accept different interpretations, discuss what she has learned by reading the book, interrogate the text, question the author's motives, and wonder if there is another point of view. By listening to and talking about one novel with the class, the teacher can foreground different ways of responding personally to and questioning or interrogating the text. Some of these whole-class demonstrations have been described in earlier chapters. Such demonstrations build within the children a rich repertoire of ways to engage with literature.

Developing a Love of Literature

There are many reasons we want children to love reading literature. Through reading, we want them to participate by enjoying and feeling and empathizing. Through the lives of book characters, we want them to learn about their own lives and the lives of others. We want them to delight in the craft and the magic of writers and illustrators and be inspired to be writers and illustrators themselves.

Through literature, children learn about themselves, their communities, the wider world. They are introduced to other people, other lands, other times, and other ways of being.

> My whole argument is that the world of this text—of any text—is not the real world. For the space of time that I exist within the world of this text, I get to try on alternative frameworks for reality that might not be on anyone's cultural map. I get to navigate my thinking with a literary map which might introduce me to places within myself that I have never visited before. (Rosenthal 1995, 115)

Those of us who are committed readers know what it's like to be hooked on a book. I spend some days at work in my office, which happens to be in my home. There's many a day I want to leave my desk and lie on my bed to continue whichever novel I am reading at the moment. It's such a wicked thought! But it's that feeling of being drawn into the book or pulled along by a book, of not wanting to put a book down, of reading until 1 A.M. in the morning when I have an early start on the following day . . . it's that feeling that I want to pass on to my students when I'm teaching literature. If I can develop this, then I know the children will be lifelong readers.

MISS BOOKWORM

Miss Bookworm lives for reading
She reads a book a week
She reads before she comes to school
And before she goes to sleep

She reads aloud each morning
When we first come inside
Seated on the carpet
Snuggled side by side

All is hushed and silent
Just her voice we hear
We go on wondrous journeys
Adventures far and near

All too soon she's closing
The book upon her knee
And thirty grade six children
Face reality

We love to hear her reading
She brings the text to life
She lives the stories with us
She groans, she laughs, she cries

Now we all live for reading
We read a book each week
We read before we come to school
And before we go to sleep

—LORRAINE WILSON

In this current time, increased mechanization in the workplace means fewer jobs and less people in full-time employment. This means longer leisure hours. One hopes that young people might read away some of this increased leisure time. When I see young people in the video arcades, pulling handles as bells ring and lights flash, I wonder if those same young people ever read novels. I guess for these children, playing in the arcades is social. Several friends can stand around the same machine at the same time. Through the teen years, when the need for friends and acceptance is strong, the book might be seen as a lonely, isolating experience. Perhaps reading centers could be established with Coke machines and comfortable couches, books, and magazines! Has anyone seriously looked at the needs of teenagers and reading? How many teenagers regularly visit libraries? Are homeless youth welcome in libraries?

I just know when I arrive at school and one of the older boys wants to stop me and talk about his current novel—"Have you read the next chapter Lorraine? What did you think . . . ?"—that something is right about our school literature program.

The Electronic Book

I wonder, too, about electronic books. Will one get this same feeling of being inside the text and transported to other places, when staring at the cold computer screen? Is touching a glass screen analogous with curling up with a book?

> I am sitting in front of the computer. I keep on wanting to touch it, to pull it towards me: I feel as if I'm in a scene from a prison movie, I'm in the visitor's room seated on one side of a glass screen, trying to reach out and touch the person on the other side. All I'm trying to do is read a story. But I want to get closer to it. I want to hold it. (Hawker 2000, 3)

Here, Phillippa Hawker describes the cold separation she feels from the story, from the author, in trying to read a Stephen King novel that was published only online. Perhaps I'm too old to change my habits: I'll continue to take my literature from books. On the other hand, if many of those boys so hypnotized by the computer screens as they play noisy, explosive computer games could be weaned to literature via the same screens, I'd welcome that!

Teacher as Reader

I find it hard to conceive how teachers who do not read literature, who do not enjoy reading, could develop children who are passionate about books, about authors, about literature. How sincere can we be in our teaching if we are trying to have children do that which we do not do or that which we do not value? It is important that teachers are seen by their students as readers who enjoy reading. At silent reading times in classrooms, teachers should be seen lost in their books, not wanting to end this quiet interlude. As well as reading adult novels, this is a time when teachers can catch up on professional reading and the latest children's novels or sometimes the daily newspaper.

When a teacher sits reading in a classroom, she is demonstrating that she is not only a teacher of reading but also a practicing reader. Similarly, if we wish for children to use literature journals for genuine reflections and learning, then we the teachers must demonstrate this.

Recently, I have been working in a grade 4–6 classroom, establishing the classroom routines for shared literature teaching for a teacher new to the school. Six of the older boys chose to read *Martin the Warrior*. I chose to read this novel with them because it was one I had not seen before. In the first session, I struggled to get through the introduction and was wondering if the group members would wish to continue with their selection at discussion time. Only one of the boys, Tristan, a very accomplished reader, was not enjoying the book. In my own journal entry toward the end of the session, I expressed some of my frustrations.

2/9 *Martin the Warrior,* Brian Jacques

Oh why did I choose this book!!! I am struggling. I find I am constantly re-reading to try to make sense. This book is set several centuries ago and uses many words I am not familiar with, e.g., damson. As well all the characters are ANIMALS. I'm not into animals!

Is this book one of a series? Perhaps one builds up the necessary knowledge to understand by reading all the series. Joshua advises me to keep reading. He says that the book gets better in Chapters 1 and 2 and you start forgetting the characters are animals. Here's hoping!

2/16 *Martin the Warrior*, Brian Jacques

Joshua was right: the introduction was more difficult to understand than the chapters. I am now actually getting into the story. I like the ingenuity of the writer regarding the ways the small creatures defend themselves and their friends (e.g., the mouse with the slingshot). I find now that I am just skipping over words and expressions from some earlier period which I do not understand.

My responses here are not contrived. I was really frustrated by this novel. My response, which I shared with the children, demonstrates that I don't expect every child to like every book and that initial access into books is not always easy.

Some Principles for Literature Teaching

There is no one right interpretation of literature. Individuals interpret the same literature differently because of the differing life and cultural experiences they bring to bear on what they read.

> Response is personal. Therefore literature has multiple interpretations. The text does not provide a meaning but offers many possibilities as each reader brings an individual set of experiences to the transaction. Responding to literature becomes not finding the meaning sanctioned by teacher, class or critic but finding one's own personal experience with the text. Response must still be grounded in text, but that grounding permits a wide range of possible responses. (Spiegel 1996, 333)

Self-motivated readers need choice over the books they read. What would happen if you had no choice of the book you read each evening? I wonder how long you would keep reading. Think for a moment of your close friends. Think of what it is they enjoy reading. Who chooses their leisure reading material? Being told what it is we are to read removes the pleasure of choosing and anticipating. In life situations when readers are told what to read, the purposes for the reading are also often determined for them.

Of course, in school when a group is to read the same title, not every child in the group gets his first choice each time, but the group titles can be selected by the group rather than the teacher. Some teachers doubt children's capacity to select their literature titles. I think trust is an issue here. Children will not select titles that are too easy for them or from which they will gain nothing, whether it be it enjoyment or further understanding of the ideas. If through our whole-class demonstrations we are introducing a variety of genres and authors, children will not continue reading the same material, choice after choice after choice.

A first-grade child's journal entry at the conclusion of a literature session was a poignant reminder to me of the importance of children having a say over the books they read. (See Figure 7–1.) On this particular day, I had selected the books.

It was too easy because I have read it before. Everyone knows about cars.

Figure 7–1 Michael

Book talk is essential. Literature teaching includes book talk.

> And while independent reading is a goal, reading with children and talking about books is also necessary. Not only does talking about books motivate children to read, it enhances their development of important cognitive strategies. In fact, classroom studies are showing that social interaction as well as strategy instruction is strongly related to the amount and breadth of students' reading. (Guthrie et al., quoted in Braunger and Lewis 1998, 64)

It is through talk that we clarify our ideas, broaden our understandings, and share our insights. In engaging in book talk, children pose questions, develop interpretations, explore hunches, and discuss issues. Importantly, they also compare texts and writing styles. They come to know that there is no one right way to interpret text.

Book talk in which the participants take the lead and are free to raise the issues of concern and interest to them is crucial in literature participation and interpretation. Such activity contrasts dramatically with some follow-up literature activities that stultify individual interpretation and have students guessing the teacher's preferred answers.

Children should be allowed to generate their own questions. If we want children to enjoy reading, if we want children to see purpose in reading, if we want children to know there is value in reading, we must encourage them to generate their own questions and seek answers through rereading, discussion, and reflection. This does not exclude the teacher from asking questions. But children must not believe that the purpose for reading is to answer someone else's questions.

The teacher has an important role in modelling different types of questions (and also different ways of commenting about and responding to literature):

I wonder what will happen in the next chapter?

How did this author let us know what sort of character Jimbo was?

It appears that this main character is very like the main characters in the other books by this author. What do you think?

If you had been that character, how would you have handled that situation?

What do you think of the ending to the story? Was it a satisfactory ending?

What might an alternative ending have been?

Has this ever happened to you?

What does this book tell us about the life of the early pioneers?

Is this view consistent with the other books on this topic?

Why do you think this author wrote this book?

Why is the main character a girl/boy?

What do you think of the representation of the grandmother in this story?

The teacher might raise such questions as part of serial reading with her class or ask one or two such questions when joining in a small literature group discussion. However, the children's questions must be listened to and respected and form the basis for class discussion. (See Chapter 4 for some examples of child-generated questions.)

Shared Book Activities

It sometimes happens in classrooms that children engage in activities following the reading of a book that take more time than did the reading of the book and contribute nothing to the further understanding of the book. Any activity undertaken while reading a novel should be for the purposes of clarifying meanings, sharing insights, and understanding the author's purposes and writing style. Generally, this involves discussion and reflective notes. The guiding rule, though, for any literature-related activity is whether or not it will contribute to the child's understanding, interpretation, and response. Certainly sometimes a story map can help show the order or complexity of a plot, as a sketch to stretch (see page 161) helps identify underlying themes, but many classroom art and construction activities I observe children engaging with following the completion of a book are simply busywork, freeing the teacher to work with another group.

Certainly with five or six groups reading five or six novels simultaneously, it is difficult for one teacher to fully interact with each group and check on their participation and engagement with each of their respective novels. Having all children make an entry in their literature journals each session is one way the teacher can follow the depth of involvement of individual children. If a teacher is uncertain of a child's commitment, she can then read recent journal entries and ask to speak with that child.

I believe a certain level of trust must be given to children: where different groups are reading different novels, we may not have time to discuss in detail each book with each group. But we can certainly spend some time with each group, and for every second or third book, we can speak in depth with a particular group. If children are observed all reading silently or discussing quietly and their journals reveal they are engaging with their books, they surely are making better use of literature time than if they were making large three-dimensional constructions of a book character or even designing book covers!

Shared Literature Groups

Shared literature occurs when a small group of children sits together in the classroom and reads the same title. The value of shared literature is the group discussion that is possible when four to six children read the same book. When each child reads a different title, in-depth book discussion is not always possible.

Shared literature reading is one of many reading activities, so it should not occur each day but it may occur twice per week. While younger children complete a picture book in one session, reading once per week is not frequent enough to maintain the story lines of chapter books and novels. Having shared literature twice per week allows time for the children to read to targets set at the end of each classroom session.

Shared literature is possible with all ages. It works well for young children in multiage classes, where the range of reading abilities will encompass emergent to independent readers. Sometimes one of the older children or the teacher may work with the emergent readers while the others work independently, reading a book chosen by a representative of their group.

Suggested Organization for K–2 Shared Literature Session

Whole-Class Immersion   The teacher reads aloud a quality picture book. It may be the recent recipient of an award, a title from an author study, or a well-loved favorite.

Small-Group Work   Before sending the small groups away to read in their groups, the teacher has the children read the instructions on the cue cards (see examples on pages 154–55), copies of which are on display at the front of the classroom.

Beginning Emergent Readers   These children are not yet reading. They may enjoy activities with books read aloud to them or some language experience activities where texts are created about their direct experiences. Appropriate activities include

- repeated readings of a book
- repeated readings of a picture book and story recomposition with sentence strips
- listening to a story at the listening center
- reviewing and talking about a class experience and creating a text about it
- completing artwork for a class-made big book

Emergent and More Advanced Readers   These children are beginning to read print. When they read, their eyes are on the words. Of course, their eyes move backward and forward from the print to the artwork, but they know that they must focus on the print. They are developing a bank of words they can recognize automatically. They expect texts to make sense. They make sensible predictions about what will happen next.

These children work in groups of four or five. Each group has a different book to read. Each group has a leader. The groups are rough-ability groups. (Note that at other times during the week, the children will be working in mixed-ability groups or friend-ship groups.) The more advanced readers in the grade may be able to move between different groups, choosing books they are interested in, but the children generally read at this time a book with which they will be able to experience success. At the conclusion of each session, one or two children take responsibility for choosing their group's book set for the next session.

Each group has a specific cue card related to its ability that guides the group leader. For example, the following cue card is ideal for those young children who are beginning to read early repetitive texts for themselves.

Literature

1. Leader reads aloud.
2. All read together.
3. Talk about the book. Has this happened to you? Talk about it.
4. Read silently.
5. Read in turn.
6. Make a journal entry: date, title, author. Fill in a face showing what you thought of the book.

The next procedure is appropriate for children who are almost reading for themselves simple texts about familiar ideas with different sentence patterns per page.

Literature

1. Look through the book.
2. Talk: What is this book about?
3. Read silently.

4. All read together.

5. Read in turn.

6. Write an entry in your literature journal.

7. Practice reading your book to share with everyone.

The first steps of looking through the book and trying to tell the story, then discussing what the book will be about, helps the children focus on the meaning and prepares them for trying to read silently (step 3). Steps 4 and 5 involve reading the book with other group members and this helps individuals who had problems with some words or phrases when reading silently.

The next cue card is suited to those children now reading picture books independently.

Literature

1. From the title, predict what is going to happen. (optional)

2. Read silently.

3. Make an entry in your literature journal: title, author's name. Write a question, an opinion, a criticism, or a puzzle.

4. Share and discuss your journal entries.

The teacher sometimes has a question on the cue cards for the children to discuss. Sometimes she directs them to consider the art style or a feature of the writing style. The teacher always encourages the children to ask their own questions, make comments, and wonder about the book.

This simple strategy of setting out expectations for each group on a cue card assists greatly in having each group stay on task. Initially, the children need assistance in reading the cue cards, but if they are pinned up at the front of the class and revisited at the start of each session, it is no time before all the children can read them.

Whole-Class Share   All groups gather on the carpet together with their books and journals. Some groups may read their book to the whole group. Others share their literature journal entries. General discussion occurs as to how well groups worked together.

Suggested Organization for Grades 2–6 Shared Literature Groups

Five or six children select a range of titles from the store of multiple book sets. They are to take into account differing interests and abilities within their class. Different children are responsible for making the book choices for each round of books. They choose four to five sets, with six to eight copies of one title in each set.

Children interested in reading the same book form a group. Sometimes it happens that one or two groups finish their books before other groups that are reading longer novels. These groups may choose another book set or engage with individual book choices. With older readers the span of reading ability can be quite wide and thus some groups will be reading longer more complex books than others. Hence not all groups finish their books on the same day. Some groups may read two or three books while one group completes just one book. However, to ensure there can be some movement between groups, it is good to organize so that several times during the year all children commence a new group novel the same day. With children having a say over their preferred title, the reading groups then do not have fixed membership. It is important that sometimes all children take part in a full range of new titles for the class so that the groups are fluid. There are two sessions per week with several days between.

Introduction to Books   Children sit in a circle while the teacher gives a brief introduction to each available title. (Remember, these have been chosen by the children.) She gives the title and the name of the author. Children may recall other books by that author. The teacher reads the blurb.

Children Peruse Books   The books from the boxes are scattered in the middle of the circle and the children have approximately seven minutes to have a quick look at each of the titles. The purpose of this is for each child to decide his or her first and second preferences. They are asked to flip through the book, read the first page, and ask themselves, "Can I read this book? Do I wish to read this book?"

Group Formation   The teacher then lists the children who wish to read each title. Sometimes more children wish to read a particular title than there are copies of the book. These children then opt for their second preference and the popular title will be repeated in the next round.

Silent Reading   As soon as children know their book groups, they move with their books to an area of the room where they can sit comfortably in a circle and read silently for almost fifteen to twenty minutes. They may sit around a cluster of tables, but they must sit in a formation that allows group discussion.

The teacher encourages the children to write any questions that occur while they read for later discussion in their group. Sometimes sticky notes can be good for this purpose. Children can stick their questions on the appropriate pages of the book.

Occasionally the teacher will give the children a particular stopping point where they will have to draw or write a prediction of what will happen next or who committed a particular action. These predictions are kept for comparison and discussion when the group meets to talk about the book.

Occasionally a child realizes he has made an inappropriate selection; perhaps the book is more difficult than he at first thought. He is permitted to join another group. When a child really wishes to read a title that is beyond his reading capabilities, another child in the group may read with him. Also, the parents of this child might be asked to read the book with their child at home.

Group Discussion   In their book groups, the children share their questions, comments, problems, hunches, wonderings, and predictions.

Literature Journal   Each session, the children make an entry in their literature journals, which becomes a record of literature books read by each child for the year. Each entry is dated with the book title and the author's name. The child does not write a book report. The entry may be the child's opinion of the book so far, a prediction about what is going to happen, a problem, a question, and so on.

Reading Target   The group agrees on a reading point for the next classroom session, for example, to the end of Chapter 4. Group members must take into account each member of the group.

Whole-Class Share   The class discusses general organizational issues, such as group cooperation, whether reading targets are appropriate, and so on. Children make general comments about their books and some individuals share their literature journal entries. At this time the teacher may share her journal entry as well. This is an excellent way to demonstrate the purpose and the value of the literature journal and different ways of responding. Sometimes she will just write a question or something that is uzzling her about the story. She takes the opportunity to express disappointment in or dislike of a book, if that is what she feels. She may pick up on comments individual children have made about the book and agree or disagree with them.

Individual Literature Books

As well as reading the same title (a shared title) as others in a small group, sometimes children read a title individually. This caters to children who have quite individual interests and tastes in literature and enables children to build confidence in of themselves as readers. Thus, while in some literature sessions all children read several shared titles in small groups, in other sessions some children may have individually chosen titles, and in occasional sessions all children could have an individual title. It might be that as part of the classroom organization of shared literature, in each session, one group of five to six children may be reading different novels and sharing a little about the individual novels within the group.

However, the value of the shared reading situation is the opportunity for discussion while the book is fresh in the mind of the readers. Such discussion can help clear up ambiguities, challenge and broaden individual children's interpretations, and expose different perspectives. When every child reads a different book in a class of thirty children, that important book talk is much harder to accommodate.

Literature Journals

The purpose of literature journals is to have children

- keep a record of books read
- reflect on books read
- formulate questions, note puzzles, list predictions, and so on as preparation for literary discussion within their groups

The entries in the journals are not meant to be book reviews, nor is their use meant to be tedious. It would be awful if the children felt that the purpose for reading were to make an entry in a literature journal. If someone is really reluctant to make an entry, all that is required is the book title, the author's name, and the date. Encourage children to write honestly in their journals. (See Figure 7–2.)

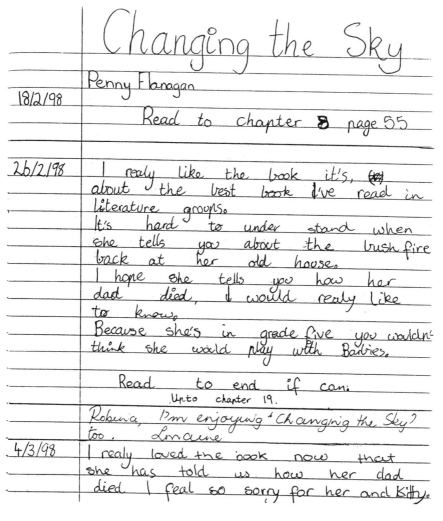

Figure 7–2 A Page from Robin's Journal, "Changing the Sky"

As I mentioned earlier, I found the book *Martin the Warrior* by Brian Jacques to be quite a complex novel. It is a fantasy genre with many small animals making up the characters. The language of some of the creatures is very hard to understand, like some very early English dialect. I include some of the journal entries of two of the grade 6 boys, Joshua and Tristan, who were reading this book. Joshua and Tristan were friends but their tastes in literature differed.

2/9 *Martin the Warrior,* Brian Jacques

I love this book! It's really great. It seems like the Hobbit and that was a great book too. It's a good story (it seems) and I like how they describe everything in detail. That's what makes a book good. I also like the language in it, sometimes it's a little bit hard to understand what they're saying but I can still enjoy it. The only thing is that I keep getting annoyed when Tristan complains about it being boring.

—JOSHUA

2/9 *Martin the Warrior,* Brian Jacques

I do not like this book. It absolutely SUX! Why you ask. I'll tell you why! (1) It's like Adolph Hitler and 65 communists all put together in a 365 page book! (2) It's from a series and you don't know which number it is. It's like making chips with no fat. (3) Is Brian a hippie? Does making a book about animals make him feel closer to Nature, well I'll tell you Brian old boy, I do Not, spelt with a capital N, do not like your book. (4) Finally it takes so long to explain one thing.

—TRISTAN

2/15

This book gets better as it goes. Oh! I like this theme and I didn't realize it was going to be a story told by someone. This Badrang guy is really mean and Druwp is such a traitor! Does he want to get out or not? I like reading about how the slaves are collecting weapons to use when Martin comes back to save them, but I also think it's sad how the little toddler collected weapons. It's sad what they get reduced to.

—JOSHUA

2/15

It's getting just a little, little, little bit good. Next thing you know I'll be saying it's the best. I don't take back what I say though. Animal pirates who would have thought! It reminds me of a totally psyched out, stuffed up version of 'Narnia.'" It's sort of the French revolution without the guillotine (unfortunately).

—TRISTAN

3/21

This book just keeps getting better every time I read. I wonder what Badrang will do about Captain Clogg? I can't believe they escaped the fort but it's unfortunate about them being split up. Oh well, they'll probably end up in Noonvale together.

This is great (as I say everytime) and I like all the characters coming into the book. The language is even harder to read since the language is all mixed together and parts are taken out.

—Joshua

2/26
I think Martin should have a new name. He's like Martin Luther King. He's trying to free everybody. Badrang is sort of like Adolph Hitler because he dreams of his own land, his own empire, a vision of supreme power and total domination.

—Tristan

Young Children and Literature Journals
From the earliest days of reading, young children can be encouraged to evaluate a book they have read from a personal enjoyment perspective. They come to know that it is all right to be critical of a book; they do not have to like everything they read. At a young age children can learn that different perspectives are valued and that there is no one right response to literature.

A simple strategy is for early writers to fill in a mouth on a face to show their opinion of a book. Their faces tell much about their enjoyment of a book! (See Figure 7–3.) If the children wish they can also write a comment about the book.

Figure 7–3 A First Goldilocks and The Three Bears

Figure 7–4 *The Sea Dog*

Sara did not write a comment about the book she had read but showed her delight in it with a picture of herself turning cartwheels. (See Figure 7–4.)

As the children become more proficient writers, they can stop drawing a face and write their reflections in full.

Sketch to Stretch

I have recently tried the sketch to stretch strategy as outlined by Phyllis Whitin (1996) in her book about this topic.

> My interest in sketching, like all good adventures, was inspired by students. I was familiar with the sketch to stretch strategy of Harste, Short and Burke (1988), but students made its potential come alive. The strategy is described as sketching what the story means to a reader. I was intrigued with the idea that colors, shapes and symbols might convey the feelings, themes and ideas in reading even though I have no artistic training myself. (xvii)

The children with whom I first worked were a multiage class of grades 4–6 students. They had a rich literature program and had much experience in personal response, mainly through talking and writing journal entries. We commenced by brainstorming commonly accepted symbols, such as those for love (heart), national pride (flag), peace (white dove), and so on. As this was a new strategy for the children, we worked as a whole group responding to four different texts over three sessions. In all three sessions, I read the texts aloud to the children, and they knew that on completion of the text they were to show what the story meant to them through sketches and the use of color and symbols. They might focus on the theme or the author message. I asked them not to just do a picture of the story or a visual retelling.

As recommended by Whitin (1996), when the children finished their first drafts, they met in small groups to explain their sketches. Group members could ask for clarification or offer suggestions. All children then had an opportunity to redraft their sketches. Figures 7–5 through 7–9 contain samples from the four texts used. The notes at the side of each sketch were written by teachers, following explanations by individual children. Here is a short synopsis of each text:

1. *Boring Mrs. Bun* by Juliet Martin: This is a picture book with a simple structure. The two sides of Mrs. Bun's existence are contrasted on alternate pages. Mrs. Bun works in a cake shop. She is always depicted as a dull, gray character while at work. The alternate pages reveal her private life—quite a contrast!

- She has a dark side and a happy side.
- She has two sides to her personality.
  - Brightness is represented by bright colours (left side).
  - The boring side is represented by dull colours (right side).

Figure 7–5 Alex's Sketch of *Boring Mrs. Bun* (Juliet Martin)

2. *Wrestling* by Eric Kupers: The central character in this story is a young boy called Eric. Feeling pressured by his school peers, Eric agrees to wrestle Marco, the social misfit of the school group. Eric likes Marco but is not strong enough to stand up to the noisy majority. He does as they want. He wrestles and hurts Marco and at the end of the story is left standing alone. Although he has won, he does not feel like a winner.

3. "Protection" by Eva Johnson and "Lawful Kidnapping" by Margaret Brusnahan: These poems are both about the stolen generation of Australian aboriginal children.

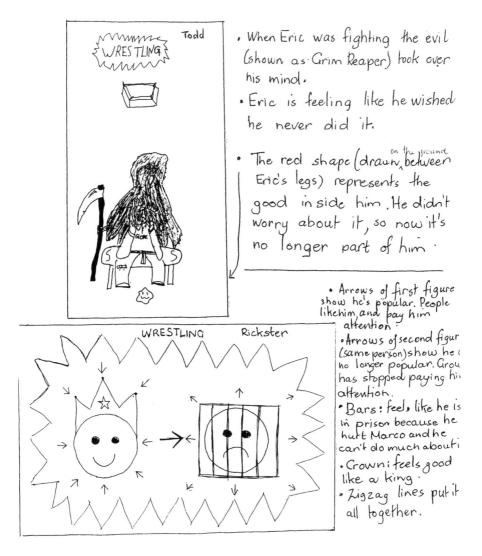

Figure 7–6 Todd's and Rickster's Sketches of *Wrestling* (Eric Kupers)

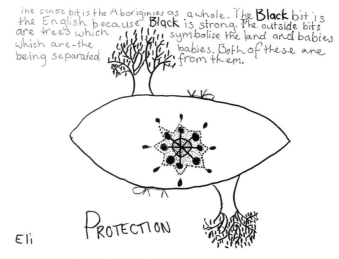

The centre bit is the Aboriginies as a whole. The **Black** bit is the English because **Black** is strong. The outside bits are trees which symbolise the land and babies which are the babies. Both of these are being separated from them.

Eli

PROTECTION

Figure 7–7 Eli's Sketch of "Protection" (Eva Johnson)

Emma

Emma explained that in her sketch, the two hands represent the white taking the black away; the two houses represent the homes of the aboriginal and white families. Note the love in the aboriginal home. Emma said that even though the white house was posh, there was no love in it. She explained that there is only half of the aboriginal flag on the right-hand side because the child is now only half aboriginal.

Figure 7–8 Emma's sketch of *Lawful Kidnapping* (Brusnahan)

On reviewing the children's sketches, the homeroom teachers and I agreed that the sketches showed insights of understandings not always evident in written journal entries. The sketching, allied with the request to use symbols and colors thoughtfully, meant the children were not just retelling the stories and poems. Rather, they were developing insightful personal interpretations. I feel the sketch to stretch strategy should be an option for children when responding in literature journals.

Sketch to Stretch with Younger Children

More recently I have used this same strategy with grade 2 children. Their teachers and I at first worried that the strategy might be too advanced for them cognitively. But at the end of three sessions where I read aloud the stories and the children responded by trying to use sketching, symbols, and colors to depict the theme or the author's intended meaning, I believed there was value in introducing this strategy. While these children did not have the range of symbols to draw upon that the older children did, they really did think carefully about what they included in their sketches in comparison to just drawing a picture of the story. They were focused on what the author might have been saying. (See Figures 7–10 and 7–11.)

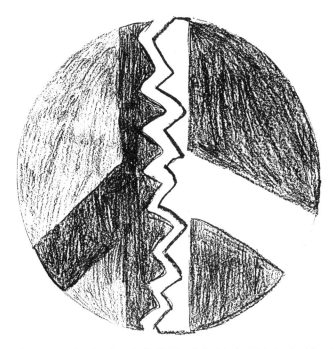

Maddie's sketch is the peace sign broken in half. The left side (which had a blue background) represents the aboriginal people running around free. The right side, which is crossed by a broad white band, signifies the coming of the white people.

Figure 7–9 Maddie's sketch of *Lawful Kidnapping* (Brusnahan)

Figure 7–10 Camilla's Sketch of *Boring Mrs. Bun* (Juliet Martin)

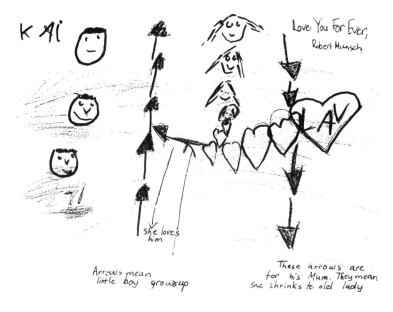

Figure 7–11 Kai's Sketch of *Love You Forever* (Robert Munsch)

Summary: Literature Teaching

In this chapter I have focused on some organizational strategies for the teaching of literature. As said in the introduction, in all literature lessons the children are engaging with the four reader practices of Freebody and Luke's model (1999), as illustrated in earlier chapters. In whole-class literature sessions the teacher demonstrates strategies that engage the reader in these practices. As well, the children are required to try out these strategies. When reading in small shared literature groups, the children have the time, the opportunity, and the know-how to read as code breakers, text participants, text users, and text analysts.

References

Braunger, J., and J. Lewis. 1998. *Building a Knowledge Base in Reading*. Portland, OR: Northwest Regional Educational Laboratory's Curriculum and Instruction Services, NCTE, and IRA.

Commeyras, M., and G. Sumner. 1996. "Literature Discussions Based on Student-Posed Questions." *The Reading Teacher* 50 (3): 262–65.

Freebody, P., and A. Luke. 1999. "A Map of Possible Practices: Further Notes on the Four Resources Model." *Practically Primary*, 4 (2): 5–8.

Hawker, P. 2000. "Readers Get the Bullet: Will Books Too?" *The Age Newspaper*. Melbourne, 25 March: 3.

Langer, J. 1994. "A Response-Based Approach to Reading Literature." *Language Arts* 71 (3): 203–11.

Spiegel, D. L. 1996. "The Role of Trust in Reader-Response Groups." *Language Arts* 3 (5): 332–39.

Rosenthal, I. 1995. "Educating Through Literature: Flying Lessons from Maniac Magee." *Language Arts* 70 (2): 113–19.

Whitin, P. 1996. *Sketching Stories, Stretching Minds*. Portsmouth, NH: Heinemann.

Children's Books

Brusnahan, M. 1992a. "Lawful Kidnapping." In *Raukkan and Other Stories*, 2. Western Australia: Magabala Books.

Flanagan, P. 1994. *Changing the Sky*. Hodder and Stoughton. New South Wales.

Jacques, B. 1993. *Martin the Warrior*. London: Red Fox.

Johnson, E. 1993. "Protection" in *Spirit Song: A Collection of Aboriginal Poetry*, compiled by Lorraine Mafi-Williams. South Australia: Omnibus Books.

Kupers, E. 1994. "Wrestling." In *Boyhood, Growing Up Male: A Multicultural Anthology*. Ed. F. Abbot, 31–33. California: Crossing Press.

Martin, J. 1986. *Boring Mrs. Bun*. New Zealand: Childerset.

Munsch, R. 1986. *Love You Forever*. Ontario, Canada: Firefly Books.

THE READING-WRITING CONNECTION

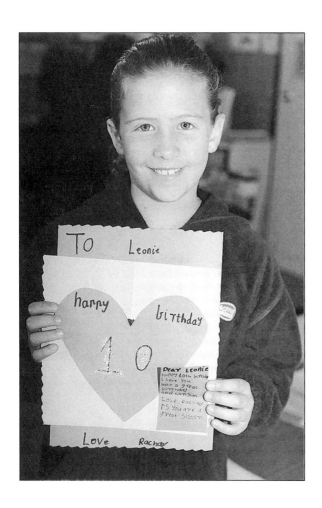

I urge us to see our tasks in schools as helping students read literature to understand the culture, to speculate on the ideas and the imaginative vision, and to speculate on the nature of and use of the language that is the medium of the artistic expression. We should help them read literature in order to understand themselves as readers, who they (and we) are, what our habits are, how our culture defines us and how we define it. We should help them use this understanding to build a sure sense of the audience for writing and to develop a sense of the importance of the craft. This means helping them learn about the uses of the language, about the culture and about the concerns and issues that cause people to enter into the transaction with text and into the imaginative uses of language that are designed to give pleasure. It means helping them connect the way they read to the way they write, to develop a sense of pleasure in the medium of the language, and to explore the cultures of the writer and of the community of readers in the classroom.

—ALAN PURVES (1993, 360)

Reading and writing are inextricably intertwined. To say that every time a child writes, that child is reading is to say the obvious. Likewise, every time a child reads, that child is learning about writing. He learns not only about different types of texts and the different purposes served by writing but also about letters, words, sentences, paragraphs, headings, labels, and directional features of written language.

In fact, reading nourishes writing. To read any text type is to inform our understandings of that text type and thus inform our attempts to write that text type. To teach writing divorced from a rich reading program is to feed writers a nutritionally poor diet.

Writing Acquisition

Writing acquisition, like oral language acquisition, is a process of hypothesis, or rule, formulation and testing. Pre-school-age children witness adults around them writing as part of their life routines and these children pick up pens and "write." Their early writing may be large circular scribbles or scribbles moving across a page. It may consist of separate letterlike symbols or strings of conventional letters. Numerals may be interwoven with the letters. Importantly, as young children learn to write through this process of experimentation, they simultaneously use their writing for some real-life purpose. They scribble on a sheet from a writing pad as their loved parent writes to a grandparent, and later, the child's letter is enclosed in the envelope along with that of the parent. They write a sign to place on a block construction, warning others not to touch. They scribble a signature under a painting.

The more experience these young children have with writing, with observing experienced writers writing, with demonstrations of print artifacts such as storybooks or street signs, and with experienced writers responding to these children's writing, the more information these young writers have to draw upon in the process of formulating rules about writing and how it works, and the more inspiration, confidence, and purpose they have to continue writing.

Five-year-old Charlotte voluntarily wrote a letter of congratulations to her cousin on the occasion of her marriage. Later in class time, after some help with some of the spelling, she wrote the congratulatory letter out on good-quality paper for delivery to the happy couple. (See Figure 8–1.)

Notice how her inability to spell some of the words conventionally did not prohibit her from using them.

CaNgragalases   congratulations
MariD   married

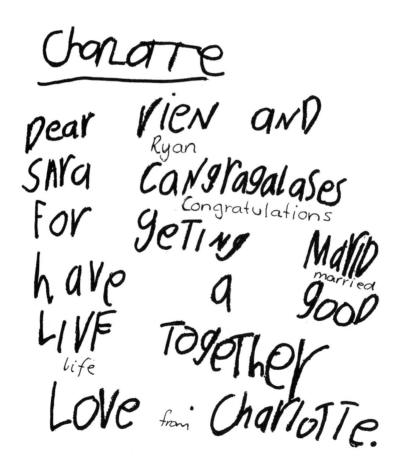

Figure 8–1 Charlotte's Letter

The Composing and Editorial Roles

Writing involves both the formulation of ideas and the application of editorial skills (spelling, punctuation, word usage) necessary to get the ideas onto paper. At the start of each new school year in any early primary classroom, one sees new starters who have learned that writing involves just the editorial role: they know they can't spell words correctly, they believe writing is spelling words correctly, and they fear making mistakes, so they write nothing in their early writing sessions. Sometimes they copy a few words from a classroom chart or they list words they have been taught at home.

> Mom
>
> Dad
>
> cat

However, in that same classroom there are children who know the purpose of writing, and even though they cannot spell conventionally, they take on the role of composer with much gusto.

Such a writer was James. From his first days at school he had much to say by writing. (See Figure 8–2.) As the weeks passed, the pages of his writing book were

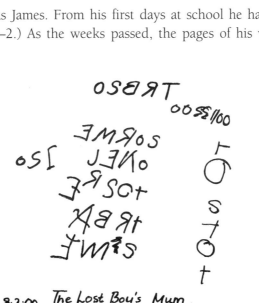

Figure 8–2 James' Sample 1

covered with line upon line of his strings of letters and always they told a great story. James' composing abilities were in advance of knowledge of the conventions of written language. One day in October, he wrote a short recount about a visit to a park. At the start of this piece there were some evident sound-letter connections. (See Figure 8–3.)

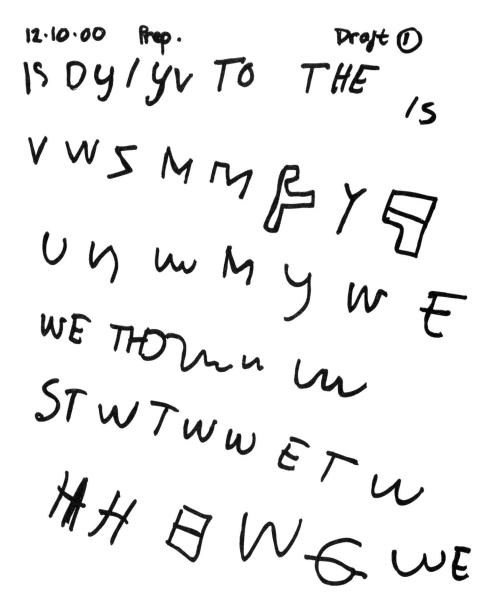

One day I went to the park and I saw a grasshopper. I catched it.

Figure 8–3 James' Sample 2

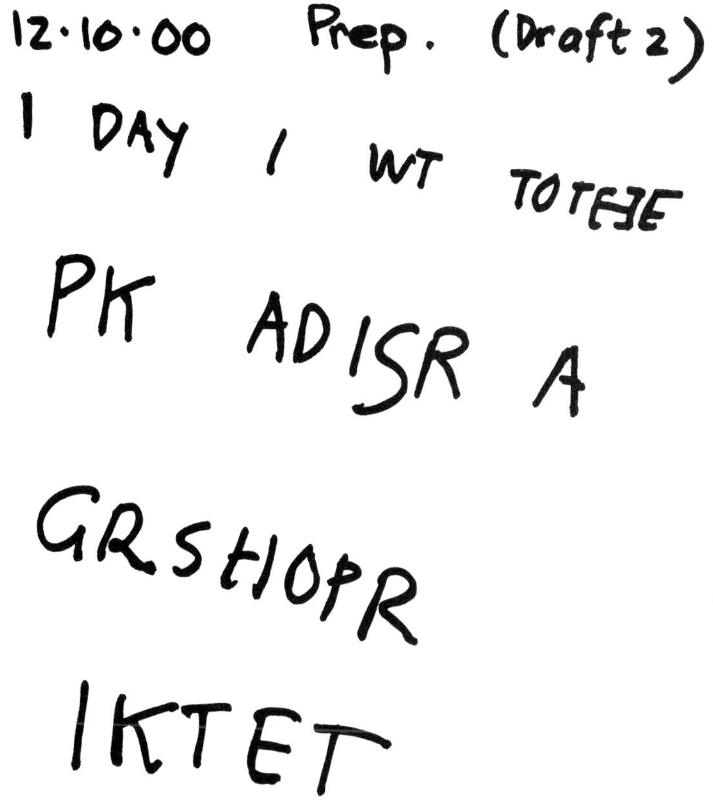

12·10·00   Prep. (Draft 2)

I DAY I WT TO THE

PK AD ISR A

GRSHOPR

IKTET

Figure 8–4 James' Sample 3

After he read the completed recount to his teacher, Jenny Hodges, she asked him to try to write it again on the facing page, but this time to focus on the spelling of each word, especially the sounds he could hear in each word. (See Figure 8–4.) This is an example of a teacher taking the opportunity to extend a child's knowledge of sound-letter relationships and word spacing skills, after the exhausting process of composing is completed.

How much easier it is for the teacher to teach at the point of need with children who compose freely. Their enthusiastic writings reveal their understandings about letters, directional features, punctuation, words, and spelling.

Reading Informs Writing

When each one of us writes, we draw upon our understandings about written text. The more widely we read, the greater depth and breadth of knowledge we have about the different written text types—how they are constructed and how writers appeal to and try to influence audiences.

Just imagine being asked to write a text type you have never seen, heard, or read. For example, imagine how difficult it would be to write a fairy tale if you had never listened to fairy tales or read one yourself. How would you know an appropriate beginning? How would you know appropriate characters, settings, and plots? Consider the following student sample:

> Once upon a time there was a palace in the middle of the forest. There was a King, a Queen, prince and princess. A mile away there lived a dragon. Almost every day the dragon came and tried to destroy the palace but the guards always chased him away. Once the dragon went to the palace and destroyed it. The poor King and Queen looked sadly at the wreckage because the prince and princess had been trapped. For many years the King and Queen looked sadly at the wreckage. Once a strange singing came from the sky. The rocks of the wreckage became lighter. So the prince and princess escaped. That same day the dragon died because he was 202 years old. Everyone was happy, especially the King and Queen.
>
> —RAJAN, GRADE 4

Was Rajan familiar with fairy tales? Obviously he was. He began with the traditional beginning, "Once upon a time." He outlined his characters, the King, the Queen, the Prince, the Princess, and the villain, the dragon. As in other fairy tales such as *Sleeping Beauty*, people can wake after many years of sleep or death, released by mysterious sources of power such as that of a kiss in *The Frog Prince* or the strange singing from the sky in Rajan's story. In his ending, the villain dies and everyone else is happy.

While it might be easy to be critical of the development of Rajan's plot—How come the dragon suddenly got past the guards?—it is also easy to see that Rajan has experienced many fairy tales. The knowledge gleaned from such reading has informed his writing.

Reading That Accompanies Text Composition

The reading-writing connection is not just about all the reading that occurs before a writer commences writing. The reading that precedes writing informs the writer about how to write. The reading an author does in the act of writing serves a different but very important purpose. It challenges the author's ideas and helps clarify his thinking about the subject of his writing.

> The reading which occurs in association with writing is of two kinds. Firstly there is the reading and re-reading of the written text as it is being constructed, or **reading which accompanies the text**. Secondly there is the sum total of all the reading that the writer has carried out prior to writing the actual text. Whenever writers sit before a blank page and begin to write, they call upon the knowledge that the reading of other texts has stored in their linguistic data pools. This is **reading which precedes the writing of a text.** (Cambourne 1988, 186)

This connection between writing and learning has implications for how teachers see the writing process. Because it is in the process of drafting that writers refine their ideas, teachers should not be aiming for the perfect first draft. It is as we struggle to get our ideas down that we learn more. Subject teachers who have students write about social and scientific issues should be fostering writing, rereading, and redrafting if they wish for their students to extend existing understandings and assume new insights. This is writing across the curriculum.

Building upon the Reading-Writing Connection

Because of this reading-writing connection, it is quite artificial to teach reading and writing separately. Where teachers spot gaps or weaknesses in children's writing, they might read aloud an example of effective writing from a published text. For example, if some children are not writing satisfactory and convincing endings to their narratives, the teacher might read several short stories as part of the introduction of a writing lesson and have the children discuss the different ending techniques. Authors can't get away with writing "The End" as many children do!

In reading sessions, children may be writing literature responses and in the process of this writing learn more about themselves and the ideas met through reading. It is very logical that at any one time children in the same class may be both writing and reading.

Classroom Strategies for Building upon the Reading-Writing Connection

Reading Aloud Different Types of Texts

Rationale   One way of informing children about different text types is to read completed examples aloud to them. When children listen to a text read aloud, be it a fairy tale or a sports report from a newspaper, they are immersed in that language and informed about it.

By reading aloud, one explicitly demonstrates how not all texts are read in the same way. One reads a storybook from the beginning and proceeds through to the end. However, one does not have to read an information text in its entirety.

Purpose   The aim of this activity is to demonstrate by thinking and reading aloud how different texts are written.

Strategies   *Factual Text*   In the context of a class study, identify something you want to learn about. For example, during a unit about sea creatures, you might say you want information about saltwater crocodiles. Turn to the table of contents in a factual text about sea creatures and read it aloud. When you find "saltwater crocodiles," note the page number and turn to that page. Then read aloud the relevant section.

Here you are demonstrating the use of the table of contents and the way information is grouped around topics in information report books. While reading such books, use of the index and the glossary may be similarly demonstrated.

Dialogue Narrative   In recent years I have been exploring the use of dialogue—just dialogue with no other language—in children's books. I have developed some simple narratives. In each story two characters talk to solve a problem. I cite an example. (Note: In the books, the artwork indicates which character is speaking.)

Billy Come Inside

MUM: Come inside Billy.

BILLY: I don't want to.

MUM: Billy it's raining.

BILLY: I don't mind.

MUM: You're getting wet.

BILLY: I don't care.

MUM: Billy your hair is wet.

BILLY: I can't see it.

MUM: Billy your jumper is wet.

BILLY: I can't feel it.

MUM: Billy, you'll catch cold.

BILLY: I'm not cold. I'm hot.

MUM: Billy, come inside right now.

BILLY: OK Mum.

BILLY: Mum, I'm wet.

—LORRAINE WILSON (1997)

The accompanying artwork by Stephen Axelsen shows a little boy desperately trying to fix his guinea pig's cage in the trunk of a tree, safe from the household dogs, before retreating into the house. This is the reason he delays going in from the rain.

Early last year I used these dialogue stories as immersions at the start of personal writing sessions with young children. I also demonstrated the writing of these stories. I have been amazed at the impact this has had on the children's writing. I include a sample written by Madison in the second week of her first year at school. (See Figure 8–5.)

Analyzing Writing Style

Rationale   Different authors use different strategies to convey information about settings, time periods, or characters.

Purpose   The purpose of this activity is to have children understand through the analysis of a published story that authors inform their readers about their characters through their actions, their thoughts and speech, their descriptions, or the accompanying artwork.

Strategy   After listening to *The Paper Bag Princess,* children in a K–2 class were asked to describe the characters of the Prince and the Princess and then to write how the author conveyed this. The children filled out charts about the characters. Here are Tom and Ed's responses.

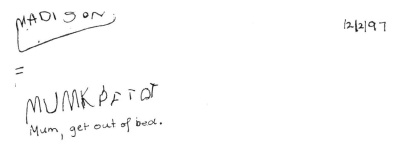

MADISON   12|2|97

=

MUMKρFTσT
Mum, get out of bed.

MUM KTON MUM KDDTᛁOO
Mum, get out of bed right this instant.

EᗷᏅD(
Why darling?.

ᗺᏅT
Because it's breakfast time.

DᏳ MUM
So get out of bed Mum

ᏒᏅᏒᐱ ᏅᏁᏅᐯ
OK, darling.

Mum, get out of bed.
Mum, get out of bed right this instant.
Why, darling?
Because it's breakfast time.
So get out of bed Mum.
OK, darling.

Figure 8–5 Madison's Writing

Tom		
	What sort of character?	How do we know?
Princess	cuning (cunning) Butuful (beautiful)	She Mad The dragon Tird The author told us She war cloths That were expensiv
Prince	Selfish	Bicos He Spoke To her in a selfish way

Ed		
	What sort of character?	How do we know?
Princess	mesind (messy) Nise hanse (handsome)	pica (picture) rist hor lif (risked her life) picar (picture)
Prince	hansem (handsome) sases (selfish) not brav	picar (picture) wot he sed picar (picture)

Innovating on Text

Rationale   To innovate on a text is to look more closely at the structure of that text. How did the author construct this text? What are the special features? Are repetition or rhyme features of this text? Both poems and stories may be used for innovating upon.

Purpose   This activity helps students understand the structure of a text by innovating upon it.

Strategies   *"Mary Had a Little Lamb"*   This activity can be done with grades 4–6 students. Begin by putting a large copy of the rhyme on display. Say the rhyme with the children. Check whether any of the children are unfamiliar with the rhyme.

    Next, identify the pattern of the rhyme:

    four lines

    lines two and four rhyme

    lines one and three have four beats

    lines two and four have three beats

Now read some published innovations on the rhyme to the children. (See *Far Out Brussel Sprout*, compiled by June Factor, 1983.) Discuss the notion of innovation, that is, constructing a new rhyme with the same structure as the first.

Then have the children work in pairs. They should choose a different pet for Mary and write a new version of the rhyme while retaining the same rhyme structure. For example:

> Mary had a little bird
> But feathers it had none.
> On sunny days the bird got warm
> By standing in the sun.

Possum Magic   I had a class of grade 4–6 children innovate on Mem Fox's *Possum Magic*. In trying to draft our first line, we came to appreciate how Mem tried many, many lead sentences before settling on "Once upon a time but not very long ago, deep in the Australian bush lived two possums." Our innovation was called *Seagull Magic*. Our lead sentence was "Once upon a time but not so very long ago, on a hot Australian beach lived two seagulls."

Trying to innovate on a wonderfully successful poem or story really makes children look carefully at how those authors crafted their writing: how they savored their carefully chosen words.

Jointly Writing Big Books

Rationale   Rather than innovate on another author's story structure, here the children and teacher jointly write a whole text. Working alongside an experienced writer supports young children in the construction of texts they would not be able to write for themselves. The teacher, as experienced writer, demonstrates the process involved in successfully completing a manuscript. A text that children have helped compose and redraft becomes a text the children can read.

Purpose: Recount   The purpose of this activity is to jointly construct a recount to demonstrate the structure of recount and to have a permanent record of a shared classroom experience.

Strategy   On a large paper chart, record as you and the children jointly compose a recount of a classroom experience. A recount is an outline of an event that has happened, so ask questions to determine the sequence: "What did we do first?" and "What did we do next?"

While jointly writing with the children, explicitly demonstrate how important rereading is to a writer. Say, "Let's reread and see if that makes sense," or "Let's reread and check the sequence. Have we left anything out? Is everything in the right place?"

Purpose: Fiction   The purposes of this activity include the following:

- demonstrating how to write narrative, beginning with a real situation
- demonstrating the importance of problems or complications in fiction and the need to bring them to resolution in the writing
- developing a classroom text that on completion will be a meaningful addition to the class library

Strategy   Use an actual class experience as the starting point for a fictional narrative. The class experience might be the construction of paper kites, for example.

You could begin the piece of writing as a recount, but at a given point interrupt and say, "At this point something very strange happened." Have the children think in pairs about what strange event occurred (e.g., one kite began to speak or the kites all flew in formation and began to dance). Have children share ideas and vote for the strange event they most wish to use in the story.

The joint construction of the story will continue over many sessions. Where there are several ideas for the course the story might take, discuss them and let the children vote for their preferred option. When the story is finished, publish it as a class big book and make smaller individual copies for each child to read.

I detail now a very recent example of this strategy: my writing demonstrations in Lisa Hoban's grade 1–3 classroom following the older children's first school camp experience. My purpose was to inform the children of the writing of narrative. Some of the grades 2–3 children in this room were writing narratives but they were not well-constructed. Some of these narratives went on and on and on, the writers not knowing when to finish. Other writers were regurgitating videos they had watched.

Hence, on large sheets of paper, I started writing about the children's trip to the camp. However, after the introductory paragraph, I stopped and said quite dramatically, "Girls and boys, I'm telling you that at this point something quite frightening happened on this first night at camp. What was it?" Here I asked all the children to talk with the person sitting next to them on the carpet. Their task was to come up with a "quite frightening event" for the first night of camp. I listed the children's events on the chalkboard and asked them to vote for the preferred event, which I would then incorporate into the story. The children so liked three of the frightening events that they persuaded me to include all three of them. Those three frightening events were (1) a loud series of knocks on the camp door, (2) a ghost in the kitchen, and (3) a violent storm.

We completed the draft over eight or nine sessions, taking about seven minutes at the start of each personal writing session. When the first draft of this story was completed, instead of doing the editing from the large chart, I typed the text, double spaced, and copied it on 11x17-inch paper. All children then worked in pairs editing the story.

I asked them to focus on meaning and on the language use. Did the story make sense? Could the language be improved? Had the best words been used?

I was impressed by the fact that having their own draft copies to work on, rather than focusing on one large draft, drew much more editing from many more children. They picked up not only spelling errors but also inconsistencies in the story.

When we were all happy with the draft, I typed it for publication. Again, I included the children in the decisions that were made. They nominated and voted for particular design features of the book, for example, they decided to have borders for all pages. As well as the beautifully bound and published big book, all children received a smaller typed version of *Noisy Night Camp* that they were free to illustrate and take home. Here is the text of the final version:

Noisy Night Camp

Last week Rooms 1 and 2 took a dare to go to Sunnystones Camp. We travelled by bus. The bus shook up and down like a wheel had fallen off. You'll never guess what happened on the first night!!!!

Around midnight Rachael heard a noise. She listened. Knock! Knock! Knock! There it was again. She crept out of bed. Knock! Knock!

Someone was at the front door. Rachael opened the front door and there was a big red kangaroo.

Meantime Jake was thirsty. He went to the kitchen. What a shock Jake got! A ghost was getting a drink from the water dispenser.

Then . . . Crash! Bang! BOOM! A lightning bolt hit Sunnystones Camp and all of the children fell out of bed.

"Ouch" said Susie. "That REALLY hurt." She touched a large lump on her head.

"That hurt," said Chris, getting up from the floor. "What was it?"

"OOOOOOOOWW," said Lisa as she hit her head on the chair by the bed.

"OOOOOOOOOOOWWW," said Jake as he was hit by a flying cup.

There was such a commotion the ghost turned pale.

"I'm going to leave this madhouse," murmured the ghost and he floated away as fast as he could toward the front door.

However blocking the doorway were Rachael and the big red kangaroo.

"OOOOOOOHHH Mr. Kangaroo," said the ghost.

"D-don't go in there. It's not safe."

"Okay Mr Ghost. Hop into my pouch and we'll escape."

As Jake, Chris, Lisa, Rachael and Susie were looking for the medicine cabinet, another loud noise hit Sunnystones Camp.

"What's making *that* terrible noise?" said Rachael.

They huddled together and listened.

"ZZZZZZZZZZZZZZZzzzzzzzzZZZZZZZZZZZZZZZzzzzzzzzZZZZZZZZZ."

"Let's follow the sound," said Susie.

As they tiptoed down the passage the sound got louder and louder.

"ZZZZZZZZZZZZZZZZZZZZZZZZZZZZZZZZZZZZZZZZ."

Near the end of the passage, they found one bedroom door was closed.

"That's strange," whispered Rachael.

"Let's look in there," said Jake.

"I've just noticed that James, Katherine, Harry and Nick are missing," said Lisa.

Jake opened the door. SURPRISE, SURPRISE!

James, Katherine, Harry and Nick were still sleeping. James, Harry, Katherine and Nick were snoring their heads off!

"Let's leave them sleeping," said Lisa. "They'll wake at sunrise."

"We'll all go to the kitchen for hot chocolate."

"Hot chocolate," said James, Harry, Katherine and Nick. "We LOVE hot chocolate."

They all drank hot chocolate before returning to bed.

We now think Sunnystones camp should be renamed "Noisy Night Camp."

Such texts, jointly constructed with the children and having the children themselves at the center of the adventures, help build a sense of classroom community and positive self-images for the individual children. We had such fun writing this book together and we all so love rereading this big book we published.

I am delighted to report that this joint construction has had a dramatic impact on the children's writing. Five or six of the children have voluntarily written narratives that began with known, familiar situations but which then veered into fantasy, and they have taken them through to publication. I include just the opening of Nathan's story, *My Roller Blades*.

My Roller Blades

I got some roller blades. My sister got them for me from a garage sale. They were in good condition. The shoelaces were purple and green. The shoes were black and the wheels were purple. I know how to ride them but one day my roller blades started talking to me. They said, "Your feet stink."

—NATHAN, GRADE 2

While it has been exciting to watch the children gain confidence in writing these fictional stories, the most exciting outcome was a piece written by Alice, a grade 1 girl. Although the grade 1 children did not go to the school camp, they had all joined in the writing of *Noisy Night Camp*. Alice is an emergent writer using strings of letters. Hence her writing is as yet not readable. However, in the writing session at which I presented the beautifully bound copy of *Noisy Night Camp*, Alice wrote the piece in Figure 8–6. The power of meaningful demonstrations! As she read this, she actually sang the line "Sometimes there was a farmer." Note the impact the line of *z*s from the story had on her writing. She explained to me that here the frog had gone to sleep. Note also how she borrowed from the class story the idea of renaming her frog to Noisy Night Frog.

Reading Demonstrations in a Writing Lesson

Rationale Reading informs writing. Where a teacher notices a need in children's writing she may read aloud a published text at the start of a writing session to demonstrate

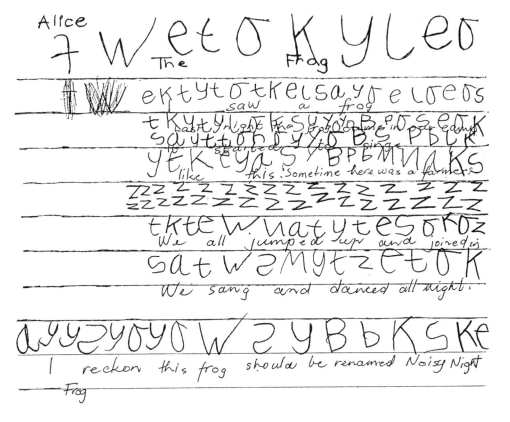

The Frog

I saw a frog.
Last night the frog came in our camp.
It started to sing like this. "Sometimes there was a farmer."
ZZZZZZZZZZZZZZZZZZZZZ
ZZZZZZZZZZZZZZZZZZZZZ
We all jumped up and joined in.
We sang and danced all night.
I reckon this frog should be renamed Noisy Night Frog.

Figure 8–6 Alice's Writing

that with which the children are struggling. Reading demonstrations may inform about different ways of beginning narrative, different ways of ending narrative, ways of introducing information report texts, the crisp abbreviated language of advertisements, and so on.

Purpose   This activity encourages students to vary the way they write, in this case, the way they commence the writing of narrative, and specifically, to try beginning with dialogue.

Strategy   Read just the opening paragraph from *Charlotte's Web* by E. B. White: "'Where's papa going with that axe?' said Fern to her mother as they were setting the table for breakfast." Discussion might center around any of the following:

- What do the children think of the opening?
- What do they think is going to happen?
- How would they describe that opening sentence?
- How has the story commenced? (with dialogue, or someone speaking)
- Has any of the boys or girls ever started a story with dialogue? (A child might retrieve a story of his that he commenced with dialogue and share it.)
- Can students recall any other books that begin in this way?

In later conferences, observe, and encourage children when you find them beginning a narrative with dialogue.

Identifying High- and Low-Interest Points

Rationale Narratives have high- and low-interest points as problems develop and solutions unfold. Many young children write narratives that are quite flat because there is no excitement, no high- and low-interest points.

Purpose By focusing on the highs and lows of published stories, this activity aims to improve the quality of children's narratives.

Strategy A simple strategy for developing children's awareness of the structure of narrative and the need for high- and low-interest points is to have them raise and lower their hands, showing increasing or waning interest, as a story is read aloud.

Read a story aloud to the children. Tell the children to raise their hands as the story becomes more interesting or exciting. Have them lower their hands as the story becomes less interesting.

Once the children as a class have identified high- and low-interest points in other author's stories, they can do the same with their own stories.

Brainstorming: What Makes a Story Interesting?

Rationale Stories are developed with high- and low-interest points, with complications and resolutions. Authors use different strategies to hook readers and keep them reading.

Purpose This activity draws children's attention to the different features of published narratives that hook them and keep them reading until the end.

Strategy I outline here an example from a grades 3–4 classroom.

On a large chart I wrote at the top: "What makes a story interesting?" Here are the children's responses:

a lot of action (Joh)
if you resemble a character (Hugh)
some scary parts (Alison)

when it makes sense (Sarah)

when it's unusual (Elliot)

excitement (Megan)

when it's funny (Drew)

when it's silly (Jesse)

I then read aloud a well-known Australian short story titled "The Drover's Wife" by Henry Lawson. This story tells of a long, lonely night spent by a drover's wife one time when her husband is away droving. A large black snake is seen disappearing under her house. The rough bush home has a slab floor, and the woman fears for the safety of her children as she keeps a vigil through the night.

The children listened intently as the drama unfolded. I then added to our list a further entry: tension (Lorraine).

Compiling this chart helped focus the children's attention on elements of that draw them in. In fact, we drew a fishing hook on a line in the top corner of the chart. At writing conference time I now ask them, "What makes your story interesting?" or "What hooks the reader into your story?"

Summary: Teaching the Reading-Writing Connection

Reading informs and teaches about writing. Rereading our own writing clarifies our thinking and extends our understanding. To teach writing and reading as if they are two separate subjects is to waste the tremendous potential of the one to inform the other. Many lessons about writing are to be learned by reading. In the process of teaching writing, the teacher may explicitly make connections between published texts the children have read and texts the children are writing. Those texts important to children in their out-of-school lives may form important bridges for them to writing in their classroom lives. In the process of rereading that which he has written, the writer is code breaker, text participant, text user, and, hopefully, text analyst.

References

Cambourne, B. 1988. *The Whole Story: Natural Learning and the Acquisition of Literacy in the Classroom.* New Zealand: Ashton-Scholastic.

Purves, A. 1993. "Toward a Re-evaluation of Reader Response and School Literature." *Language Arts* 70 (5): 348–60.

Children's Books

Factor, J., comp. 1983. *Far Out Brussel Sprout.* Melbourne: Oxford University Press.

Fox, M. 1983. *Possum Magic.* Adelaide, Australia: Omnibus Books.

Lawson, H. 1986. "The Drover's Wife." In *The Victorian Readers Fifth Book,* Reprint, Victoria, Australia: Ministry of Education (Schools Division).

White, E. B. 1963. *Charlotte's Web.* Australia: Puffin Books.

Wilson, L. 1997. *Billy Come Inside.* Australia: Nelson ITP.

The Writing Classroom

Ours is a writing classroom
We write some time each day.
Letters, novels, diaries,
We write in different ways.

Our teacher is a writer too,
(Although she's no Bill Peet),
She shares with us when she wants help
We try to be discreet.

She reads to us from published works,
We talk about the authors,
How did they start? Do they get stuck?
How did this pass the censors?

As we read the works of others
We learn the writing art,
Of how to hook a reader
By mind and soul and heart.

—Lorraine Wilson

PLANNING FOR CLASSROOM READING

If there is a unifying theme in all these prescriptions and a common characteristic of the very best classrooms, it is that kids are taken seriously. The educators (and parents) who do the most for children are those who honor, and work hard to find out, what children already know. They start where the student is and work from there. They try to figure out what students need and where their interests lie. Superb teachers strive constantly to imagine how things look from the child's point of view, what lies behind his questions and mistakes. All of this represents a decisive repudiation of the Old School, where, as Dewey observed, "the center of gravity is outside the child. It is in the teacher, the textbook, anywhere and everywhere you please except in the immediate instincts and activities of the child himself."

—ALFIE KOHN (1999, 131)

Any curriculum that takes children seriously and starts with the children requires the most professional, most knowledgeable teachers. Such teachers are able to tap their students' existing knowledge—to observe their interests, questions, and approximations—and plan from this. Planning to teach thus, that is, planning so that curriculum, and specifically reading, is relevant to children's lives, is a far cry from following a state-prescribed curriculum with teacher manuals ensuring that teachers of similar grade levels teach the same content, words, letters, and sounds; that children of similar ages read the same texts; and that all children are driven toward the same narrow outcomes.

In this latter approach, the children are quite irrelevant. In this latter approach, teachers are deprofessionalized. When systems make curriculum decisions that are best made by on-site professionals who know their students and their communities, and when systems monitor student performance with the statewide testing of trivia that can be tested and marked by machines, they are dumbing down education: they are dumbing down, or deprofessionalizing, our teaching force.

> Teaching is a social activity. Pre-desiFgned programs cannot take the place of teachers, even when the programs are administered by teachers.
>
> Teaching involves decisions made on the spot, not decisions to move from one instructional goal to the next, but decisions about the condition of the learner. Such conditions might include the learner's (and also the teacher's) physical, emotional, and psychological state at that particular time, together with interest, comprehension, past experience, self image, feelings about the task at hand, and feelings about the teacher (or about the student).
>
> All these considerations require teachers to interact with and be responsive to learners *personally*, as individuals, not as items on an instruction chart or data on an achievement record. (Smith 1999, 151)

Planning for the Big Picture

When planning for a class of children, it is most important to plan for the big picture. This is where we draw upon our belief systems about living, about learning, about language, and about reading. As teachers, we must consider why we wish for our students to be literate. We must ponder the type of lives we hope for our students and then consider which literacies they will need to attain such lives. Once we have answers to these questions, we can plan our particular class literacy programs.

I think of an Australian teacher named Thinh Hoang, who was born in Vietnam and has spent her school holidays travelling around Vietnam collecting children's books, traditional rhymes, and stories. Thinh teaches at Footscray Primary School in Melbourne, where most of the children are Vietnamese. Thinh appreciates the link between bringing children to literacy in their first language with later success in literacy in the community language. In her teaching, the Vietnamese rhymes and tales are very important components. How relevant are these texts not only to these children but also to their families!

Hence, before we can plan reading activities for our classrooms, we need to address the following questions. Ideally a whole school staff would address these questions together so that in the school teaching program there would be some consistency and continuity.

Which sort of literate lives do we wish for the children we teach?

Which literacies are important in these children's communities?

Which reading practices are important for these children: do they need to be code breakers *and* text participants *and* text users *and* text analysts?

How do we describe the reading process?

What is our definition of reading?

Do we value personal response to literature?

What are the different purposes for reading?

What are the different text types?

Which of these purposes and text types will be necessary in these children's lives?

Which community events could be the subject of classroom literacy? (local book fair, community agricultural show, sports team success, etc.)

How can we work together with the school community to promote literacy?

What are these children's current understandings about literacy?

What are these students' needs and interests?

What are the resources (both human and material) we need for our preferred literacy program?

Hopefully, the teacher will plan a program designed to make children comfortable and confident in all four practices of Luke and Freebody's Four Resources Model.

Different emphases may be desirable and necessary in the reading programs of different school communities. Catering to such different emphases and to differing children's interests and existing knowledge will mean that *no* commercial teaching manual will possibly be right for all teachers of the same grade level across the same country. If reading instruction is to be relevant to children's lives, reading programs are best developed at individual school sites. Teachers must be free to tune in to their students' conversations, to observe them at play and in the community, for the purpose of planning reading that will matter to them.

Planning for Authentic Reading

We do not read to read. We read to do something else. Therefore, classroom reading should never be for its own sake, for example, to get to a higher level or to keep quiet while the teacher works with another group. Classroom reading should serve the same purposes as reading done in the big wide world, for example, reading to learn, reading to follow directions and make something, reading for relaxation and enjoyment, reading some social communication from a friend, reading about some local community event, and so on. We must remember that reading is social practice.

Last Saturday evening, Nicholas came for tea with his mom and dad. During the previous week, Jaqueline (his mother) had offered to bring dessert. She said she would let Nicholas choose. Dessert that Saturday was a chocolate brownie slice with fresh strawberries. Jaqueline explained that she had given her dessert recipe book to Nicholas and told him to sit down and select a dessert. She reflected later that it might have been the enticing photograph that influenced his choice rather than the written recipe. But how often are we adult cooks tempted by the photographs in recipe books? Why else would full-color photos be included?

No wonder this little boy is reading. This is just one example of many of the authentic purposes for reading to which he has been exposed. We see also the expectation and trust that he will make an acceptable choice of dessert.

I wondered later about cooking in school. Usually, we teachers choose the recipes. We copy just one recipe on the board for all to see. How easy it would be to have some attractive recipe books in the classroom library from which the children could make cooking choices.

Integrated Curriculum

If one is planning to take account of differing cultural, economic, and geographic characteristics of particular communities, if one is planning for the interests and the needs of pupils, and if one is planning for authentic language use in the school curriculum, then it follows that the curriculum is integrated. Language is not learned divorced from content or context.

Integrated curriculum involves integrating children's lives into their curriculum, integrating the learning of symbol systems and skills with learning about the world, and integrating the development of children's listening, speaking, reading, and writing.

> If language is learned best when it is whole and in natural context, then integration is a key principle for language development and learning through language. In fact language development and content become a dual curriculum. For learners it's a single curriculum focusing on what is being learned, what language is used for. But for teachers there is always a double agenda: to maximize opportunities for pupils to engage in authentic speech and literacy events while they study their community, do a literature unit on Lloyd Alexander, carry out a scientific study of mice, or develop a sense of fractions and decimals. Speaking, listening and writing and reading are all happening in context of the exploration of the world of things, events, ideas and experiences.
>
> The content curriculum draws on the interests and experiences children have outside of school, and this incorporates the full range of oral and written functions. It becomes a broad, rich curriculum that starts where the learners are in language and knowledge and builds out from there. (Goodman 1986, 30)

Integrating Children's Lives into the Classroom

Integrated curriculum is more than a series of integrated topics or investigations. A curriculum that is inclusive of all children's culture, race, religion, and economic status and that plans learning from children's interests and current knowledge integrates the children's lives into the classroom programs. Time is planned for children to explore personal concerns, personal interests, and family happenings via writing and the arts. At personal writing time, which is scheduled at least twice per week, the children choose the writing form, the topic, and whether or not the work goes to publication. Children of all ages may use this time to recount those things they have been doing both in and out of school. They may also take the opportunity to write about issues that are concerning them or to pen letters to family members.

Letter diaries in which the teacher and one student exchange letters approximately once per week provide opportunities for children to raise ideas, suggestions, and personal worries. Each letter diary is the joint property of the teacher and one student and is an excellent vehicle for incorporating each child's life into the classroom.

Integrated Themes or Topics

Integrated curriculum will in part involve integrated themes or topics. Such topics arise from children's questions and interests and follow children's inquiries. In planning integrated topics, the teacher should be mindful of possible content outcomes of the unit as well as the type of language texts that will be necessary for the content objectives to be met. When planning an integrated topic, ask:

What is it the children wish to find out?

Which conceptual understandings of the content disciplines will be important through this unit?

Which language uses and which text types will be necessary for the children to come to the content understandings?

How will I plan for the literacy needs of individual children when using these texts during this unit of study?

For example, in an integrated study of clothing with young children, many of whom are learning English as a second language, language aims for the unit might include the following:

oral labelling of clothing

oral recounts of clothing worn on special occasions

listening to members of national groups tell about national costumes

reading class experience stories (recounts) of visiting community members who knit or sew labelling diagrams as part of the literacy curriculum (in the context of learning the names of items of clothing)

reading procedural genre (in the context of children making paper dolls and clothes to fit and following simple patterns to make simple garments)

Any integrated unit that starts with the children's existing knowledge, follows the children's lines of inquiry, and incorporates an inquiry process, cannot be done in two weeks. Where children are genuinely involved in asking questions and researching information by reading, interviewing, experimenting, visiting, using the Internet and so on, such integrated units spread over nine or ten weeks or longer. This allows time for children to process and refine new information. Generally, teachers conclude such units knowing the work could have continued. Perhaps it is positive that one unit of study finishes with children being enthused and still generating questions. Is this not developing enthusiasm for learning?

Teachers I know generally plan to conduct four integrated studies per year: one each term in their four-term year. They try to ensure that two of the units are science-oriented and two are more socially oriented, although some units include the study of both the social world and the physical world.

The children take part in listing topics they would like to investigate and questions they want to answer. Where children have not been accustomed to having their inquiries valued, it sometimes occurs that their ideas of possible class investigations are limited and reflect previous class studies in which they have participated. The teacher may then suggest possible topics or investigations. The children then vote on the topic of investigation to be undertaken.

Then the teacher discusses possible lines of investigation and possible related excursions with the class. Initially in the unit development, teachers tap the children's existing knowledge. At the commencement of an integrated study of living things, Mary Kadyra, a K–2 teacher, asked her students to define on paper a living thing, Her words to the children were "Show on your paper what you think a living thing is. You can write or draw." Figures 9–1 through 9–3 show responses to this task from three children in her class. Note the different conceptual understandings these children have.

The Crowded Curriculum

Today we hear teachers speak of the crowded curriculum. Schools are being asked to teach curricula to cure societal ills, such as drug education, bike education, and family education, to name just a few. As more and more special subjects are included, teachers are finding it harder to have long uninterrupted teaching blocks for integrated studies. Teachers are constantly pressed for time. Classroom sessions are never quite finished properly. I think we all need to slow down and perhaps attempt less, in more time. If we teachers are feeling frazzled and rushed, how must the children be feeling? No one gains from feeling frazzled or from never completing anything properly.

NAME. JOSIE
(Prep)

LIVING THINGS

DATE. 26-1
26·2·1996

What is a living thing?

A person

Figure 9–1 Josie's Response

NAME. Joel S
(Gn 2)

DATE

LIVING THINGS

What is a living thing?

MaMes — mammals

RaPTIL LeZZd — reptiles - lizard

Sack

feyh SaykC — A shark is a fish

WhaLES

PBaJu-fieh — puffer fish

Sodfieh — sword fish

BaJe budgie — sword fish

YeBBes — yabbies

BoldS — birds

SideS — spiders

Figure 9–2 Joel's Response

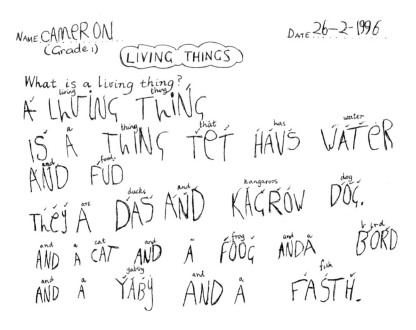

NAME CAMERON
(Grade 1)   (LIVING THINGS)   DATE 26-2-1996

What is a living thing?
A LIVING THING
IS A THING TET HAVS WATER
AND FUD
THEY A DAS AND KAGROV DOG.
AND A CAT AND A FOOG ANDA BORD
AND A YABY AND A FASTH.

Figure 9–3 Cameron's Response

The Schedule

Professional teachers do not need someone else to plan their daily and weekly class routines for them. Professional teachers make judgments about what occurs where and when, taking into account the needs of the children (Are they hungry, sleepy, cold, upset?), the availability of resources, special subject schedules, and special events.

The schedule is a servant of curriculum: it reflects the philosophical stance of the school or the teacher. Teachers on-site in their classrooms with their students are the best people to determine what happens when during the school day.

Designing the daily schedule is a delicate balance between being flexible in adapting to daily curriculum foci and children's needs and providing regular routines that give the children some stability and security. In the state of Victoria today, it is expected that all K–2 classes have a two-hour literacy block each morning. The first hour is for the teaching of reading and the second hour is for the teaching of writing. (Yes, the teaching of reading is separated from the teaching of writing.) The large majority of schools start this two-hour literacy block at 9 A.M., to fit it in before the morning recess break at 11. School begins at 9, and so the very first thing the children experience each day is reading instruction. Educationally, how sound is this? Are all Victorian four- and five-year-olds ready for instruction in reading the moment the school day starts?

Of course they're not. I think of schools where I have taught and where some children had to get themselves up and off to school. Their parents started work at 6 A.M. in the factories. Sometimes the children did not hear their alarm clock and came late. All children are tired on some mornings. Is it not better to let them sleep a little longer than to have them at school by 9 A.M. and have them be tired and cranky throughout the day? And why should the school day start so formally for young children?

Starting the School Day

Let us consider an alternate way of starting the school day. The room is prepared with a variety of activities available for the children: a home area with dolls, beds, and tea sets; building equipment; art tables; computer games; a book corner; a writing table; puzzle center; and a farm or zoo animal area. Where the school room is prepared with such developmental activities, children may arrive before the bell and enter the room with a parent who will perhaps help the child settle into an activity. Children who arrive a few minutes after the bell are not obviously late. The teacher is able to greet each child individually as he or she enters the room. Because the children are all busily engaged with a variety of educational activities, the teacher is able to spare a minute or two for any parent wanting her ear or for any distressed child.

And what about the children? The children find something they wish to do. They are engaged in hands-on activities with others. They are able to socialize with their classmates and make friends. As well, all the activities have educational value; they are not time fillers.

Any classroom is a social unit. Learning is social by nature. Beginning each school day on the first bell with instruction in reading is extremely regimented and sends a message about authority and the power of the teacher in controlling learning. This is in conflict with the notion of children being active in the learning process. With such a regimented start to the school day, where is there allowance for personal greetings between teacher and students, students and students, parents and teacher?

Starting the school day with a choice of activities is equally valid for older students. Similarly, they too may enter their classroom before the first bell, have a chat or exchange a greeting with their teacher, and then find something to do. The choice may not include dolls and motor cars, but certainly eleven- and twelve-year-olds have much to gain from constructional kits; independent time on the classroom computers; extra time to continue writing and publishing; games such as Monopoly, checkers, and chess; an opportunity to complete unfinished work; the challenge of fitting a few more pieces into a large class jigsaw puzzle; a chance to add further strands to a class weaving; and, of course, time to curl up with a book or a magazine.

Weekly Planning

Weekly planning for reading includes the following:

- the teacher reading aloud quality literature, big books, poems, rhymes, songs, factual texts, school notices, daily schedules, routines, etc.
- all children reading some of the same texts, such as rhymes and songs

- members of small groups reading the same texts (e.g., a small-group literature book or a factual text to find answers to research questions)
- individual children choosing texts around personal interests
- children reading both commercial and classroom-made texts
- children reading fiction and nonfiction texts
- children revisiting texts
- children meeting new texts
- children working in different group structures
- children working in shared literature groups twice weekly
- children borrowing take-home books (maybe a literature book or a library book)
- the teacher leading a study of print features arising in the context of a text being read or needs revealed in children's writing (a particular letter, capital letters, sound-letter patterns, morphemic spelling patterns, items of punctuation)
- the teacher conducting at least one reading conference per child. This may include the child reading aloud to the teacher or discussing books read with the teacher. (With some large classes, the teacher may conference with each child once every two weeks.)
- the teacher making an evaluative comment about most children on the children's reading profiles

Over a week, reading sessions *might* include the following:

	For Early Inexperienced Readers	For More Experienced Young Readers
Two integrated reading sessions	For example, compilation of class experience story about class experience (excursion, experiment, visitor, etc.) OR Reading and illustrating individual copies of the class-compiled book. AND/OR	
	Recomposition of class story using sentence strips.	
	AND/OR	
	Listening at listening center to story or factual text related to topic. Children write what they have learned or children tell what they have learned and teacher records on master list.	Children read and examine individual copies of illustrated factual text or news report and write what they have learned.
	AND/OR	
	In mixed-ability groups, brainstorming predictions for forthcoming excursions. Class list is compiled and read.	

	For Early Inexperienced Readers	For More Experienced Young Readers
	AND/OR	
	Repeated readings of book related to topic.	Sorting of topic words.
Two small-group literature sessions (see Chapter 7)	In small matched-ability groups, children read books of their choosing. They respond in literature journals, giving personal reflections, sharing responses, posing questions, and taking a critical literacy stance.	
One whole-class session with teacher introducing a way of responding to text **OR**	Personal response, critical literacy, sketch to stretch, note-taking from factual text.	
One innovation on a text **OR**	After teacher demonstration with all children, children complete a second innovation by working with the teacher.	After teacher demonstration, children work with a partner or individually on their own innovations.
One readers theatre session	All children work in small mixed-ability groups. (see page 204)	

In addition, there are two personal writing sessions each week. As mentioned earlier, reading may be part of the demonstration of writing that occurs at the start of the writing session. At personal writing time, children choose the topic they write about and the audience they write for. Some of their writing is published. The published works become part of the reading stock of the classroom. Of course, the children write every day, but the writing on other days will be for more specific purposes, e.g., write a prediction before a science experiment; write a recount of a school outing.

Daily Planning

While some routines occur each day, e.g., sustained quiet reading, the daily literacy program is not the same each day. Each day:

The teacher reads aloud.

Children read privately.

Everyone reads silently.

In early literacy classes, some familiar text is revisited.

In any one literacy session, writing, reading, listening, and speaking activities may be occurring at one time.

Children read a variety of text types.

The teacher makes anecdotal comments about several children in evaluative files. Some children's samples of writing or literature responses are added to their evaluation files.

Small-Group Literature Sessions

For K–2 students, a small-group literature session can take place twice a week. The session outlined below is for a class with some emergent readers and others beginning to read picture books for themselves.

1. Whole-class immersion/demonstration
   Teacher reads a familiar big book aloud with children joining in. She also reads aloud a new picture book, big book, or title of author under study.

2. Small group work
   Three to four small groups, each of four to five children, move to independent work areas to read titles of their choosing. Each group of children has a leader, who follows instructions on a cue card, outlining the expectations for each group. (See Chapter 7.) The teacher works with the remaining nine to ten children who are emergent readers. She engages them in repeated readings of a big book or a picture book where each child has a copy.

   or

   Teacher and children engage with language experience work.

   or

   Emergent readers follow a story at the listening center. The teacher works with this group, demonstrating the workings of the cassette player and how to follow the text in the book, so in the future this group might work independently.

3. Whole-class share
   Children sit in a circle to share what they have done. Some books are read aloud. Some literature journals are shared.

Alternatives to Sustained Quiet Reading

In many grades there are one or two children who do not enjoy or who do not make good use of sustained quiet reading time. It is purposeless, then, to make them engage in this activity. Since most children make good use of this reading time, it should not be stopped because of a few. Therefore, alternate reading arrangements need to be made for the few. For example, if two or three classes took sustained reading at the same time, a reading support teacher might read aloud to this group or involve them in repeated readings outside the children's classrooms. Alternatively, the children who cannot sustain silent reading could listen to a taped book. Another idea is that a parent might volunteer to read aloud high-interest books to this small group.

Evaluation

If the teacher intends to develop lifelong readers who engage with the four reading practices described throughout this book, then evaluation will involve reference to how the children (1) code break, (2) make meaning, (3) use text, and (4) critically analyze text. When evaluating children, the teacher should keep the following question in mind.

Code Breaking

Do the reader's miscues make sense?

What does the reader do when a miscue does not make sense? Does the reader self-correct?

Are the miscues generally of a visual nature?

Do the miscues make sense semantically and syntactically?

What does the reader do when he encounters an unknown word?

Does the reader refer to pictorial information to confirm meaning?

Does the reader sometimes refer to earlier sections of the text to confirm meaning?

Does the reader stop and sound out each unknown word?

Does the reader skip an unknown word, read on, draw upon context, and return to insert a word?

Does the reader start the sentence again and draw upon context to insert a word?

Does the reader's retelling indicate that the reader is reading for meaning?

Text Participant

Does the reader read to make meaning?

Does the reader volunteer commentary on the book as he reads?

Does the reader laugh or cry as he reads?

Does the reader respond personally by reflecting on some related life experience?

Can the reader retell in his own words?

Does the reader choose to reread favorite books?

Can the reader discuss different themes from the book?

Does the reader peep to the last pages to see how the story ends?

Text User

What is the reader reading and why? (Hopefully he is not reading a book only because he was told to! This is not reading for living.)

Does the reader read to pursue personal interests? (e.g., to learn more about sharks, to work out how to play a particular game, to check the position of his favorite team on the sports page, to escape and relax in a good book)

Does the reader interact with others who read the same material?

Does the reader make appropriate use of the features of the texts he is reading? (e.g., table of contents, glossary, quantities in a recipe)

Does the student choose to read on his own time?

Does the student choose to borrow from the school library?

Text Analyst

Is the reader able to identify author motives?

Does the reader present a point of view that is in conflict with that of the author?

Does the reader question decisions made by authors of fiction?

Does the reader question the accuracy of nonfiction writing?

Is the reader able to perceive how different social groups are portrayed in the writing? Does he sometimes question this portrayal?

Does the reader perceive how particular texts position the reader?

Does the reader understand how authors and illustrators use particular words and colors in texts to position the reader?

Does the reader identify those voices not being heard?

Does the reader write to authors, querying their motives/portrayal of particular groups/why some points of view were not included?

Evaluation will also include notes on the children's interest and participation in regular classroom reading.

How do they participate at silent reading time? What do they choose to read at silent reading time?

How well do the children participate in small literature groups? Are they involved with the reading? Do they engage in book discussions?

In class book constructions, do the children contribute ideas? Are they able to identify inconsistencies in the text being constructed?

Do the children regularly borrow take-home books? Which types of books do the children borrow?

When reading factual texts, are the children able to find answers to their questions?

Which nonbook materials do the children read?

Importantly, each child's reading profile should include notes about the child's attitude toward reading.

Equipment

Classroom Library

Following are some suggestions for your classroom library. Have a wide range of books written in different styles and about different subjects on display. The books must be authentic texts: they have been written to tell a story or written to inform. They have not been written to teach reading. The books come from the school library or reading resource room and are changed regularly. The library shelves must be inviting with room to display book covers, to make selection easier for the children. The shelves should not be overcrowded and the books should not be worn.

Depending on the age of the children, magazines can be included, as well as a copy of the daily newspaper. There should be comfortable cushions, seats, mats, or a carpet to sit on. There should be displays about authors, illustrators, or particular types of books, for example, nursery rhyme books.

It is important that children are made responsible for caring for the books from the first days of the school year. When children use the book corner, they must be responsible for packing the books away. Books are not to be left on the floor and walked upon. At the end of each reading session, it is wise to quietly ask all children to turn their eyes to the book corner. Is it tidy? If it isn't, those children who were reading there must either tidy it then and there or during their lunch period.

Caregivers will need to be advised that their children will be borrowing books of their choice, around their interests and hence may not be able to read these books independently. The caregivers are to read the books aloud to their children and engage them in discussions about the books.

The class library will also contain books published in the classroom. These books will be about the children and their classroom experiences, and these titles may also be borrowed by the children as take-home books.

Book Sets

A book set contains six to eight copies of a book for shared reading. These sets of books should be stored outside classrooms in a central area. Children take turns borrowing particular sets for their classroom. They choose a title that they would like to read and are able to read. The book sets are kept in the classroom after they have been used in shared literature sessions so that the children may borrow from them for take-home books. Books purchased for shared reading in multiple numbers must meet certain criteria:

- Meaning must be central (as opposed to controlled vocabulary and phonic texts).
- All books must be written by an author.
- Both fiction and nonfiction may be included.
- Books must be in good condition.

- Books must be accessible to the children.
- Books must be easily found and returned.

Finally, where possible, involve the children in the purchase of new book titles. When new books are to be purchased, a display can be mounted at school where the children peruse the possibilities and recommend their preferred titles. Older children can be involved in the selection of new titles for the early grades. I find they remember very clearly those books they enjoyed at an earlier age and they take great pride in advising teachers about the selection of books for younger children.

Big Books
The school big book collection should include folktales, narratives, poems, factual, and procedural texts. Because big books are to be used with a group, rather than an individual child, the print should be large enough for the group members to read from their position in front of the teacher. Where possible, the same books should be purchased in smaller editions as well, for individual children to borrow as take-home books, or use for individual research.

Big Book Stand
This makes life so much easier. It should have a shelf on which to stand the book that is wide enough that the book does not fall off when being read to the class. As well, it should include storage space for several big books at any one time.

Blank Big Books
These are essential for teacher-modelled writing (e.g., teacher's diary, teacher's modelled literature reflections), collections of favorite classroom rhymes, and collections of favorite classroom songs. Writing done in these large blank books does not go astray as easily, as when done on separate sheets of paper.

Listening Center
I believe a listening center is a must in each early primary classroom. It means that a group of eight children can be profitably engaged in listening to a good story or a factual text or participating in repeated readings of a text while the teacher is busy with another group.

Taped Book Sets
Popular books may be read onto audiotapes by parents. Many commercially taped books are read too quickly and do not leave time for the child to browse at the pictures. When taping books, do not read too quickly, but do not read so slowly that the listening becomes tedious. Always give some sort of signal when it is time to turn the page. At the start of a new page, wait a few seconds before beginning to read. When you have finished reading a page, wait again for a few seconds before giving the signal to turn the page. This allows time for children to examine the artwork.

Classroom Published Books

These are books the children have either written individually or jointly constructed. These should be on display in the classroom.

Copies of the Daily Newspaper(s)

Display the newspaper in grades 3–6 classrooms. Some children are avid followers of particular sports and enjoy reading the sports sections of newspapers. In rural areas, the local newspapers often feature photos of people the children know, with accompanying articles.

Literature Journals

These are exercise books that are the property of each individual child for the purpose of reflecting on books read. (See chapter 7.) They are introduced when children are starting to write in a way that is almost readable.

Dictionaries

A classroom should have several different dictionaries. These should include an adult dictionary that the children will witness the teacher refer to and several different children's dictionaries for the children to use once they are able to check their own spelling.

The Alphabet

The alphabet should be on display in classrooms in a format that's large enough for children to refer to from their tables. This applies not only to kindergarten, first- and second-grade classrooms but also to third- and fourth-grade rooms, for there are always some eight- and nine-year-olds who are not confident with the order of the letters of the alphabet. In grades 5–6, where children are learning English as a second language, it might be that their first written language features an alphabet other than the English one. Here, too, the English alphabet should be clearly in view. I would like to see the alphabet painted on school playgrounds, like a long snake or trail, so children could walk along it.

Writing Paper

On the writing shelves there should be a variety of paper: recycled paper for draft writing; plain paper and lined paper; and good white printer paper for publishing.

Publishing Materials

Good-quality publishing materials for the class publishing program include quality white paper, multicolored cover paper and cardboard, rolls of clear contact for covering books, a heavy-duty stapler and book tape for bookbinding, several small staplers, a small paper cutter (for the teacher's use), publishing pens for the children to hand letter their books, a variety of materials for artwork (felt pens, paint, colored pencils, food coloring, colored paper for collage), glue, scissors, special felt pens (multicolored, silver, gold), glitter, correction pens, and so on. Note that special publishing materials are only used for publishing. They are not to be used for draft work.

Display Accessories

Keep on hand a collection of clothes pegs, binder clips, pins, strong magnets, reusable adhesives, and so on, for displaying children's work.

Grouping Children

Throughout the week children should experience flexible grouping. Groups can be formed according to interest, friendship, mixed ability, need/ability, and social cohesion.

Interest Groups

Interest groups work well for science or social studies research. Where a group of children have identified a topic that they all wish to learn more about, they can work together. For example, in an integrated study of the sea, those children wanting to find out more about sharks might work together. They might listen to a taped reading of a factual text about sharks. Either the children could follow this with a group brainstorming of what they have learned or each individual child could make some notes about sharks based on the taped book. They could also discuss questions and puzzles they have after listening to the tape.

Friendship Groups

All of us enjoy working with our friends. Sometimes it is appropriate for groups of friends to work together. An example might be after the teacher has read aloud from the class serial and ask children to consider a critical literacy issue. For example, "Discuss in your group who exercised power in this story. Who was without power? Support your opinions with examples from the book."

Mixed-Ability Groups

Mixed-ability groups work well with readers theatre. The procedures are introduced to the whole class and many different small groups rehearse different rhymes and then share them with the class. When the children are comfortable and confident in the routines of readers theatre, small groups can work independently while the teacher works with other groups.

To prepare for this activity, make multiple copies of nine to ten rhymes and mark them for part reading (e.g. Reader 1, Reader 2, Reader 3, All, etc.). Then explain readers theatre as scripted theatre. The purpose is to entertain an audience, but the players read their scripts. Voices must be clearly audible and expressive.

Now have proposed leaders read the group instructions from an enlarged cue card:

Readers Theatre

1. Leader reads aloud.
2. All read together.
3. Leader reads aloud.

4. Leader gives out parts.

5. Practice reading in parts.

6. Practice with expression.

7. Perform to everyone.

Hand out copies of rhymes to groups, each of which has a competent reader as its leader. (If there are four parts to be read, then the group consists of four children.) Let the children gather in small groups so the leaders can take their groups through the routine as set out on the cue cards (ten to twelve minutes). Then have each group present to the whole class. Finally, encourage evaluation from the audience: Could the voices be heard? Did the group introduce its particular rhyme? Was the rhyme presented in an interesting way?

Need/Ability Groups

Sometimes children of all ages will be grouped according to need. In younger age groups, repeated readings are appropriate for those children not yet able to read an early text for themselves. To include in such a group children who can read those texts for themselves would be to waste their time.

Socially Cohesive Groups

In any classroom, a teacher has the right to form groups on the basis of children's ability to work cooperatively together. Of course, the children must know the reason for the group membership and be given an opportunity to prove they can work well with friends of their choosing. However, where individual children are constantly disruptive, not only the teacher but also the other children have the right to exercise some control over which group those children work with.

In all small-group activities, the children must be engaged in educationally worthwhile activities. Busywork that is an end in itself is not acceptable.

Summary: Planning for Classroom Reading

In planning for classroom reading, there is much for the teacher to consider. As reading is social practice, it is wise for the teacher to begin by looking beyond the classroom and to think about the children's lives and their futures. She must know and consider her students, their abilities, and their interests. She must be strong in her view of herself as a professional educator and her capacities to plan a curriculum for her students. She must plan to integrate the teaching of reading with children's individual interests as well as with the class integrated units of study. She must plan to have the physical resources necessary to implement her desired program.

Sometimes it happens that as teachers, we become bogged down with matters imposed by our systems, such as compulsory statewide testing.

When teachers are told, either explicitly or implicitly, that their major responsibility is to improve test scores, they may understandably be driven to spend precious class time on the option that leads to short-term results. Nevertheless research backs up the majority opinion of teachers in the study who believe that, in the long run, students' intellectual development and reading achievement are better served by practices that foster the desire to read. (Worthy, Turner, and Moorman 1998, 302)

I suggest that when that happens, it is time for us to pause and question:

How strong am I professionally?

What are the big issues?

Is my class program enthusing my children for reading?

Is the class reading program relevant to the children's lives?

Am I developing readers who are not only code breakers but also text participants, text users, and text analysts?

Are my children reading to live?

References

Goodman, K. 1986. *What's Whole in Whole Language?* New York: Scholastic.

Kohn, Alfie. 1999. *The Schools Our Children Deserve.* New York: Houghton Mifflin.

Smith, F. 1999. "Why Systematic Phonics and Phonemic Awareness Instruction Constitute an Educational Hazard." *Language Arts* 77 (2): 150–55.

Worthy, J., M. Turner, and M. Moorman. 1998. "The Precarious Place of Self-Selected Reading." *Language Arts* 75 (4): 296–304.

LAST WORD

Read to Live

They say,
we are what we eat.
I say,
we are what we read.

Think for a moment.
List all you have read
this past week.

Your list tells about
  your work
  your home
  your family
  your friends
  your worries
  your dreams
  your hobbies
  your passions
  your compassion.

Your list tells about you.

I say,
we are
what we read.
We read to live.

        —LORRAINE WILSON